USER INTERFACES IN C++ AND OBJECT-ORIENTED PROGRAMMING

MARK GOODWIN

ADVANCED
COMPUTER
BOOKS

MIS: PRESS

MANAGEMENT INFORMATION SOURCE, INC.

COPYRIGHT

DEDICATION

To Ryan and Matthew: the best children in the whole world.

ACKNOWLEDGMENTS

I would like to express my most sincere thanks to the following companies:

- Guidelines Software, Inc., Orinda, CA
- Microsoft Corporation, Redmond, WA
- Zortech, Inc., Arlington, MA

Without their generous contributions, this book would not have been possible.

TABLE OF CONTENTS

DISK ORDER FORM
ON LAST PAGE
OF BOOK

INTRODUCTION

Perhaps the most important and challenging phase in an application program's development is the construction of the program's user interface. Essentially, a user interface is the method an application program uses to interact with the computer operator. Today's application programmers use such state-of-the-art features as windows, pull-down menus, pop-up menus, dialog boxes, and on-line help to construct highly attractive and efficient user interfaces. In fact, a well-constructed user interface can almost eliminate the need for external manuals. Typically, computer operators will need to consult accompanying reference manuals only when they use an unfamiliar program feature.

To effectively construct an application program's user interface, most programmers rely heavily on user interface toolboxes. These user interface toolboxes provide all of the routines for building state-of-the-art user interfaces. However, because the C++ programming language is so new to the world of IBM PCs and compatibles, commercially produced C++ user interface toolboxes aren't yet readily available. Therefore, C++ programmers must either make do with a C user interface toolbox or write their own C++ user interface toolbox. Although purchasing a C user interface toolbox will certainly relieve application programmers from writing their own user interface routines, the generic functions supplied in commercially available user interface toolboxes aren't always the best choice for all programs. On the other hand, a self-written C++ user interface toolbox will provide the C++ programmer with routines that are easily customized to fulfill an application program's specific needs. Furthermore, C++'s object-oriented programming techniques allow the programmer to quickly customize a self-written user interface toolbox by making a few minor changes to the toolbox's low-level routines.

The biggest stumbling block in writing a C++ user interface toolbox is the programmer's lack of knowledge in the area of low-level display programming. To remedy this knowledge gap, this book provides the C++ programmer with the necessary knowledge for quick and easy implementation of today's user interface techniques on the IBM PC and compatibles. Furthermore, this book presents a C++ user interface toolbox called **windows.lib** (hereinafter referred to as WINDOWS). WINDOWS includes user interface functions for opening and closing text windows, pop-up menus, dialog box menus, pull-down menus, and more. When used properly in an application program, the WINDOWS functions will produce a user interface that is truly state of the art in appearance. Additionally, the WINDOWS functions can be easily customized to satisfy an application program's special needs.

USER REQUIREMENTS

The programs in this book require an IBM PC or compatible, Zortech C++ or an equivalent C++ translator and C compiler combination, and the Microsoft Macro Assembler (MASM) or equivalent. Although its use is strictly optional, the WINDOWS toolbox provides extensive support for a Microsoft-compatible mouse. To fully understand the information in this book, an intermediate level of programming knowledge is required. However, all of the WINDOWS routines can be easily incorporated into an application program by even a novice C++ programmer. Thus, *User Interfaces in C++ and Object Oriented Programming* provides something for everybody.

CHAPTER OVERVIEWS

Chapter 1 explains how the MS-DOS video functions, the IBM PC ROM BIOS functions, and direct memory access techniques are used to perform display input/output.

Chapter 2 presents the low-level assembly language routines for filling portions of the display screen with a specific character, setting the attributes for a portion of the display screen, saving a portion of the display screen in a memory buffer, redisplaying a previously buffered screen display, drawing a single-lined or a double-lined border around a portion of the display screen, and retrieving keyboard input.

Chapter 3 presents the low-level C++ functions for turning the cursor on and off, positioning the cursor, displaying single characters, and setting individual character attributes.

Chapter 4 presents the low-level C++ mouse routines and defines a class of pointer objects.

Chapter 5 presents the routines for implementing a class of dynamic window objects.

Chapter 6 presents the routines for constructing three distinct classes of menu objects.

Chapter 7 presents the routines for displaying and retrieving dates, dollar values, numeric values, telephone numbers, Social Security numbers, and strings.

Chapter 8 presents SIMPLE LEDGER, a complete general ledger accounting system that illustrates how the WINDOWS toolbox is used to build an application program.

APPENDIX OVERVIEWS

Appendix A presents a complete reference guide for the WINDOWS toolbox. A syntax summary, a description of its purpose, and a coding example are given for each of the WINDOWS functions.

Appendix B presents a reference guide for the IBM PC ROM BIOS video functions.

Appendix C presents a reference guide for the Microsoft mouse driver functions.

Appendix D explains how the WINDOWS toolbox is compiled with either the Zortech C++ compiler or the Guidelines C++ translator.

THE IBM PC DISPLAY

Although the IBM PC family of computers supports a wide variety of display adapters, there are only three basic methods for reading from and writing to the display screen: the MS-DOS video services, the ROM BIOS video services, and direct memory access. While all three display methods can be used to build effective program displays, such considerations as program portability, speed, and ease of programming should be considered before selecting a method for a particular application program. This chapter takes a further look at all three of the display methods to help you fully understand how and why the WINDOWS toolbox performs display input/output the way it does.

1

THE MS-DOS VIDEO SERVICES

Without a doubt, the MS-DOS video services offer the highest degree of program portability. Not only do they offer portability across all IBM PCs and compatibles, they provide compatibility for any computer that is capable of running the MS-DOS operating system. Because the MS-DOS video services are called as MS-DOS function calls (calls to INT 21H), their ease of use is quite high. Indeed, most high-level languages use the MS-DOS video services to implement their generic display output commands (i.e., C++'s and C's printf functions, Pascal's Writeln procedure, and BASIC's PRINT statement).

Although the MS-DOS video services' high degree of compatibility makes them an excellent choice for writing highly portable programs, their lack of speed and versatility, coupled with their lack of such essentials as display reading functions and cursor control functions, makes them entirely unsuitable for windowing environments such as WINDOWS. Except for their use by a C++ compiler's run-time library, the MS-DOS video services are not used by the WINDOWS toolbox.

THE ROM BIOS VIDEO SERVICES

Because of the MS-DOS video services' shortcomings, many programmers have gone elsewhere to find video routines that offer the speed and versatility required by today's application programs. Fortunately, the ROM BIOS video services offer a wide variety of routines that are quite capable of meeting almost any application program's demands. Use of the ROM BIOS video services does limit a program's portability to IBM PCs and true compatibles, but because of a strong commitment by IBM and other manufacturers to maintain ROM BIOS compatibility, all of today's PC compatibles have ROM BIOSes that are upwardly compatible with the original IBM PC's ROM BIOS. Therefore, use of the ROM BIOS video services does not impose any real problems in porting a program from one member of the PC family to another.

```
 ┌─────────────────────────────────────────────────────┐
 │ Function Name              Function Code             │
 ├─────────────────────────────────────────────────────┤
 │ Set Video Mode                  00H                  │
 │ Set Cursor Type                 01H                  │
 │ Set Cursor Position             02H                  │
 │ Read Cursor Values              03H                  │
 │ Read Light Pen Position         04H                  │
 │ Select Display Page             05H                  │
 │ Scroll Window Up                06H                  │
 │ Scroll Window Down              07H                  │
 │ Read Character/Attribute Pair   08H                  │
 │ Write Character/Attribute Pairs 09H                  │
 │ Write Characters                0AH                  │
 │ Set Color Palette               0BH                  │
 │ Write Graphics Pixel            0CH                  │
 │ Read Graphics Pixel             0DH                  │
 │ Write Character in Teletype Mode 0EH                 │
 │ Get Video Mode                  0FH                  │
 └─────────────────────────────────────────────────────┘
```

Figure 1.1   The IBM PC ROM BIOS video functions

Using the ROM BIOS video services is as simple as loading a few parameters into the CPU's registers and making a call to INT 10H. Figure 1.1 outlines the ROM BIOS video services. Furthermore, Appendix B provides a complete description for all of the ROM BIOS video services. The following code fragment shows how the ROM BIOS **Set Cursor Position** function could be used to move the cursor to the upper left corner of the display screen:

Example 1.1

```
        .
        .
        .
mov     ah,2            ;AH=Set cursor position function code
mov     bh,0            ;BH=Page 0
mov     dh,0            ;DH=Top row of the display
mov     dl,0            ;DL=Left column of the display
int     10h             ;Set the new cursor position
        .
        .
        .
```

Perhaps the most important point to make about the previous program fragment is that the ROM BIOS video services' function code is always passed in register AH. Furthermore, when the video page number is required, it is usually passed in register BH. Instead of the two separate statements used in the previous code, a **mov dx,0** statement could have been used to pass the new cursor position. For that matter, an **xor dx,dx** statement would be an even more efficient way to pass the Row 0, Column 0 cursor position. Remember, any number **xor**ed with itself will always produce a result of zero. Thus, **xor**ing the DX register with itself will result in the correct coordinates being passed to the ROM BIOS video services.

DIRECT MEMORY ACCESS

Although the WINDOWS toolbox could be completely developed using the ROM BIOS video services, the ROM BIOS video services do not offer the speed required by certain time-critical functions (i.e., reading and writing to large portions of the display screen). Therefore, all time-critical WINDOWS functions will use direct memory access techniques to provide the necessary lightning-fast response times.

To understand how display memory is directly accessed, consider a detailed look at the IBM PC display adapters. The three major display adapters used by the IBM PC are the Monochrome Display Adapter (MDA), the Color Graphics Adapter (CGA), and the Enhanced Graphics Adapter (EGA). Although these three display adapters have a wide variety of differences, they share the important feature of all being memory-mapped devices. When a display adapter is a memory-mapped device, programs, with a few restrictions, can directly read from and write to the display adapter's memory by simply reading from and writing to a specific area of the computer's memory. Figure 1.2 presents a simple memory map for the IBM PC and the three display adapters just mentioned.

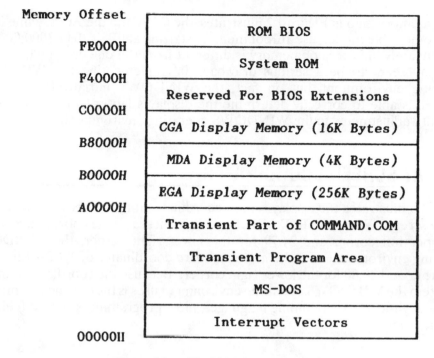

Memory Offset

	ROM BIOS
FE000H	System ROM
F4000H	Reserved For BIOS Extensions
C0000H	CGA Display Memory (16K Bytes)
B8000H	MDA Display Memory (4K Bytes)
B0000H	EGA Display Memory (256K Bytes)
A0000H	Transient Part of COMMAND.COM
	Transient Program Area
	MS-DOS
	Interrupt Vectors
000000H	

Figure 1.2   The IBM PC memory map

The Monochrome Display Adapter

The MDA is the most basic of the three display adapters. It only offers an 80-column by 25-row black-and-white text mode. The memory map in Figure 1.2 shows that the MDA uses 4K of memory, starting at 0B0000H (B000:0000H).

The Color Graphics and Enhanced Graphics Adapters

The CGA offers four text modes: 40-column by 25-row black-and-white, 40-column by 25-row color, 80-column by 25-row black-and-white, and 80-column by 25-row color. The CGA offers three graphics modes: 320-horizontal-pixel by 200-vertical-pixel four-color graphics, 320-horizontal-pixel by 200-vertical-pixel four-color graphics (without color burst), and 650-horizontal-pixel by 200-vertical-pixel two-color graphics. The EGA offers all seven CGA modes and more. Because this book deals with the 80-column by 25-row text modes, only the CGA compatible modes will be discussed in detail.

As the memory map in Figure 1.2 illustrates, the CGA and the EGA, while in the CGA compatible modes, use 16K of memory starting at 0B8000H (B800:0000H). Unfortunately, this area of memory is different from the one used by the MDA. This may seem to be a serious drawback in implementing the WINDOWS operating environment, but, in fact, the WINDOWS initialization function **settext80** is able to correctly determine the display adapter type and make the necessary adjustments to the WINDOWS operating environment.

DISPLAY SCREEN COORDINATES

Figure 1.3 illustrates the display screen coordinates for an 80-column by 25-row display screen. While the ROM BIOS video services use the coordinates 0,0 for the upper left corner and 24,79 for the lower right corner, the WINDOWS operating environment uses the more standard coordinates of 1,1 for the upper left corner and 25,80 for the lower right corner. Because the coordinate numbering system the WINDOWS operating environment uses is the one most commonly used by high-level programming languages, most programmers should feel right at home using it.

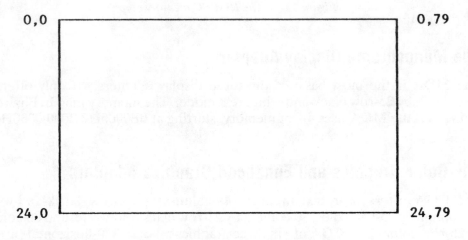

Figure 1.3   80-column by 25-row display screen coordinates

CHARACTER/ATTRIBUTE PAIRS

As shown in Figure 1.3, an 80-column by 25-row display screen is composed of 2000 individual display characters (80 columns * 25 rows = 2000); therefore, it would seem logical to assume that an 80-column by 25-row display screen would require 2000 bytes of display memory. Unfortunately, this assumption would be incorrect. The IBM PC display adapters use a system of character/attribute pairs to display each of the individual characters. The character portion of each character's character/attribute pair is simply its ASCII value. Accordingly, the first byte of screen memory would hold 4DH if an **M** is displayed in the upper left corner of the display screen. Figures 1.4 and 1.5 illustrate how the attribute byte for each display character's character/attribute pair is constructed. If the character in the upper left corner of the display screen has a normal (white character on a black background) attribute (07H), the second byte of screen memory holds the value of 07H.

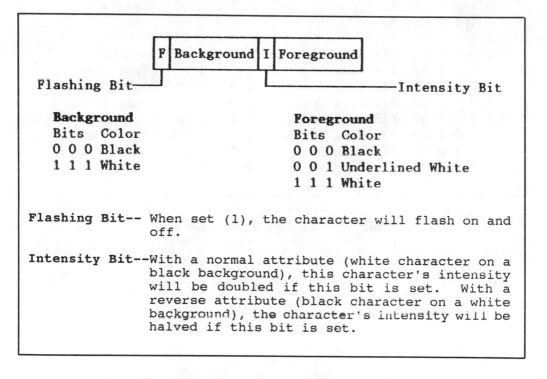

Figure 1.4   The monochrome display attributes

```
                    ┌─┬─┬─┬─┬─┬─┬─┬─┐
                    │F│R│G│B│I│R│G│B│
                    └─┴─┴─┴─┴─┴─┴─┴─┘
    Flashing Bit                    Blue Bit
         Red Bit                    Green Bit
       Green Bit                    Red Bit
        Blue Bit                    Intensity Bit
```

Background

F	R	G	B	Hex	Color
0	0	0	0	00	Black
0	0	0	1	01	Blue
0	0	1	0	02	Green
0	0	1	1	03	Cyan
0	1	0	0	04	Red
0	1	0	1	05	Magenta
0	1	1	0	06	Brown
0	1	1	1	07	White
1	0	0	0	08	Flashing Black
1	0	0	1	09	Flashing Blue
1	0	1	0	0A	Flashing Green
1	0	1	1	0B	Flashing Cyan
1	1	0	0	0C	Flashing Red
1	1	0	1	0D	Flashing Magenta
1	1	1	0	0E	Flashing Brown
1	1	1	1	0F	Flashing White

Foreground

I	R	G	B	Hex	Color
0	0	0	0	00	Black
0	0	0	1	01	Blue
0	0	1	0	02	Green
0	0	1	1	03	Cyan
0	1	0	0	04	Red
0	1	0	1	05	Magenta
0	1	1	0	06	Brown
0	1	1	1	07	White
1	0	0	0	08	Dark Gray
1	0	0	1	09	Light Blue
1	0	1	0	0A	Light Green
1	0	1	1	0B	Light Cyan
1	1	0	0	0C	Light Red
1	1	0	1	0D	Light Magenta
1	1	1	0	0E	Yellow
1	1	1	1	0F	Intense White

Figure 1.5   CGA and EGA attribute bytes

VIDEO MEMORY OFFSETS

To access a character's position in video memory, a method must be devised for figuring a character's video memory offset. A display character's video memory offset is figured by multiplying the character's row position by 160 (remember there are two bytes per character, so there are 160 bytes for each display screen row) and adding the character's column position to the result (*row* * 160 + *column*). For this method to work correctly, the ROM BIOS video services' coordinate system must be used for the row and column values. However, you can use the WINDOWS coordinate system just as easily be subtracting one from both the row and column numbers before applying them in the above formula. A display screen character's attribute offset is figured by using the above formula and adding one to the result (*row* * 160 + *column* + 1).

Although the MDA only provides enough memory for one display page, the CGA and EGA have sufficient memory for multiple display pages. To adjust the previous formulas for multiple display pages, the page number is multiplied by 4096 (each display page is allocated 4K of memory and not the minimum 4000 bytes of memory) and added to the character or attribute offset. The WINDOWS operating environment is set to page zero by its initialization routine, **settext80**. Thus, the additional complexity of having to take display pages into account is completely eliminated.

AVOIDING INTERFERENCE

To access a character's position in video memory, a method must be devised for figuring a character's video memory offset. A display character's video memory offset is figured by multiplying the character's row position by 160 (remember there are two bytes per character, so there are 160 bytes for each display screen row) and adding the character's column position to the result (*row* * 160 + *column*). For this method to work correctly, the ROM BIOS video services' coordinate system must be used for the row and column values. However, you can use the WINDOWS coordinate system just as easily by subtracting 1 from both the row and column numbers before applying them in the above formula. A display screen character's attribute offset is figured by using the above formula and adding 1 to the result (*row* * 160 + *column* + 1).

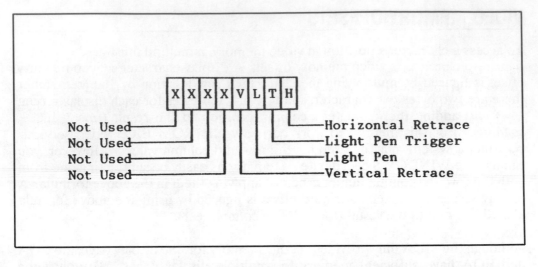

Figure 1.6   Video controller status register (port 03DAH)

The Horizontal Retrace Interval

Whenever the video controller is in the horizontal retrace interval, one byte of display memory can be safely accessed without unwanted snow appearing on the display screen. Figure 1.6 shows that bit 0 of the video controller's status register (port 03DAH) is set to 1 whenever the video controller is in the horizontal retrace interval. The following code fragment illustrates how this bit is used to successfully display a byte in AH to the display memory address in ES:DI.

Example 1.2

```
            .
            .
            .
            mov     dx,03dah        ;DX=Status port address
            cli                     ;Disable the interrupts
horizontal1:    in      al,dx           ;Get the controller's status
            and     al,1            ;Loop if already
            jnz     horizontal1     ; in horizontal retrace
horizontal2:    in      al,dx           ;Get the controller's status
            and     al,1            ;Loop till start
            jz      horizontal2     ; of horizontal retrace
            mov     es:[di],ah      ;Display the byte
            sti                     ;Enable the interrupts
            .
            .
            .
```

Because the horizontal retrace occurs in such a short period of time, the previous program fragment disables the interrupts before attempting to access display memory. If the interrupts weren't disabled, an interrupting routine (such as the system clock) could steal valuable execution speed from the previous algorithm. Thus, an ill-timed interrupt would defeat the algorithm's purpose by causing snow to appear on the display. Additionally, the previous code does not interrupt any horizontal retrace intervals that are already in progress. Attempting to access display memory during a partial horizontal retrace interval would almost certainly result in unwanted display interference.

The Vertical Retrace Interval

Although the horizontal retrace interval is useful for reading and writing a limited number of display characters, the inherent overhead in the previously mentioned algorithm makes it too slow to use for reading and writing an extensive amount of display characters. Fortunately, the vertical retrace interval is very well suited for displaying and reading a large number of characters in one operation. Figure 1.6 shows that bit 3 of the video controller's status register is set to 1 whenever the video controller is in its vertical retrace interval. Whenever the video controller goes into the vertical retrace interval, large areas of display memory can be accessed by disabling the video controller, performing the necessary display memory accesses, and re-enabling the video controller. Because the video controller's vertical retrace interval only lasts 1.25 milliseconds, the video memory accesses must be completed as quickly as possible, or a flickering screen could result. Because many of its low-level video functions are coded in assembly language, the WINDOWS operating environment totally eradicates screen flickering. The following program code demonstrates how to move an entire screen display from the memory buffer pointed to by DS:SI to the display memory pointed to by ES:DI.

Example 1.3

```
                    .
                    .
                    .
                mov     dx,3dah         ;DX=Controller status port
disable_cga1:   in      al,dx           ;Get controller status
                and     al,8            ;Loop if not
                jz      disable_cga1    ; in vertical retrace
                mov     dl,0d8h         ;DX=Control select register
                mov     al,25h          ;Disable
                out     dx,al           ; the CGA
        rep     movsw                   ;Move buffer contents
                push    ds              ;Save DS
                mov     ax,40h          ;Set DS to
                mov     ds,ax           ; ROM BIOS data segment
                mov     bx,65H          ;BX=Ctr mode select value pointer
                mov     al,[bx]         ;AL=Ctr mode select value
                out     dx,al           ;Reenable the CGA
                pop     ds              ;Restore DS
                    .
                    .
                    .
```

A few points of interest in the previous code fragment are the methods used to disable and re-enable the CGA. After determining that the video controller is in the vertical retrace interval, the CGA is disabled by simply sending a value of 25H to the video controller's select register (port 03D8H). As soon as the desired operation has been fully carried out, the video controller is re-enabled by sending the previous controller's select value to the video controller's select register. Fortunately, the ROM BIOS video driver stores the last value sent to the video controller select register at memory location 0040:0065H; therefore, the code in Example 1.3 retrieves the previously saved select value and sends it to the video controller to restore the controller's previous state.

THE WINDOWS APPROACH TO DISPLAY INPUT/OUTPUT

After examining the three basic text display methods, you can see that the MS-DOS video services do not provide sufficient speed and versatility for the WINDOWS operating environment. Although the ROM BIOS video services have sufficient versatility, their lack of speed in a number of areas limits their usefulness when implementing certain time-critical functions. Therefore, the WINDOWS operating environment uses a mixture of the ROM BIOS video services and direct memory access techniques. Such functions as display initialization, cursor positioning, and turning the cursor on and off will use the ROM BIOS video services. Other operations, such as reading from and writing to large segments of the display screen, filling large segments of the display screen with one particular character, and displaying strings, will be handled by direct memory access techniques. The WINDOWS operating environment uses a mixture of the available tools for the best possible blend of speed and programming ease.

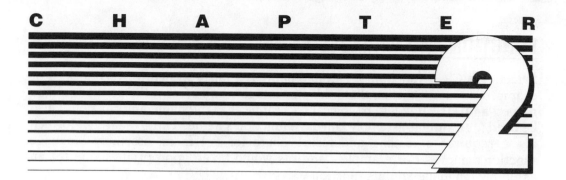

THE LOW-LEVEL ASSEMBLY LANGUAGE FUNCTIONS

As explained in Chapter 1, the time-critical WINDOWS functions must be coded in assembly language. Furthermore, a general-purpose keyboard input function must also be coded in assembly language. Although the low-level WINDOWS functions are coded using fairly simple assembly language programming techniques, their implementation is complicated by the way C++ calls an assembly language function. The C++ calling conventions require strict syntactic conformity with the C++ compiler's method of implementing function and variable names. Additionally, the C++ compiler's method of passing parameters to a function and returning values from a function must be strictly observed.

This chapter presents low-level assembly language routines to accomplish the following tasks: filling portions of the display screen with a specific character, setting the attributes for a portion of the display screen, saving a portion of the display screen in a memory buffer, redisplaying a previously buffered screen display, drawing a single- or double-line border around a portion of the display screen, and retrieving keyboard input.

FUNCTION AND VARIABLE NAMES

Selecting a C++ function or variable name is a fairly straightforward task. For example, a C++ function that adds two integers and returns the result could be named **addints**. It would be logical to assume that the name **addints** could also be used for a similar assembly language function's name. Unfortunately, Zortech C++ requires a leading underscore character (_) in an assembly language function's name. For example, _**addints** would be an appropriate name for an assembly language **addints** function.

In addition to adhering to the C++ compiler's naming conventions, an assembly language function or variable name must be made global before a C++ program can either call the function or reference the variable; therefore, all global assembly language function and variable names are declared **public**. By using a **public** declaration, the linker will be able to correctly link the assembly language functions and variables to any C++ functions that employ them.

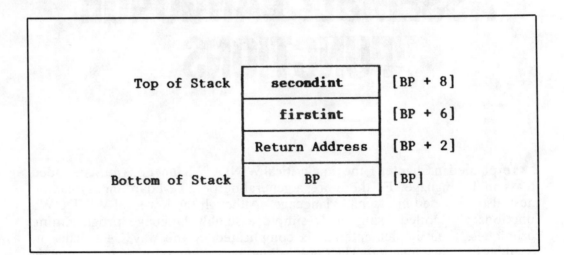

Figure 2.1   addints stack frame

PARAMETER PASSING

To pass parameters to an assembly language function, C++ builds a stack frame. Upon entry to the assembly language function, the stack frame consists of a return address (two bytes for **near** calls or four bytes for **far** calls) followed by the first parameter and the last parameter. An example stack frame for the **addints** function is presented in Figure 2.1. This stack frame assumes that **addints** is to be used with a compact or large memory model program and has a function prototype of **int addints(int firstint, int secondint);**. Because **addints** is accessed with a **far** call, the C++ compiler puts a four-byte return address on the bottom of the stack. To reference the passed parameters, the assembly language function first saves and then points register BP to the bottom of the stack as follows:

Example 2.1

```
                .
                .
                .
_addints proc   far
                push    bp              ;Save BP
                mov     bp,sp           ;Point it to the stack frame
                .
                .
                .
```

With register BP pointing to the bottom of the stack frame, **firstint** can be referenced by using the offset 6[bp]. Remember, register BP was pushed onto the stack below the four-byte return address; therefore, the first parameter is located six bytes from the bottom of the stack. Additionally, **secondint** can be referenced by using an offset of 8[bp]. By accessing the parameters through register BP offsets, the coding of the **addints** function can be continued as follows:

Example 2.2

```
              .
              .
              .
          mov     ax,6[bp]            ;Get the first integer into AX
          add     ax,8[bp]            ;Figure the result
              .
              .
              .
```

RETURNING TO THE CALLING PROGRAM

Now that **addints** has performed its intended function, it must return to the calling program with the calculated result. With Zortech C++, a value is returned to the calling program by placing the return value in a CPU register or combination of CPU registers. In the case of the **addints** function's integer result, the result is returned in the AX register. Because the **addints** function's result is already in register AX, no further steps are necessary to pass the value back to the calling program. However, suppose the result ended up in register BX instead of register AX. To return the value to the calling program, the **addints** function would be required to execute a **mov ax,bx** instruction before returning control to the calling C++ program.

In addition to preparing the return value, the **addints** function must clean up the stack before returning to the calling program. Because register BP was pushed onto the stack, it must be retrieved with a **pop bp** instruction. After retrieving register BP from the stack, the stack has been restored to its entry condition. Therefore, the **addints** function returns to the calling program by executing a **ret** instruction. The following program illustrates the remainder of the **addints** function's code:

Example 2.3

```
                  .
                  .
                  .
              pop     bp              ;Restore BP and the stack
              ret                     ;Return to the calling program
  _addints    endp
                  .
                  .
                  .
```

OTHER CONSIDERATIONS

Although not required by the **addints** function, many assembly language functions will require space for local variables. Local variable space is allocated by subtracting the required number of bytes from the stack pointer. Suppose the **addints** function had required local variable space for two integers (*row* and *col*). The following revision to the **addints** function would allocate the necessary local variable space:

Example 2.4

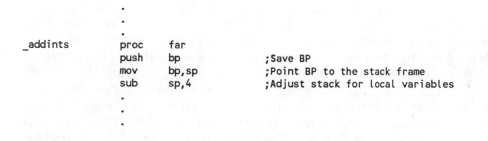

```
                 .
                 .
                 .
_addints         proc    far
                 push    bp              ;Save BP
                 mov     bp,sp           ;Point BP to the stack frame
                 sub     sp,4            ;Adjust stack for local variables
                 .
                 .
                 .
```

With the necessary local variable space allocated, the local variables can be referenced as negative offsets to the BP register. Thus, *row* and *col* could be referenced by the offsets -2[bp] and -4[bp]. It doesn't matter which location is selected for a variable; however, a variable's location must remain constant once it has been assigned.

Because the stack pointer is moved by the local variable space allocation, the assembly language function must deallocate the local variable space before attempting to restore register BP. Deallocation of the local variable space is accomplished by a simple **mov sp,bp** instruction. Recall that before the local variable space was allocated, registers BP and SP were pointing to the same memory location. Therefore, loading register SP with the pointer in register BP effectively removes the local variable space from the stack. The following code fragment shows how the modified **addints** function deallocates its local variable space before returning to the calling program:

Example 2.5

```
              .
              .
              .
        mov    sp,bp          ;Restore the stack pointer
        pop    bp             ;Restore BP
        ret                   ;Return to the calling program
_addints endp
              .
              .
              .
```

One last consideration must be taken into account by an assembly language function. Zortech C++ requires that certain CPU registers remain unaltered by an assembly language function; therefore, any unalterable registers used in an assembly language function must be saved on the stack at the start of the function and retrieved from the stack before returning to the calling program. Functions that do not require local variable space allocation should save the necessary registers just after the stack frame pointer has been set by the **mov bp,sp** instruction. The saved registers must be retrieved before register BP is restored during the function's exiting routine. Functions that do require local variable space allocation should save the required registers after the local variable space allocation has occurred. Accordingly, all of the saved registers must be retrieved before the assembly language function deallocates the local variable space. If the local variable space is deallocated first, the registers' contents will be lost, and erratic program execution is almost certain to result.

THE 80286 AND OTHERS

The 80286, 80386, V20, and V30 microprocessors all have additional assembly language instructions for handling stack frames. These instructions are the **enter** and **leave** instructions. The **enter** instruction automatically sets up register BP as the stack frame pointer and will allocate any necessary local variable space. The **leave** instruction will deallocate any previously allocated local variable space and restore register BP to its original value. Because the **enter** and **leave** instructions use less memory and are faster than their equivalents, they should be used whenever the computer is known to have a supporting microprocessor; further-more, using **enter** and **leave** greatly simplifies the implementation of the stack frame coding requirements. The following program fragment illustrates how the **addints** function could be rewritten to take advantage of the **enter** and **leave** instructions:

Example 2.6

```
            .
            .
            .
_addints proc   far
            enter   0,0           ;Set up the stack frame
            mov     ax,6[bp]      ;AX=First integer value
            add     ax,8[bp]      ;Figure the result
            leave                 ;Restore the stack
            ret                   ;Return
_addints endp
            .
            .
            .
```

Note that the code in the previous example does not allocate local variable space. To allocate local variable space with the **enter** instruction, the programmer indicates the required number of bytes with the first value in the **enter**'s operand field. Thus, four bytes of local variable space could be allocated with an **enter 4,0** instruction.

SOURCE LISTING: video.asm

Listing 2.1, **video.asm**, contains all of the low-level assembly language functions. To provide support for a wide variety of memory models and the 80286 microprocessor, **video.asm** makes extensive use of conditional assembly directives.

Listing 2.1: video.asm

```
;
; VIDEO.ASM - For the WINDOWS Toolbox
;             Low-Level Input/Output Assembly Language Routines
;
;

;
; Set BIGCODE and BIGDATA as follows:
;
; Memory Model   BIGCODE BIGDATA
;
; Small          0       0
; Medium         1       0
; Compact        0       1
; Large          1       1
```

continued...

```
BIGCODE          equ     0
BIGDATA          equ     0

                 ifdef   cpu286
                 .286
                 endif

;
; ROM BIOS Locations
;
bios_data        equ     40h
crt_mode_set     equ     65h


DGROUP           group   _DATA
_DATA            segment word public 'DATA'
                 assume  ds:DGROUP

                 public  __nonibm

__nonibm         dw      1
displayseg       dw      0b800h

_DATA            ends


                 if      bigcode
VIDEO_TEXT       segment word public 'CODE'
                 assume  cs:VIDEO_TEXT

                 extrn   _show_mouse:far, _hide_mouse:far

                 else
_TEXT            segment word public 'CODE'
                 assume  cs:_TEXT

                 extrn   _show_mouse:near, _hide_mouse:near

                 endif


                 public  _settext80,_fillscreen,_setattrib
                 public  _savescreen,_restorescreen,_drawbox
                 public  _printstring,_waitkey

;
; Set to 80 x 25 text mode
;
                 if      bigcode
_settext80       proc    far
                 else
_settext80       proc    near
```

continued...

```
                endif
                mov     ah,15           ;Get the
                int     10h             ; video mode
                cmp     al,2            ;Jump
                je      settext801      ; if
                cmp     al,3            ;   it's
                je      settext801      ;     already
                cmp     al,7            ;       a 80 x 25
                je      settext801      ;         video mode
                mov     ax,3            ;Set it to
                int     10h             ; 80 x 25 color
settext801:     mov     ax,0500h        ;Set the
                int     10h             ; page to 0
                mov     ah,12h          ;Check
                mov     bl,10h          ; for
                int     10h             ;   EGA
                cmp     bl,10h          ;Jump
                jne     settext803      ; if EGA
                mov     ah,15           ;Get the
                int     10h             ; video mode
                cmp     al,7            ;Jump
                je      settext802      ; if MDA
                mov     __nonibm,0      ;Flag IBM CGA
                jmp     short settext803 ;Jump
settext802:     mov     displayseg,0b000h ;Set the display segment address
settext803:     ret                     ;Return
_settext80      endp


;
; Fill text window
;
                if      bigcode
_fillscreen     proc    far
row1            equ     <6[bp]>
col1           equ     <8[bp]>
row2           equ     <10[bp]>
col2           equ     <12[bp]>
char           equ     <14[bp]>
att            equ     <16[bp]>
                else
_fillscreen     proc    near
row1            equ     <4[bp]>
col1           equ     <6[bp]>
row2           equ     <8[bp]>
col2           equ     <10[bp]>
char           equ     <12[bp]>
att            equ     <14[bp]>
                endif
rows           equ     <-2[bp]>
```

continued...

```
cols            equ     <-4[bp]>
                call    _hide_mouse     ;Hide the mouse pointer
                ifdef   cpu286
                enter   4,0             ;Set up the stack frame
                else
                push    bp              ;Save BP registers
                mov     bp,sp           ;Point it to the stack
                sub     sp,4            ;Reserve local space
                endif
                push    di              ;Save
                push    es              ; the registers
                mov     ax,row1         ;Figure
                mov     bx,col1         ; the
                call    fig_vid_off     ;  video offset
                mov     di,ax           ;DI=Video offset
                mov     es,displayseg   ;ES=Video segment
                mov     ax,row2         ;Figure
                sub     ax,row1         ; the number
                inc     ax              ;  of rows
                mov     rows,ax         ;Save it
                mov     ax,col2         ;Figure
                sub     ax,col1         ; the number
                inc     ax              ;  of columns
                mov     cols,ax         ;Save it
                cld                     ;Flag increment
                mov     al,byte ptr char ;AL=Display character
                mov     ah,byte ptr att ;AH=Display attribute
                call    disable_cga     ;Disable the CGA if necessary
fillscreen1:    push    di              ;Save the video offset
                mov     cx,cols         ;CX=Number of columns
        rep     stosw                   ;Display the row
                pop     di              ;Restore the video offset
                add     di,160          ;Point it to the next row
                dec     word ptr rows   ;Loop
                jnz     fillscreen1     ; till done
                call    enable_cga      ;Enable the CGA if necessary
                pop     es              ;Restore
                pop     di              ; the registers
                call    _show_mouse     ;Restore the mouse pointer
                ifdef   cpu286
                leave                   ;Restore the stack
                else
                mov     sp,bp           ;Reset the stack pointer
                pop     bp              ;Restore BP
                endif
                ret                     ;Return
_fillscreen     endp

;
; Set attributes
;
                if      bigcode
```

continued...

```
_setattrib      proc    far
row1            equ     <6[bp]>
col1            equ     <8[bp]>
row2            equ     <10[bp]>
col2            equ     <12[bp]>
att             equ     <14[bp]>
                else
_setattrib      proc    near
row1            equ     <4[bp]>
col1            equ     <6[bp]>
row2            equ     <8[bp]>
col2            equ     <10[bp]>
att             equ     <12[bp]>
                endif
rows            equ     <-2[bp]>
cols            equ     <-4[bp]>
                call    _hide_mouse     ;Hide the mouse pointer
                ifdef   cpu286
                enter   4,0             ;Set up the stack frame
                else
                push    bp              ;Save BP
                mov     bp,sp           ;Point it to the stack
                sub     sp,4            ;Save space for local data
                endif
                push    di              ;Save
                push    es              ; the registers
                mov     ax,row1         ;Figure
                mov     bx,col1         ; the
                call    fig_vid_off     ;  video offset
                mov     di,ax           ;DI=Video offset
                inc     di              ;Bump it to the first attribute
                mov     es,displayseg   ;ES=Video segment
                mov     ax,row2         ;Figure
                sub     ax,row1         ; the number
                inc     ax              ;  of rows
                mov     rows,ax         ;Save it
                mov     ax,col2         ;Figure
                sub     ax,col1         ; the number
                inc     ax              ;  columns
                mov     cols,ax         ;Save it
                cld                     ;Flag increment
                mov     al,byte ptr att ;AL=Display attribute
                call    disable_cga     ;Disable the CGA if necessary
setattrib1:     push    di              ;Save the video offset
                mov     cx,cols         ;CX=Number of columns
setattrib2:     stosb                   ;Set the attribute byte
                inc     di              ;Bump the video pointer
                loop    setattrib2      ;Loop till done
                pop     di              ;Restore the video offset
                add     di,160          ;Point it to the next row
                dec     word ptr rows   ;Loop
```

continued...

```
                jnz     setattrib1          ; till done
                call    enable_cga          ;Enable the CGA if necessary
                pop     es                  ;Restore
                pop     di                  ; the registers
                call    _show_mouse         ;Show the mouse pointer
                ifdef   cpu286
                leave                       ;Restore the stack
                else
                mov     sp,bp               ;Reset the stack pointer
                pop     bp                  ;Restore BP
                endif
                ret                         ;Return
_setattrib      endp

;
; Save screen
;
                if      bigcode
_savescreen     proc    far
row1            equ     <6[bp]>
col1            equ     <8[bp]>
row2            equ     <10[bp]>
col2            equ     <12[bp]>
array           equ     <14[bp]>
                else
_savescreen     proc    near
row1            equ     <4[bp]>
col1            equ     <6[bp]>
row2            equ     <8[bp]>
col2            equ     <10[bp]>
array           equ     <12[bp]>
                endif
rows            equ     <-2[bp]>
cols            equ     <-4[bp]>
                call    _hide_mouse         ;Hide the mouse pointer
                ifdef   cpu286
                enter   4,0                 ;Set up the stack frame
                else
                push    bp                  ;Save BP
                mov     bp,sp               ;Point it to the stack
                sub     sp,4                ;Make room for local data
                endif
                push    di                  ;Save
                push    si                  ; the
                push    es                  ;  registers
                mov     ax,row1             ;Figure
                mov     bx,col1             ; the
                call    fig_vid_off         ;  video offset
                mov     si,ax               ;SI=Video offset
                mov     ax,row2             ;Figure
                sub     ax,row1             ; the number
```

continued...

```
                inc     ax              ;  of rows
                mov     rows,ax         ;Save it
                mov     ax,col2         ;Figure
                sub     ax,col1         ; the number
                inc     ax              ;  of columns
                mov     cols,ax         ;Save it
                cld                     ;Flag increment
                call    disable_cga     ;Disable the CGA if necessary
                push    ds              ;Save DS
                if      bigdata
                les     di,array        ;ES:DI=Array Pointer
                else
                push    ds              ;Point ES
                pop     es              ; to the data segment
                mov     di,array        ;ES:DI=Array pointer
                endif
                mov     ds,displayseg   ;DS:SI=Video pointer
savescreen1:    push    si              ;Save the video offset
                mov     cx,cols         ;CX=Number of columns
        rep     movsw                   ;Save the row
                pop     si              ;Restore the video offset
                add     si,160          ;Point it to the next row
                dec     word ptr rows   ;Loop
                jnz     savescreen1     ; till done
                pop     ds              ;Restore DS
                call    enable_cga      ;Enable the CGA if necessary
                pop     es              ;Restore
                pop     si              ; the
                pop     di              ;  registers
                call    _show_mouse     ;Restore the mouse pointer
                ifdef   cpu286
                leave                   ;Restore the stack
                else
                mov     sp,bp           ;Reset the stack pointer
                pop     bp              ;Restore BP
                endif
                ret                     ;Return
_savescreen     endp

;
; Restore screen
;
                if      bigcode
_restorescreen  proc    far
row1            equ     <6[bp]>
col1           equ     <8[bp]>
row2           equ     <10[bp]>
col2           equ     <12[bp]>
array          equ     <14[bp]>
                else
_restorescreen  proc    near
row1           equ     <4[bp]>
```

continued...

```
col1            equ     <6[bp]>
row2            equ     <8[bp]>
col2            equ     <10[bp]>
array           equ     <12[bp]>
                endif
rows            equ     <-2[bp]>
cols            equ     <-4[bp]>
                call    _hide_mouse         ;Hide the mouse pointer
                ifdef   cpu286
                enter   4,0                 ;Set up the stack frame
                else
                push    bp                  ;Save BP
                mov     bp,sp               ;Point it to the stack
                sub     sp,4                ;Make room for local data
                endif
                push    di                  ;Save
                push    si                  ; the
                push    es                  ;  registers
                mov     ax,row1             ;Figure
                mov     bx,col1             ; the
                call    fig_vid_off         ;  video offset
                mov     di,ax               ;DI=Video offset
                mov     es,displayseg       ;ES=Video segment
                mov     ax,row2             ;Figure
                sub     ax,row1             ; the number
                inc     ax                  ;  of rows
                mov     rows,ax             ;Save it
                mov     ax,col2             ;Figure
                sub     ax,col1             ; the number
                inc     ax                  ;  of columns
                mov     cols,ax             ;Save it
                cld                         ;Flag increment
                call    disable_cga         ;Disable the CGA if necessary
                if      bigdata
                push    ds                  ;Save DS
                lds     si,array            ;DS:SI=Array pointer
                else
                mov     si,array            ;DS:SI=Array pointer
                endif
restorescreen1: push    di                  ;Save the video offset
                mov     cx,cols             ;CX=Number of columns
        rep     movsw                       ;Save the row
                pop     di                  ;Restore the video offset
                add     di,160              ;Point it to the next row
                dec     word ptr rows       ;Loop
                jnz     restorescreen1      ; till done
                if      bigdata
                pop     ds                  ;Restore DS
                endif
                call    enable_cga          ;Enable the CGA if necessary
                pop     es                  ;Restore
```

continued...

```
                pop     si              ; the
                pop     di              ;  registers
                call    _show_mouse     ;Restore the mouse pointer
                ifdef   cpu286
                leave                   ;Restore the stack
                else
                mov     sp,bp           ;Reset the stack pointer
                pop     bp              ;Restore BP
                endif
                ret                     ;Return
_restorescreen  endp


;
; Draw box
;
                if      bigcode
_drawbox        proc    far
row1            equ     <6[bp]>
col1            equ     <8[bp]>
row2            equ     <10[bp]>
col2            equ     <12[bp]>
flag            equ     <14[bp]>
att             equ     <16[bp]>
                else
_drawbox        proc    near
row1            equ     <4[bp]>
col1            equ     <6[bp]>
row2            equ     <8[bp]>
col2            equ     <10[bp]>
flag            equ     <12[bp]>
att             equ     <14[bp]>
                endif
rows            equ     <-2[bp]>
cols            equ     <-4[bp]>
                call    _hide_mouse     ;Hide the mouse pointer
                ifdef   cpu286
                enter   4,0             ;Set up the stack
                else
                push    bp              ;Save BP
                mov     bp,sp           ;Point it to the stack
                sub     sp,4            ;Save space for local data
                endif
                push    di              ;Save
                push    es              ; the registers
                mov     ax,row1         ;Figure
                mov     bx,col1         ; the
                call    fig_vid_off     ;  video offset
                mov     di,ax           ;DI=Video offset
                mov     es,displayseg   ;ES=Video segment
                mov     ax,row2         ;Figure
                sub     ax,row1         ; the number
```

continued...

```
            dec     ax                      ;  of rows - 2
            mov     rows,ax                 ;Save it
            mov     ax,col2                 ;Figure
            sub     ax,col1                 ; the number
            dec     ax                      ;  of columns - 2
            mov     cols,ax                 ;Save it
            cld                             ;Flag increment
            mov     ah,att                  ;AH=Display attribute
            call    disable_cga             ;Disable the CGA if necessary
            push    di                      ;Save the video offset
            mov     al,201                  ;AL=Double line character
            cmp     word ptr flag,0         ;Jump if
            je      drawbox1                ; double line
            mov     al,218                  ;AL=Single line character
drawbox1:   stosw                           ;Save the character/attribute pair
            mov     al,205                  ;AL=Double line character
            cmp     word ptr flag,0         ;Jump if
            je      drawbox2                ; double line
            mov     al,196                  ;AL=Single line character
drawbox2:   mov     cx,cols                 ;CX=Line length
       rep  stosw                           ;Display the line
            mov     al,187                  ;AL=Double line character
            cmp     word ptr flag,0         ;Jump if
            je      drawbox3                ; double line
            mov     al,191                  ;AL=Single line character
drawbox3:   stosw                           ;Save the character/attribute pair
            pop     di                      ;Restore the video pointer
            add     di,160                  ;Point it to the next row
drawbox4:   push    di                      ;Save the video pointer
            mov     al,186                  ;AL=Double line character
            cmp     word ptr flag,0         ;Jump if
            je      drawbox5                ; double line
            mov     al,179                  ;AL=Single line character
drawbox5:   stosw                           ;Save the character/attribute pair
            add     di,cols                 ;Point to
            add     di,cols                 ; the right side
            stosw                           ;Save the character/attribute pair
            pop     di                      ;Restore the video pointer
            add     di,160                  ;Point it to the next row
            dec     word ptr rows           ;Loop till the
            jnz     drawbox4                ; sides are complete
            mov     al,200                  ;AL=Double line character
            cmp     word ptr flag,0         ;Jump if
            je      drawbox6                ; double line
            mov     al,192                  ;AL=Single line character
drawbox6:   stosw                           ;Save the character/attribute pair
            mov     al,205                  ;AL=Double line character
            cmp     word ptr flag,0         ;Jump if
            je      drawbox7                ; double line
            mov     al,196                  ;AL=Single line character
```

continued...

```
drawbox7:        mov     cx,cols             ;CX=Line length
         rep     stosw                       ;Display the line
                 mov     al,188              ;AL=Double line character
                 cmp     word ptr flag,0     ;Jump if
                 je      drawbox8            ; double line
                 mov     al,217              ;AL=Single line character
drawbox8:        stosw                       ;Save the character/attribute pair
                 call    enable_cga          ;Enable the CGA if necessary
                 pop     es                  ;Restore
                 pop     di                  ; the registers
                 call    _show_mouse         ;Show the mouse pointer
                 ifdef   cpu286
                 leave                       ;Restore the stack
                 else
                 mov     sp,bp               ;Reset the stack pointer
                 pop     bp                  ;Restore BP
                 endif
                 ret                         ;Return
_drawbox         endp


;
; Display string
;
                 if      bigcode
_printstring     proc    far
row              equ     <6[bp]>
col              equ     <8[bp]>
string           equ     <10[bp]>
                 else
_printstring     proc    near
row              equ     <4[bp]>
col              equ     <6[bp]>
string           equ     <8[bp]>
                 endif
                 call    _hide_mouse         ;Hide the mouse pointer
                 ifdef   cpu286
                 enter   0,0                 ;Set up the stack frame
                 else
                 push    bp                  ;Save BP
                 mov     bp,sp               ;Point it to the stack
                 endif
                 push    si                  ;Save
                 push    di                  ; the
                 push    es                  ;  registers
                 mov     ax,row              ;Figure
                 mov     bx,col              ; the
                 call    fig_vid_off         ;  video offset
                 mov     di,ax               ;DI=Video offset
                 mov     es,displayseg       ;ES=Video segment
                 cld                         ;Flag increment
                 cmp     word ptr __nonibm,0 ;IBM CGA?
```

continued...

```
               if     bigdata
               push   ds                 ;Save DS
               lds    si,string          ;DS:SI=String pointer
               else
               mov    si,string          ;DS:SI=String pointer
               endif
               je     print_string2      ;Jump if IBM CGA
print_string1: lodsb                     ;Get the next character
               or     al,al              ;Jump
               jz     print_string6      ; if done
               stosb                     ;Display the character
               inc    di                 ;Bump the video pointer
               jmp    print_string1      ;Loop till done
print_string2: mov    dx,03dah           ;DX=Video status register
print_string3: lodsb                     ;Get the next character
               or     al,al              ;Jump
               jz     print_string6      ; if done
               mov    ah,al              ;Put it in AH
               cli                       ;Disable the interrupts
print_string4: in     al,dx              ;Loop
               and    al,1               ; if in
               jnz    print_string4      ;   horizontal retrace
print_string5: in     al,dx              ;Loop
               and    al,1               ; if not in
               jz     print_string5      ;   horizontal retrace
               mov    es:[di],ah         ;Display the character
               sti                       ;Reenable the interrupts
               inc    di                 ;Bump the
               inc    di                 ; video pointer
               jmp    print_string3      ;Loop till done
print_string6: if     bigdata
               pop    ds                 ;Restore DS
               endif
               pop    es                 ;Restore
               pop    di                 ; the
               pop    si                 ;   registers
               call   _show_mouse        ;Restore the mouse pointer
               ifdef  cpu286
               leave                     ;Restore the stack
               else
               pop    bp                 ;Restore BP
               endif
               ret                       ;Return
_printstring   endp

;
; Get a Key
;
               if     bigcode
_waitkey       proc   far
               else
```

continued...

```
_waitkey         proc    near
                 endif
                 mov     ah,01h              ;Has a key
                 int     16h                 ; been pressed?
                 jz      _waitkey            ;Loop if not
                 mov     ah,0                ;Get
                 int     16h                 ; the key
                 or      al,al               ;Jump if
                 jz      wait_key1           ; extended key
                 xor     ah,ah               ;Erase the scan code
                 jmp     short wait_key2     ;Jump
wait_key1:       xchg    ah,al               ;AX=Scan code
                 inc     ah                  ;AX=Scan code + 256
wait_key2:       ret                         ;Return
_waitkey         endp


;
; Figure video offset
;
fig_vid_off      proc    near
                 push    dx                  ;Save DX
                 push    bx                  ;Save the column
                 dec     ax                  ;Decrement the row
                 mov     bx,160              ;Figure the
                 mul     bx                  ; row offset
                 pop     bx                  ;Restore the column
                 dec     bx                  ;Decrement it
                 sal     bx,1                ;Figure the column pair offset
                 add     ax,bx               ;AX=Video offset
                 pop     dx                  ;Restore DX
                 ret                         ;Return
fig_vid_off      endp


;
; Disable CGA
;
disable_cga      proc    near
                 cmp     __nonibm,0          ;Jump if it
                 jne     disable_cga2        ; isn't an IBM CGA
                 push    ax                  ;Save the
                 push    dx                  ; registers
                 mov     dx,3dah             ;DX=Video status port
disable_cga1:    in      al,dx               ;Wait
                 and     al,8                ; for
                 jz      disable_cga1        ;  vertical retrace
                 mov     dl,0d8h             ;DX=Video select register port
                 mov     al,25h              ;Disable
                 out     dx,al               ; the video
                 pop     dx                  ;Restore
                 pop     ax                  ; the registers
disable_cga2:    ret                         ;Return
disable_cga      endp
```

continued...

```
;
; Enable CGA
;
enable_cga      proc    near
                cmp     __nonibm,0      ;Jump if it
                jne     enable_cga1     ; isn't an IBM CGA
                push    ax              ;Save
                push    bx              ; the
                push    dx              ;  registers
                push    ds              ;
                mov     ax,bios_data    ;Set the
                mov     ds,ax           ; data segment
                mov     bx,crt_mode_set ;BX=Video mode set value pointer
                mov     al,[bx]         ;AL=Video mode set value
                mov     dx,03d8h        ;DX=Video select register port
                out     dx,al           ;Reenable the video mode
                pop     ds              ;Restore
                pop     dx              ; the
                pop     bx              ;  registers
                pop     ax              ;
enable_cga1:    ret                     ;Return
enable_cga      endp

                if      bigcode
VIDEO_TEXT      ends
                else
_TEXT           ends
                endif

                end
```

Function Description: settext80

The **settext80** function initializes the WINDOWS operating environment. Its implementation is illustrated by the following pseudocode:

if (current video mode ! = 80 x 25 text mode)
*   set video mode to 80 x 25 color text mode*
switch (display adapter) {
*   case CGA:*
*   _nonibm = IBM CGA*
*   case MDA:*
*   display segment = 0xb000*
}

As the previous pseudocode and the actual program code illustrate, the **settext80** function could easily have been coded in C++ instead of in assembly language; however, good programming practice dictates that related functions should be grouped into a single program module. This keeps the linking requirements to a minimum and makes the WINDOWS toolbox easier to maintain.

Function Description: fillscreen

The **fillscreen** function fills a text window with a specified character/attribute pair. Its implementation is illustrated by the following pseudocode:

```
hide the mouse pointer
figure the video offset
figure the number of rows
figure the number of columns
disable the display adapter if it's an IBM CGA
for (i = 0; i < number of rows; i + +) {
    for (j = 0; j < number of columns; j + +) {
        display the character/attribute pair
    }
}
re-enable the display adapter if it's an IBM CGA
restore the mouse pointer
```

Function Description: setattrib

The **setattrib** function sets an entire text window's attributes to a specified attribute value. Its implementation is illustrated by the following pseudocode:

```
hide the mouse pointer
figure the video offset
bump the video offset to point to the first attribute byte
figure the number of rows
figure the number of columns
disable the display adapter if it's an IBM CGA
for (i = 0; i < number of rows; i + +) {
    for (j = 0; j < number of columns; j + +) {
        set the position's attribute
    }
}
re-enable the display adapter if it's an IBM CGA
restore the mouse pointer
```

Function Description: savescreen

The **savescreen** function saves the entire contents of a text window to a specified buffer area. Its implementation is illustrated by the following pseudocode:

```
hide the mouse pointer
figure the video offset
figure the number of rows
figure the number of columns
disable the display adapter if it's an IBM CGA
for (i = 0; i < number of rows; i + +) {
    for (j = 0; j < number of columns; j + +) {
        save a character/attribute pair in the buffer
    }
}
re-enable the display adapter if it's an IBM CGA
restore the mouse pointer
```

Function Description: restorescreen

The **restorescreen** function redisplays a previously buffered text window. Its implementation is illustrated by the following pseudocode:

```
hide the mouse pointer
figure the video offset
figure the number of rows
figure the number of columns
disable the display adapter if it's an IBM CGA
for (i = 0; i < number of rows; i + +) {
    for (j = 0; j < number of columns; j + +) {
        display a character/attribute pair
    }
}
re-enable the display adapter if it's an IBM CGA
restore the mouse pointer
```

Function Description: drawbox

The **drawbox** function draws a border around a text window. Its implementation is illustrated by the following pseudocode:

```
hide the mouse pointer
figure the video offset
figure the number of interior rows
figure the number of interior columns
disable the display adapter if it's an IBM CGA
display the upper left corner
for (i = 0; i < number of interior columns; i+ +) {
    display a horizontal line character
}
display the upper right corner
for (i = 0; i < number of interior rows; i+ +) {
    display the left side character
    display the right side character
}
display the lower left corner
for (i = 0; i < number of interior columns; i+ +) {
    display a horizontal line character
}
display the lower right corner
re-enable the display adapter if it's an IBM CGA
restore the mouse pointer
```

Function Description: printstring

The **printstring** function displays a string at a specified display screen position. Its implementation is illustrated by the following pseudocode:

```
hide the mouse pointer
figure the video offset
while (!(end of string)) {
    if (display adapter ! = IBM CGA) {
        display a character
    }
    else {
        while (in horizontal retrace) ;
        while (not in horizontal retrace) ;
        disable the interrupts
        display a character
        enable the interrupts
    }
}
restore the mouse pointer
```

Function Description: waitkey

The **waitkey** function waits for the operator to press a key. Once a key is pressed, the key's ASCII code is returned for nonextended keys or the key's scan code + 256 is returned for extended keys. The **waitkey** function's implementation is illustrated by the following pseudocode:

```
while (key not pressed) ;
get the key's value
if (extended key)
    return(scan code + 256)
else
    return (ASCII code)
```

Function Description: fig_vid_off

The **fig_vid_off** function is used internally by the other WINDOWS video functions to calculate video offsets. Its implementation is illustrated by the following pseudocode:

```
decrement the row number
figure the row offset (row * 160)
decrement the column number
figure the column offset (column * 2)
figure the video offset (row offset + column offset)
```

Function Description: disable_cga

The **disable_cga** function is used internally by the other WINDOWS video functions to disable IBM CGA display adapters. Its implementation is illustrated by the following pseudocode:

```
if (display adapter = = IBM CGA) {
    while (not in vertical retrace) ;
    disable the CGA
}
```

Function Description: enable_cga

The **enable_cga** function is used internally by the other WINDOWS video functions to enable a previously disabled IBM CGA. Its implementation is illustrated by the following pseudocode:

```
if (display adapter = = IBM CGA) {
    enable the CGA
}
```

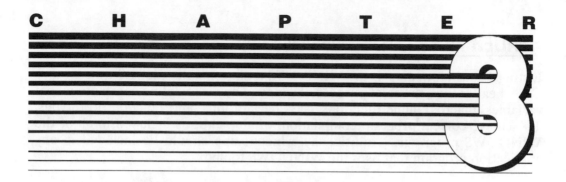

C H A P T E R

3

THE C++ INPUT/OUTPUT FUNCTIONS

Although Chapter 2 presented a diverse collection of low-level input/output functions, the WINDOWS toolbox implementation requires a number of other low-level input/output functions before it can support the higher level window and menu functions. Unlike the assembly language code used in Chapter 2, the remainder of the low-level input/output functions can be completely coded using C++. Thus, the remaining low-level input/output functions are easier to code and offer a much higher degree of portability. This chapter presents the low-level C++ functions for turning the cursor on and off, positioning the cursor, displaying single characters, and setting individual character attributes.

HEADER FILE LISTING: windows.hpp

Listing 3.1, **windows.hpp**, is the WINDOWS toolbox header file. Like most other
C++ header files, the chief purpose of **windows.hpp** is to define constants, global
variables, macros, inline functions, class declarations, and function prototypes.
To achieve correct program compilation, **windows.hpp** is included in all of the
WINDOWS programs. Additionally, **windows.hpp** should be included in any
application program that uses the WINDOWS toolbox.

Listing 3.1: windows.hpp

```
/******************************************************************************
* windows.hpp - For the WINDOWS Toolbox
*                Definition File
******************************************************************************/
#ifndef WINDOWS
#define WINDOWS

/* define NULL if not already defined */
#ifndef NULL
#ifdef LPTR
#define NULL 0L
#else
#define NULL 0
#endif
#endif

/* logic constants */
#define TRUE 1
#define FALSE 0

/* display type constants */
#define _IBM_CGA 0
#define _NONIBM_CGA 1

/* border line constants */
#define _DOUBLE_LINE 0
#define _SINGLE_LINE 1
#define _NO_BORDER 2

/* window constants */
#define _NO_CLEAR 0
#define _CLEAR 1
#define _NO_SCROLL 0
#define _SCROLL 1
#define _UP 0
#define _DOWN 1
#define _LEFT 2
#define _RIGHT 3
```

continued...

```
/* boolean data type */
typedef int boolean;

/* structure declarations */
typedef struct {
        char *string;
        int hotkey;
        void (*function)(void);
        void (*help)(void);
} MENU;

typedef struct {
        char *heading;
        int hotkey, number;
        MENU *mptr;
} MENU_HEAD;

typedef struct {
        int month, day, year;
} date;

typedef struct {
        int area, exchange, no;
} phone ;

typedef struct {
        int no1, no2, no3;
} ssn ;

/* class declarations */
class pointer {
public:
        pointer();
        ~pointer();
        void on(void);
        void off(void);
        void read(void);
        int row(void);
        int col(void);
        boolean lbutton(void);
        boolean rbutton(void);
};

class window {
private:
        int row1, col1, row2, col2, watt, bflg;
        char *buffer;
        boolean oflag, sflag;
        int orow, ocol, ostart, oend;
        int crow, ccol;
        int b_adj(int cols) { return(bflg != _NO_BORDER ? cols : 0); }
```

continued...

```
          int urow() { return(row1 + b_adj(1)); }
          int lcol() { return(col1 + b_adj(1)); }
          int brow() { return(row2 - b_adj(1)); }
          int rcol() { return(col2 - b_adj(1)); }
public:
          window(int r1 = 1, int c1 = 1, int r2 = 25, int c2 = 80, int w = 7,
                  int b = _NO_BORDER, int s = _NO_SCROLL);
          window(window &);
          ~window();
          void draw(void);
          void open(void);
          void close(void);
          void setcurpos(int, int);
          int currow(void) { return(crow); }
          int curcol(void) { return(ccol); }
          int p_row(int row) { return(urow() + row - 1); }
          int p_col(int col) { return(lcol() + col - 1); }
          void cls(void);
          void clreol(void);
          void scroll(int, int, boolean);
          void horizontal_bar(int, int);
          void vertical_bar(int, int);
          void print(char *);
          void println(char *);
          void printat(int, int, char *);
          void printlnat(int, int, char *);
};

class popup {
private:
          int row, col1;
          boolean ESC_flag;
public:
          popup(int, int, boolean e = FALSE);
          popup(popup &);
          int get(int, MENU *);
};

class dialog {
private:
          int row, col;
          boolean ESC_flag;
public:
          dialog(int, int, boolean e = FALSE);
          dialog(dialog &);
          int get(int, MENU *, int, ...);
};

class pulldown {
```

continued...

```
private:
        int row, number, *tabs;
        char *hotkeys;
        MENU_HEAD *menus;
        void (*menu_help)(void);
public:
        pulldown(int, int, MENU_HEAD *, void(*m_h)(void) = NULL);
        pulldown(pulldown &);
        void display(void);
        int get(int);
};

/* external variable declarations */
extern int _nonibm;
extern int _mouse_x, _mouse_y;
extern _left_button, _right_button;
extern pointer mouse;
extern int _menu_att, _menu_hotkey, _menu_highlight;

/* macro definitions */
#define clearone(row, col, att) fillone(row, col, ' ', att)
#define clearscreen(row1, col1, row2, col2, att)\
        fillscreen(row1, col1, row2, col2, ' ', att)

/* inline function definitions */
#ifndef max
inline int max(int a, int b) { return(a > b ? a : b); }
#endif
#ifndef min
inline int min(int a, int b) { return(a < b ? a : b); }
#endif

/* function prototypes */
void cursoroff(void);
void cursoron(void);
char *date_string(char *, date &);
void display_date(int, int, date &);
void display_dollar(int, int, int, double &);
void display_number(int, int, int, unsigned long &);
void display_phone(int, int, phone &);
void display_ssn(int, int, ssn &);
void display_string(int, int, int, char *);
void drawbox(int, int, int, int, int, int);
void fillone(int, int, int, int);
void fillscreen(int, int, int, int, int, int);
void hide_mouse(void);
void hotstring(int, int, int, char *);
int input_date(int, int, date &);
int input_dollar(int, int, int, double &);
int input_number(int, int, int, unsigned long &);
int input_phone(int, int, phone &);
int input_ssn(int, int, ssn &);
```

continued...

```
int input_string(int, int, int, char *);
void getcurpos(int *, int *, int *, int *);
char *phone_string(char *, phone &);
void printcenter(int, int, char *);
void printone(int, int, int);
void printstring(int, int, char *);
void read_mouse(void);
void reset_mouse(void);
void restorescreen(int, int, int, int, char *);
void save_initial_video(void);
void savescreen(int, int, int, int, char *);
void setattrib(int, int, int, int, int);
void setone(int, int, int);
void setcurpos(int, int);
void setcursor(int, int);
void settext80(void);
void show_mouse(void);
char *ssn_string(char *, ssn &);
int waitkey(void);

#endif
```

SOURCE LISTING: lowlevel.cpp

Listing 3.2, **lowlevel.cpp**, contains all of the low-level C++ video functions. These functions support such diverse operations as turning the cursor on and off; positioning the cursor; displaying single characters, attributes, and character/attribute pairs; and centering strings.

Listing 3.2: lowlevel.cpp

```
/**************************************************************************
* lowlevel.cpp - For the WINDOWS Toolbox
*                Low-Level Input/Output Routines
**************************************************************************/
#include <stdio.h>
#include <dos.h>
#include <string.h>
#include "windows.hpp"

static void initcur(void);

static int cursorstart = -1, cursorend = -1;
```

continued...

```
void cursoroff()
{
        union REGS regs;

        initcur();
        regs.h.ah = 1;
        regs.x.cx = 0x2000;
        int86(0x10, &regs, &regs);
}

void cursoron()
{
        union REGS regs;

        initcur();
        regs.h.ah = 1;
        regs.h.ch = cursorstart;
        regs.h.cl = cursorend;
        int86(0x10, &regs, &regs);
}

void setcurpos(int row, int col)
{
        union REGS regs;

        regs.h.ah = 2;
        regs.h.bh = 0;
        regs.h.dh = --row;
        regs.h.dl = --col;
        int86(0x10, &regs, &regs);
}

void setcursor(int cstart, int cend)
{
        cursorstart = cstart;
        cursorend = cend;
        cursoron();
}

void getcurpos(int *row, int *col, int *cstart, int *cend)
{
        union REGS regs;

        regs.h.ah = 3;
        regs.h.bh = 0;
        int86(0x10, &regs, &regs);
        *row = ++regs.h.dh;
        *col = ++regs.h.dl;
        *cstart = regs.h.ch;
        *cend = regs.h.cl;
}
```

continued...

```
void fillone(int row, int col, int chr, int att)
{
        union REGS regs;

        setcurpos(row, col);
        regs.h.ah = 9;
        regs.h.al = chr;
        regs.h.bh = 0;
        regs.h.bl = att;
        regs.x.cx = 1;
        int86(0x10, &regs, &regs);
}

void printone(int row, int col, int chr)
{
        union REGS regs;

        setcurpos(row, col);
        regs.h.ah = 10;
        regs.h.al = chr;
        regs.h.bh = 0;
        regs.x.cx = 1;
        int86(0x10, &regs, &regs);
}

void setone(int row, int col, int att)
{
        union REGS regs;

        setcurpos(row, col);
        regs.h.ah = 8;
        regs.h.bh = 0;
        int86(0x10, &regs, &regs);
        regs.h.ah = 9;
        regs.h.bl = att;
        regs.x.cx = 1;
        int86(0x10, &regs, &regs);
}

void printcenter(int row, int col, char *string)
{
        printstring(row, col - (strlen(string) >> 1), string);
}

static void initcur()
{
        union REGS regs;
```

continued...

```
        if (cursorstart == -1 && cursorend == -1) {
                regs.h.ah = 3;
                regs.h.bh = 0;
                int86(0x10, &regs, &regs);
                cursorstart = regs.h.ch;
                cursorend = regs.h.cl;
        }
}
```

Function Description: cursoroff

The **cursoroff** function turns the blinking cursor character off. Its implementation is illustrated by the following pseudocode:

if (called for the first time) {
*   save the cursor character's starting and ending lines*
}
use the ROM BIOS to turn the cursor off

Function Description: cursoron

The **cursoron** function turns the blinking cursor character on. Its implementation is illustrated by the following pseudocode:

If (called for the first time) {
*   save the cursor character's starting and ending lines*
}
use the ROM BIOS to turn the cursor on

Function Description: setcurpos

The **setcurpos** function sets the display screen's cursor position. Its implementation is illustrated by the following pseudocode:

decrement the row
decrement the column
use the ROM BIOS to position the cursor

Function Description: setcursor

The **setcursor** function sets the cursor character's starting and ending lines. Its implementation is illustrated by the following pseudocode:

save the cursor character's new starting line
save the cursor character's new ending line
use the **cursoron** *function to perform the action*

Function Description: getcurpos

The **getcurpos** function retrieves the cursor's row position, column position, starting line, and ending line. Its implementation is illustrated by the following pseudocode:

use the ROM BIOS to get the cursor values
bump the row position
bump the column position
return the cursor values

Function Description: fillone

The **fillone** function displays a character/attribute pair at a specified display screen position. Its implementation is illustrated by the following pseudocode:

set the cursor position
use the ROM BIOS to display the character/attribute pair

Function Description: printone

The **printone** function displays a character at a specified display screen position. Its implementation is illustrated by the following pseudocode:

set the cursor position
use the ROM BIOS to display the character

Function Description: setone

The **setone** function sets the attribute for a specified display screen position. Its implementation is illustrated by the following pseudocode:

set the cursor position
use the ROM BIOS to get the position's character
use the ROM BIOS to display the character/attribute pair

Function Description: printcenter

The **printcenter** function centers a string on a specified display screen position. Its implementation is illustrated by the following pseudocode:

use the **printstring** *function to display the string at the*
    position defined by (column - (length of the string / 2))

Function Description: initcur

The **initcur** function saves the initial cursor character's starting and ending lines. The **initcur** function is used internally only by the **cursoroff** and **cursoron** functions. Its implementation is illustrated by the following pseudocode:

if (the initial values haven't been saved) {
    use the ROM BIOS to get the cursor values
    save the cursor character's starting line
    save the cursor character's ending line
}

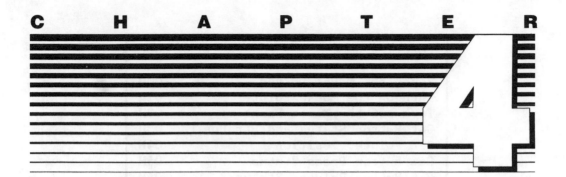

POINTING DEVICES

This chapter presents the low-level C++ mouse routines and defines a class of pointer objects. In addition to the computer keyboard, many of today's state-of-the-art application programs use pointing devices for a wide variety of input operations: program navigation, drawing, marking blocks of text, etc. Although the joystick was the first pointing device to be used with IBM PCs and compatibles, the mouse and its close cousin the trackball have usurped the joystick's position as the pointing device of choice. Because the mouse has become such an accepted part of today's computer systems, almost all of today's application programs provide at least a minimal amount of mouse support. To allow the WINDOWS application program to exploit a mouse's many desirable traits, this chapter presents the C++ functions for incorporating a Microsoft-compatible mouse into the WINDOWS operating environment. To enable you to fully understand how the WINDOWS toolbox implements the mouse functions, this chapter first takes a further look at the Microsoft mouse driver.

Function Name	Function Code
Reset the Mouse Driver	00H
Turn on the Mouse Pointer	01H
Turn off the Mouse Pointer	02H
Get Button Status and Ptr Pos	03H
Set Pointer Position	04H
Get Button Press Status	05H
Get Button Release Status	06H
Set Horizontal Limits	07H
Set Vertical Limits	08H
Set Graphic Shape	09H
Set Text Pointer Type	0AH
Get Motion Count	0BH
Set User-Defined Event Handler	0CH
Turn on Light Pen Emulation	0DH
Turn off Light Pen Emulation	0EH
Set Mickey:Pixels Ratios	0FH
Set Exclusion Area	10H
Set Double Speed Threshold	13H
Swap User-Defined Event Handlers	14H
Get Mouse Status Buffer Size	15H
Save Mouse Driver Status	16H
Restore Mouse Driver Status	17H
Set Alt Event Handler	18H
Get Alt Event Handler's Address	19H
Set Sensitivity	1AH
Get Sensitivity	1BH
Set Interrupt Rate	1CH
Set Pointer Display Page	1DH
Get Pointer Display Page	1EH
Disable Mouse Driver	1FH
Enable Mouse Driver	20H
Reset Mouse Driver	21H
Set Language	22H
Get Language Code	23H
Get Mouse Information	24H

Figure 4.1   The Microsoft mouse driver functions

THE MICROSOFT MOUSE DRIVER

The Microsoft mouse driver presents a wide variety of mouse routines that can meet the needs of even the most demanding application program. Like the ROM BIOS video services, the Microsoft mouse driver routines are called by an **INT** call. Instead of a call to the ROM BIOS video services' INT 10H, the Microsoft mouse driver routines are called by issuing a call to INT 33H. Figure 4.1 outlines the Microsoft mouse driver routines. Furthermore, Appendix C provides a complete description for all of the Microsoft mouse driver routines. Although the list of mouse routines in Figure 4.1 may seem a bit formidable, most application programs only employ a small fraction of the available mouse routines. Thus, effectively incorporating a mouse into a program's user interface is a surprisingly easy task.

SOURCE LISTING: mouse.cpp

Listing 4.1, **mouse.cpp**, presents the low-level mouse routines for resetting the mouse driver, turning the mouse pointer on and off, and retrieving the mouse's button status and pointer location.

Listing 4.1: mouse.cpp

```
/*******************************************************************************
* mouse.cpp - For the WINDOWS Toolbox
*             Text Pointer Routines
*******************************************************************************/
#include <dos.h>
#include "windows.hpp"

int _mouse_x, _mouse_y;
int _left_button, _right_button;
static boolean mouse_flag = FALSE;

void reset_mouse(void)
{
        union REGS regs;

        regs.x.ax = 0;
        int86(0x33, &regs, &regs);
        mouse_flag = regs.x.ax;
}
```

continued...

```
void show_mouse(void)
{
        union REGS regs;

        if (mouse_flag) {
                regs.x.ax = 1;
                int86(0x33, &regs, &regs);
        }
}


void hide_mouse(void)
{
        union REGS regs;

        if (mouse_flag) {
                regs.x.ax = 2;
                int86(0x33, &regs, &regs);
        }
}


void read_mouse(void)
{
        union REGS regs;

        _left_button = _right_button = FALSE;
        _mouse_x = _mouse_y = 0;
        if (mouse_flag) {
                regs.x.ax = 3;
                int86(0x33, &regs, &regs);
                if (regs.x.bx & 1)
                        _left_button = TRUE;
                if (regs.x.bx & 2)
                        _right_button = TRUE;
                _mouse_x = regs.x.cx;
                _mouse_y = regs.x.dx;
        }
}
```

Function Description: reset_mouse

The **reset_mouse** function resets the mouse driver. Additionally, the **reset_mouse** function determines whether or not a mouse is attached to the computer. Its implementation is illustrated by the following pseudocode:

call the mouse driver's reset routine
save the mouse's status in **mouse_flag**

Function Description: show_mouse

The **show_mouse** function turns on the mouse pointer. Its implementation is illustrated by the following pseudocode:

```
if (mouse is attached) {
    turn on the mouse pointer
}
```

Function Description: hide_mouse

The **hide_mouse** function turns off the mouse pointer. Its implementation is illustrated by the following pseudocode:

```
if (mouse is attached) {
    turn off the mouse pointer
}
```

Function Description: read_mouse

The **read_mouse** function retrieves the mouse's button status and pointer position. Its implementation is illustrated by the following pseudocode:

```
left button = released
right button = released
mouse x-coordinate = 0
mouse y-coordinate = 0
if (mouse is attached) {
    get the mouse values
    save the left button status
    save the right button status
    save the x-coordinate
    save the y-coordinate
}
```

SOURCE LISTING: pointer.cpp

Although the mouse functions in **mouse.cpp** are all that are necessary to incorporate a mouse into the WINDOWS operating environment, Listing 4.2, **pointer.cpp**, provides the C++ functions for an entire class of pointer objects. Because these pointer functions allow access to the mouse as an abstract data object, the higher level WINDOWS functions can be easily customized to fit a particular application program's requirements. For example, the WINDOWS toolbox could just as easily be customized for a joystick by simply making a few minor changes to the pointer object's code. This ability to easily customize the WINDOWS toolbox is a direct result of C++'s support for object-oriented programming. After all, changing the pointing device in a C implementation of the WINDOWS toolbox would require a major rewrite of the complete toolbox. Fortunately, the power of object-oriented programming will allow a major change in the WINDOWS operating environment without a corresponding need to rewrite the entire toolbox.

Listing 4.2: pointer.cpp

```
/*****************************************************************************
* pointer.cpp - For the WINDOWS Toolbox
*                Text Pointer Routines
*****************************************************************************/
#include <dos.h>
#include "windows.hpp"

pointer::pointer()
{
        reset_mouse();
}

pointer::~pointer()
{
        hide_mouse();
}
void pointer::on(void)
{
        show_mouse();
}

void pointer::off(void)
{
        hide_mouse();
}
```

continued...

```
void pointer::read(void)
{
        read_mouse();
}

int pointer::row(void)
{
        return(_mouse_y / 8 + 1);
}

int pointer::col(void)
{
        return(_mouse_x / 8 + 1);
}

int pointer::lbutton(void)
{
        return(_left_button);
}

int pointer::rbutton(void)
{
        return(_right_button);
}

pointer mouse;
```

Constructor Description: pointer::pointer

The **pointer::pointer** constructor resets the pointer object's driver. Its implementation is illustrated by the following pseudocode:

reset the mouse driver

Destructor Description: pointer::~pointer

The **pointer::~pointer** destructor turns off the pointer object's display screen pointer. Its implementation is illustrated by the following pseudocode:

turn off the mouse pointer

Function Description: pointer::on

The **pointer::on** function turns on the pointer object's display screen pointer. Its implementation is illustrated by the following pseudocode:

turn on the mouse pointer

Function Description: pointer::off

The **pointer::off** function turns off the pointer object's display screen pointer. Its implementation is illustrated by the following pseudocode:

turn off the mouse pointer

Function Description: pointer::read

The **pointer::read** function reads the pointer object's button status and display screen pointer position. Its implementation is illustrated by the following pseudocode:

retrieve the mouse's button status and pointer position

Function Description: pointer::row

The **pointer::row** function returns the pointer object's row position. Its implementation is illustrated by the following pseudocode:

return(mouse y_coordinate / 8 + 1)

Function Description: pointer::col

The **pointer::col** function returns the pointer object's column position. Its implementation is illustrated by the following pseudocode:

return(mouse x_coordinate / 8 + 1)

Function Description: pointer::lbutton

The **pointer::lbutton** function returns the pointer object's left button status. Its implementation is illustrated by the following pseudocode:

return(mouse's left button status)

Function Description: pointer::rbutton

The **pointer::rbutton** function returns the pointer object's right button status. Its implementation is illustrated by the following pseudocode:

return(mouse's right button status)

Object Description: mouse

The **mouse** object is a predefined pointer object. By employing **mouse** in an application program, the application programmer can easily incorporate the mouse into the application program by simply accessing the mouse as an abstract data object.

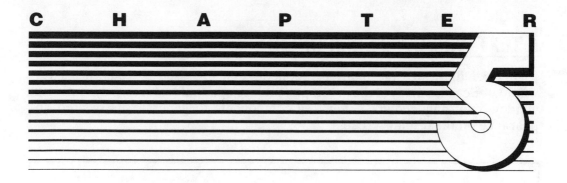

THE DYNAMIC WINDOW FUNCTIONS

Using the low-level input/output functions presented in Chapters 2 and 3 as a set of basic building blocks, this chapter presents the C++ functions for a class of dynamic text window objects. These dynamic text window functions perform such diverse operations as opening windows, closing windows, drawing windows, displaying horizontal and vertical scroll bars, scrolling windows, clearing windows, displaying window strings, and more. Text window components and the C++ dynamic memory management operators are discussed before the dynamic window functions' source code is introduced so you will better understand how these functions operate.

A TEXT WINDOW'S COMPONENTS

Figure 5.1 illustrates the many components that are used to construct a text window. Because many of these components are optional features, a dynamic text window may only require a few key components to generate its desired appearance on the display screen.

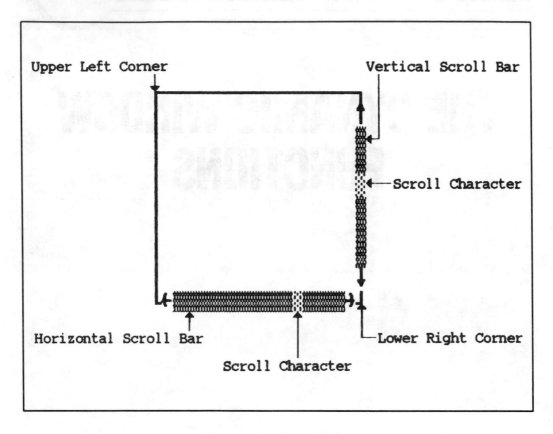

Figure 5.1   A text window

Following are more detailed explanations of these components:

- **Upper Left and Lower Right Coordinates:** The upper left and lower right coordinates are used to define a text window's size and screen position. A text window can be as small as a single character or as large as the whole screen.

- **Border:** The WINDOWS toolbox supports both single- and double-lined window borders. Note that borders are an optional text window component.

- **Horizontal Scroll Bar:** A horizontal scroll bar is used by the text window to indicate the cursor's current line position. Because a text window may not be wide enough to display an entire line, a horizontal scroll bar provides a very useful visual aid for indicating the displayed portion's relation to the whole line. Note that horizontal scroll bars are an optional text window component.

- **Vertical Scroll Bar:** A vertical scroll bar is used by the text window to indicate the cursor's current file position. Because a text window may not be tall enough to display an entire file, a vertical scroll bar provides a useful visual aid for indicating the displayed portion's relation to the whole file. Note that vertical scroll bars are an optional text window component.

THE C++ DYNAMIC MEMORY MANAGEMENT OPERATORS

Before it actually displays a text window, the WINDOWS toolbox must first save the current text window's portion of the display screen. If the current contents of the text window are not saved, the WINDOWS toolbox would not be able to properly restore a closed text window's portion of the display screen. Because the WINDOWS operating environment can't possibly know in advance the number and size of an application program's windows, the WINDOWS toolbox makes extensive use of the C++ dynamic memory management operators to obtain and release text window buffer space.

The C++ programming language provides two dynamic memory management operators called **new** and **delete**. The **new** operator is used to dynamically allocate a memory block. The following program demonstrates how **new** might be used to allocate space for a 100-element array of type **int**:

Example 5.1

```
#include <stdio.h>
#include <stdlib.h>

int *intarray;

main()
{
        /* Allocate space for a 100 element integer array */
        intarray = new int[100];
        if (intarray == NULL)
                printf("Not enough memory to allocate the requested array\n");
        else
                printf("A 100 element integer array has been allocated space\n");
        exit(0);
}
```

Example 5.1 illustrates that **new** returns a **NULL** pointer if it is unable to allocate an adequate amount of memory space; therefore, allocation errors can be easily trapped by performing a NULL pointer check.

The **delete** operator releases a previously allocated memory block. The program in Example 5.2 demonstrates how the **delete** operator might be used to deallocate a 25-element array of type **float**:

Example 5.2

```
#include <stdio.h>
#include <stdlib.h>

float *fltarray;

main()
{
        /* Allocate space for a 25 element float array */
        fltarray = new float[25];
        if (fltarray == NULL) {
                printf("Memory allocation failed\n");
                exit(1);
        }

        /* Release the array's allocated memory space */
        delete fltarray;
        exit(0);
}
```

With the dynamic memory management operators shown in Examples 5.1 and 5.2 at its disposal, the WINDOWS toolbox can dynamically open and close text windows. Before it displays a text window, WINDOWS allocates a memory block large enough to hold the current contents of the text window. After successfully allocating the memory block, WINDOWS saves the text window's current contents by using the **savescreen** function (see Chapter 2). When it is time to close the text window, WINDOWS restores the text window's former contents by using the **restorescreen** function (see Chapter 2). Redisplaying the former contents is followed by releasing the text window's dynamically allocated memory block.

SOURCE LISTING: window.cpp

Listing 5.1, **window.cpp**, presents the functions for a class of dynamic text window objects. These functions permit opening and closing text windows, drawing text windows, displaying horizontal and vertical scroll bars, scrolling text windows, clearing text windows, displaying window strings, and more.

Listing 5.1: window.cpp

```
/*****************************************************************************
 * Window.cpp - For the WINDOWS Toolbox
 *               Dynamic Window Routines
 *****************************************************************************/
#include <string.h>
#include "windows.hpp"

window::window(int r1, int c1, int r2, int c2, int w, int b, int s)
{
        row1 = r1;
        col1 = c1;
        row2 = r2;
        col2 = c2;
        watt = w;
        bflg = b;
        sflag = s;
        oflag = FALSE;
}
```

continued...

```
window::window(window &arg)
{
        row1 = arg.row1;
        col1 = arg.col1;
        row2 = arg.row2;
        col2 = arg.col2;
        watt = arg.watt;
        bflg = arg.bflg;
        sflag = arg.sflag;
        buffer = arg.buffer;
        oflag = arg.oflag;
        orow = arg.orow;
        ocol = arg.ocol;
        ostart = arg.ostart;
        oend = arg.oend;
        crow = arg.crow;
        ccol = arg.ccol;
}

window::~window()
{
        if (oflag)
                close();
}

void window::draw(void)
{
        if (!watt)
                return;
        clearscreen(row1, col1, row2, col2, watt);
        if (bflg != _NO_BORDER)
                drawbox(row1, col1, row2, col2, bflg, watt);
}

void window::open(void)
{
        buffer = new char[(col2 - col1 + 1) * 2 * (row2 - row1 + 1)];
        savescreen(row1, col1, row2, col2, buffer);
        if (watt)
                draw();
        oflag = TRUE;
        getcurpos(&orow, &ocol, &ostart, &oend);
        if (ostart < 32)
                cursoroff();
        setcurpos(1, 1);
}
```

continued...

```
void window::close(void)
{
        if (oflag) {
                restorescreen(row1, col1, row2, col2, buffer);
                delete buffer;
                oflag = FALSE;
                ::setcurpos(orow, ocol);
                if (ostart < 32)
                        cursoron();
        }
}

void window::setcurpos(int row, int col)
{
        if (oflag) {
                crow = row;
                ccol = col;
                ::setcurpos(p_row(crow), p_col(ccol));
        }
}

void window::cls(void)
{
        if (oflag) {
                clearscreen(urow(), lcol(), brow(), rcol(), watt);
                setcurpos(1, 1);
        }
}

void window::clreol(void)
{
        if (oflag)
                clearscreen(p_row(crow), p_col(ccol), p_row(crow), rcol(), watt);
}

void window::scroll(int num, int dir, boolean clear)
{
        int i, rows, cols;
        char *scrollbuffer;

        cols = (rcol() - lcol() + 1) * 2;
        rows = brow() - urow() + 1;
        scrollbuffer = new char[cols * rows];
        savescreen(urow(), lcol(), brow(), rcol(), scrollbuffer);
        switch (dir) {
                case _UP:
                        for (i = urow() + num; i < brow() + 1; i++)
                                memmove(scrollbuffer + (i - num - urow()) * cols,
                                        scrollbuffer + (i - urow()) * cols, cols);
                        break;
```

continued...

```
                case _DOWN:
                        for (i = brow(); i >= urow() + num; i--)
                                memmove(scrollbuffer + (i - urow()) * cols,
                                        scrollbuffer + (i - num - urow()) * cols, cols);
                        break;
                case _LEFT:
                        for (i = urow(); i <= brow(); i++)
                                memmove(scrollbuffer + (i - urow()) * cols,
                                        scrollbuffer + (i - urow()) * cols + num * 2,
                                        cols - num * 2);
                        break;
                default:
                        for (i = urow(); i <= brow(); i++)
                                memmove(scrollbuffer + (i - urow()) * cols + num * 2,
                                        scrollbuffer + (i - urow()) * cols,
                                        cols - num * 2);
        }
        restorescreen(urow(), lcol(), brow(), rcol(), scrollbuffer);
        if (clear) {
                switch (dir) {
                        case _UP:
                                clearscreen(brow() - num + 1, lcol(), brow(), rcol(),
                                        watt);
                                break;
                        case _DOWN:
                                clearscreen(urow(), lcol(), urow() + num - 1, rcol(),
                                        watt);
                                break;
                        case _LEFT:
                                clearscreen(urow(), rcol() - num + 1, brow(), rcol(),
                                        watt);
                                break;
                        default:
                                clearscreen(urow(), lcol(), brow(), lcol() + num - 1,
                                        watt);
                }
        }
        delete scrollbuffer;
}

void window::horizontal_bar(int current, int total)
{
        int row, col, cstart, cend;

        getcurpos(&row, &col, &cstart, &cend);
        if (cstart < 32)
                cursoroff();
        if (!total) {
                current = 0;
                total = 1;
        }
```

continued...

```
        fillone(row2, col1 + 1, 27, watt);
        fillscreen(row2, col1 + 2, row2, col2 - 2, 177, watt);
        fillone(row2, col2 - 1, 26, watt);
        fillone(row2, (int)((long)(col2 - col1 - 4) * current / total + col1 + 2),
                176, watt);
        ::setcurpos(row, col);
        if (cstart < 32)
                cursoron();
}

void window::vertical_bar(int current, int total)
{
        int row, col, cstart, cend;

        getcurpos(&row, &col, &cstart, &cend);
        if (cstart < 32)
                cursoroff();
        if (!total) {
                current = 0;
                total = 1;
        }
        fillone(row1 + 1, col2, 24, watt);
        fillscreen(row1 + 2, col2, row2 - 2, col2, 177, watt);
        fillone(row2 - 1, col2, 25, watt);
        fillone((int)((long)(row2 - row1 - 4) * current / total + row1 + 2),
                col2, 176, watt);
        ::setcurpos(row, col);
        if (cstart < 32)
                cursoron();
}

void window::print(char *string)
{
        int i, off;
        char *line = new char[rcol() - lcol() + 2];

        if (oflag) {
                if (sflag) {
                        off = 0;
                        while (off < strlen(string)) {
                                i = 0;
                                while (i + off < strlen(string) && p_col(ccol + i) <=
                                rcol()) {
                                        line[i++] = string[i + off];
                                }
                                line[i] = 0;
                                off += i;
                                printstring(p_row(crow), p_col(ccol), line);
                                ccol += strlen(line);
```

continued...

```
                            if (p_col(ccol) > rcol()) {
                                    ccol = 1;
                                    crow++;
                                    if (p_row(crow) > brow()) {
                                            scroll(1, _UP, _CLEAR);
                                            crow--;
                                    }
                            }
                            setcurpos(crow, ccol);
                    }
            }
            else {
                    i = 0;
                    while (i < strlen(string) && p_col(ccol + i) <= rcol()) {
                            line[i++] = string[i];
                    }
                    line[i] = 0;
                    printstring(p_row(crow), p_col(ccol), line);
                    ccol += strlen(line);
                    if (p_col(ccol) > rcol()) {
                            ccol = 1;
                            crow++;
                            if (p_row(crow) > brow())
                                    crow--;
                    }
                    setcurpos(crow, ccol);
            }
    }
    delete line;
}

void window::println(char *string)
{
    if (oflag) {
            print(string);
            ccol = 1;
            crow++;
            if (p_row(crow) > brow()) {
                    if (sflag)
                            scroll(1, _UP, _CLEAR);
                    crow--;
            }
            setcurpos(crow, ccol);
    }
}
```

continued...

```
void window::printat(int row, int col, char *string)
{
        if (oflag) {
                setcurpos(row, col);
                print(string);
        }
}

void window::printlnat(int row, int col, char *string)
{
        if (oflag) {
                setcurpos(row, col);
                println(string);
        }
}

static window w;

void save_initial_video(void)
{
        settext80();
        w.open();
}
```

Constructor Description: window::window

The **window::window** constructor saves the dynamic text window object's upper left coordinates, lower right coordinates, attribute, border type, and scroll type. Additionally, the **window::window** constructor flags the dynamic text window as closed. Its implementation is illustrated by the following pseudocode:

save the text window's upper left coordinates
save the text window's lower right coordinates
save the text window's attribute
save the text window's border type
save the text window's scroll type
flag the text window as closed

Destructor Description: window::~window

When a dynamic text window object goes out of scope, the **window::~window** destructor closes its corresponding text window. Its implementation is illustrated by the following pseudocode:

```
if (text window open) {
    close the text window
}
```

Function Description: window::draw

The **window::draw** function draws a text window onto the display screen. Its implementation is illustrated by the following pseudocode:

```
if (object isn't displayable) {
    return
}
clear the text window's portion of the display screen
if (border is requested) {
    draw the requested border
}
```

Function Description: window::open

The **window::open** function dynamically opens a text window. Its implementation is illustrated by the following pseudocode:

```
allocate memory for the text window's current contents
save the text window's current contents
if (object is displayable) {
    draw the window
}
flag the window as opened
save the current cursor values
if (cursor is on) {
    turn off the cursor
}
move the cursor to the text window's upper left corner
```

Function Description: window::close

The **window::close** function closes a previously opened text window. Its implementation is illustrated by the following pseudocode:

```
if (text window is open) {
    redisplay the text window's former contents
    free the text window's memory allocation
    flag the window as closed
    restore the old cursor position
    if (cursor was on) {
        turn on the cursor
    }
}
```

Function Description: window::setcurpos

The **window::setcurpos** function sets the text window's cursor position. Its implementation is illustrated by the following pseudocode:

```
if (text window is open) {
    save the cursor's new row position
    save the cursor's new column position
    move the cursor to its actual physical display screen position
}
```

Function Description: window::cls

The **window::cls** function clears a text window. Its implementation is illustrated by the following pseudocode:

```
if (text window is open) {
    clear the text window's interior contents
    home the text window's cursor
}
```

Function Description: window::clreol

Starting at the current cursor column, the **window::clreol** function clears to the end of the current cursor line. Its implementation is illustrated by the following pseudocode:

```
if (text window is open) {
    clear the remainder of the current cursor line
}
```

Function Description: window::scroll

The **window::scroll** function scrolls the contents of a text window up, down, left, or right. Its implementation is illustrated by the following pseudocode:

```
allocate memory to save the text window's contents
move the text window's contents into the buffer
switch (scroll direction) {
    case up:
        scroll the buffer up by the specified number of lines
    case down:
        scroll the buffer down by the specified number of lines
    case left:
        scroll the buffer left by the specified number of lines
    case right:
        scroll the buffer right by the specified number of lines
}
display the scrolled buffer's contents
if (clear the scrolled lines is requested) {
    switch (scroll direction) {
        case up:
            clear the specified number of scroll lines at the text  window's bottom
        case down:
            clear the specified number of scroll lines at the text window's top
        case left:
            clear the specified number of scroll lines at the text window's right
        case right:
            clear the specified number of scroll lines at the text window's left
    }
}
release the allocated buffer space
```

Function Description: window::horizontal_bar

The **window::horizontal_bar** function displays a horizontal scroll bar at the bottom of a text window. Its implementation is illustrated by the following pseudocode:

```
save the current cursor values
if (cursor is on) {
    turn off the cursor
}
trap any possible divide-by-zero errors
display a left arrow at the beginning of the scroll bar
display the scroll bar's body
display a right arrow at the end of the scroll bar
display the scroll character
restore the old cursor position
if (cursor was on) {
    turn on the cursor
}
```

Function Description: window::vertical_bar

The **window::vertical_bar** function displays a vertical scroll bar on the right side of a text window. Its implementation is illustrated by the following pseudocode:

```
save the current cursor values
if (cursor is on) {
    turn off the cursor
}
trap any possible divide-by-zero errors
display an up arrow at the scroll bar's top
display the scroll bar's body
display a down arrow at the scroll bar's bottom
display the scroll character
restore the old cursor position
if (cursor was on) {
    turn on the cursor
}
```

Function Description: window::print

The **window::print** function displays a string at the text window's current cursor position. Its implementation is illustrated by the following pseudocode:

```
if (text window is open) {
    if (scrollable text window) {
        offset = 0;
        while (character's remain in the string) {
            counter = 0;
            while (character's remain in the string && right border
                hasn't been reached) {
                move a character into the display string
            }
            flag the end of the display string
            adjust the offset
            display the display string
            adjust the cursor column
            if (right border has been reached) {
                reset the cursor column
                adjust the cursor row
                if (bottom border has been reached) {
                    scroll the text window up one line
                    adjust the cursor row
                }
            }
            move the cursor to the end of the string + 1
        }
    }
    else {
        counter = 0
        while (characters remain in the string && the right border
            hasn't been reached) {
            move a character into the display string
        }
        flag the end of the display string
        display the display string
        adjust the cursor column
```

continued...

```
    if (right border has been reached) {
        reset the cursor column
        adjust the cursor row
        if (bottom border has been reached) {
            adjust the cursor row
        }
    }
    set the new cursor position
    }
}
```

Function Description: window::println

The **window::println** function displays a string at the current cursor position and moves the cursor to the start of the next line. Its implementation is illustrated by the following pseudocode:

```
if (text window is open) {
    display the string
    reset the cursor column
    adjust the cursor row
    if (bottom border has been reached) {
        if (scrollable text window) {
            scroll the text window up one line
        }
        adjust the cursor row
    }
    set the new cursor position
}
```

Function Description: window::printat

The **window::printat** function displays a string at a specified text window position. Its implementation is illustrated by the following pseudocode:

```
if (text window is open) {
    set the cursor position
    display the string
}
```

Function Description: window::printlnat

The **window::printlnat** function displays a string at a specified text window position and moves the cursor to the start of the next line. Its implementation is illustrated by the following pseudocode:

```
if (text window is open) {
    set the cursor position
    display the string
}
```

Function Description: save_initial_video

The **save_initial_video** function initializes the WINDOWS operating environment, saves the initial cursor values, turns the cursor off, and saves the initial contents of the display screen. Its implementation is illustrated by the following pseudocode:

```
initialize the WINDOWS operating environment
define a text window object for the entire display screen
```

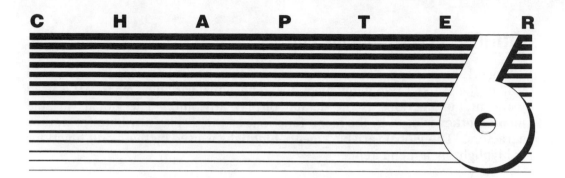

C H A P T E R

6

THE MENU FUNCTIONS

This chapter presents the WINDOWS toolbox menu functions. These menu functions implement three extremely useful menu objects: pop-up menu objects, dialog box menu objects, and pull-down menu objects. Although other menu types do exist, the three supported by the WINDOWS data objects are by far the most popular of the menu types found in today's state-of-the-art application programs. Not only do they increase operator efficiency, they also provide a much shorter training period for operators who are unfamiliar with an application program.

SOURCE LISTING: menus.cpp

Listing 6.1, **menus.cpp**, defines the global variables and a hotstring function used by all of the WINDOWS menu functions. The global variable **_menu_att** is used by the menu functions as the default display attribute. The global variable **_menu_hotkey** is used by the menu functions as the display attribute for hotkey characters. The global variable **_menu_highlight** is used by the menu functions for highlighting a menu item.

Listing 6.1: menus.cpp

```
/****************************************************************************
* menus.cpp - For the WINDOWS Toolbox
*              Menu Global Variables and Functions
****************************************************************************/
#include "windows.hpp"

int _menu_att = 0x70, _menu_hotkey = 0x7f, _menu_highlight = 7;

void hotstring(int row, int col, int hotkey, char *string)
{
        printstring(row, col, string);
        setone(row, col + hotkey, _menu_hotkey);
}
```

Function Description: hotstring

The **hotstring** function displays a menu hotstring at a specified display screen position. Its implementation is illustrated by the following pseudocode:

display the string at the specified position
set the hotkey character's attribute to **_menu_hotkey**

POP-UP MENUS

Figure 6.1 illustrates a pop-up menu's components. Essentially, a pop-up menu is a text window that lists a variety of possible menu selections.

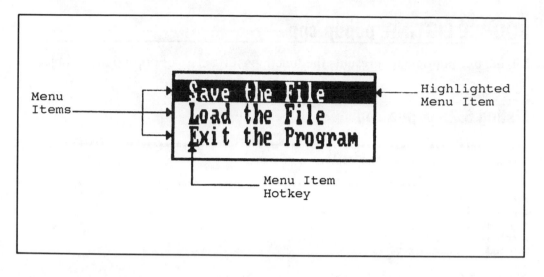

Figure 6.1 A pop-up menu

Following are more complete descriptions of a pop-up menu's components:

- **Menu Items:** A pop-up menu is composed of one or more menu items.

- **Highlighted Menu Item:** As Figure 6.1 illustrates, one of the menu's items will be highlighted. The highlighting can be moved from one item to the next by pressing the **UP ARROW** or **DOWN ARROW** key. The highlighted menu item can be selected by pressing the **ENTER** key. Furthermore, help, if it's available, can be requested by pressing the **F1** key.

- **Hotkeys:** Each of the pop-up menu items has an associated hotkey. Although Figure 6.1 shows the hotkeys as underlined characters (i.e., "S" for Save, "L" for Load, and "E" for Exit), a menu item's hotkey character will actually be displayed using a color different from the one used for the remainder of the menu item's characters. A pop-up menu item can be selected simply by pressing its corresponding hotkey.

SOURCE LISTING: popup.cpp

Listing 6.2, **popup.cpp**, presents the functions for a class of pop-up menu objects.

Listing 6.2: popup.cpp

```
/****************************************************************************
* popup.cpp - For the WINDOWS Toolbox
*              Pop-up Menu Routine
****************************************************************************/
#include <stdlib.h>
#include <string.h>
#include <bios.h>
#include <ctype.h>
#include "windows.hpp"

popup::popup(int r, int c, boolean e)
{
        row = r;
        col1 = c;
        ESC_flag = e;
}

popup::popup(popup &arg)
{
        row = arg.row;
        col1 = arg.col1;
        ESC_flag = arg.ESC_flag;
}

int popup::get(int number, MENU *menu)
{
        int i, col2, key, mlen = 0, select, mrow, mcol;
        window w1, w2;

        for (i = 0; i < number; i++)
                mlen = max(mlen, strlen(menu[i].string));
        mlen += 4;
        col2 = col1 + mlen - 1;
        w1 = window(row, col1, row + number + 1, col2, _menu_att, _SINGLE_LINE);
        w1.open();
        for (i = 0; i < number; i++)
                hotstring(row + i + 1, col1 + 2, menu[i].hotkey, menu[i].string);
        select = 0;
        while (TRUE) {
                w2 = window(row + 1 + select, col1 + 1, row + 1 + select, col2 - 1, 0);
                w2.open();
                setattrib(row + 1 + select, col1 + 1, row + 1 + select,
                        col2 - 1, _menu_highlight);
```

continued...

```
while (TRUE) {
        do {
                mouse.read();
        } while (!_bios_keybrd(1) && !mouse.lbutton()) ;
        if (mouse.lbutton()) {
                do {
                        mouse.read();
                } while (mouse.lbutton()) ;
                if (mouse.row() > row && mouse.row() < row + number + 1
                        &&
                        mouse.col() > col1 && mouse.col() < col2) {
                        key = menu[mouse.row() - row - 1].string[
                                menu[mouse.row() - row - 1].hotkey];
                        break;
                }
                else {
                        if (ESC_flag && (mouse.row() < row ||
                                mouse.row() > row + number + 1 ||
                                mouse.col() < col1 || mouse.col() >
                                        col2)) {
                                key = 27;
                                break;
                        }
                }
                continue;
        }
        key = waitkey();
        switch (key) {
                case 13:
                        key = menu[select].string[menu[select].hotkey];
                        break;
                case 27:
                        if (!ESC_flag)
                                continue;
                        break;
                case 315:
                        if (menu[select].help != NULL)
                                (*menu[select].help)();
                        continue;
        }
        break;
}
w2.close();
switch (key) {
        case 27:
                return(27);
        case 328:
                select = (--select + number) % number;
                continue;
        case 336:
                select = ++select % number;
                continue;
```

continued...

```
                    default:
                        if (key > 31 && key < 128) {
                            for (i = 0; i < number; i++) {
                                if (toupper(key) == toupper(menu[i].string
                                            [menu[i].hotkey])) {
                                    if (menu[i].function != NULL) {
                                        w1.close();
                                        (*menu[i].function)();
                                        return(0);
                                    }
                                }
                            }
                        }
                    }
                }
            }
        }
    }
}
```

Function Description: popup::get

The **popup::get** function executes pop-up menus. Its implementation is illustrated by the following pseudocode:

```
figure the menu's width
figure the menu's right column
open a text window for the menu
for (i = 0; i < number of menu items; i+ +) {
    display a menu item
}
highlighted menu item = first menu item
while (TRUE) {
    open a text window to save the highlighted menu item
    highlight the highlighted menu item
    while (TRUE) {
        do {
            read the mouse values
        } while (key not pressed && left mouse button not pressed) ;
        if (left mouse button pressed) {
            do {
                read the mouse values
            } while (left mouse button not released) ;
            if (mouse pointer is within the pop-up menu) {
                key = pointed to menu item's hotkey character
                break
            }
        }
```

continued...

```
        else {
            if (ESC flag && mouse is outside the pop-up menu) {
                key = ESC
                break
            }
        }
        continue
    }
    get a key
    switch (key) {
        case ENTER:
            key = highlighted menu item's hotkey
            break
        case ESC:
            if (!ESC flag) {
                continue
            }
            break
        case F1:
            if (highlighted menu item's help function ! = NULL) {
                call the function
            }
            continue
    }
    break
}
restore the highlighted menu item's appearance by closing its text window
switch (key) {
    case ESC:
        return(27)
    case UP ARROW:
        move the highlighting up to the previous menu item
        continue
    case DOWN ARROW:
        move the highlighting down to the next menu item
        continue
    default:
        if (key is a printable character) {
            for (i = 0; i < number of menu items; i + +) {
                if (key = menu item[i]'s hotkey) {
                    if (menu item[i]'s function ! = NULL) {
```

continued...

erase the menu by closing its text window
call the function
return(0)

```
            }
          }
        }
      }
    }
}
```

DIALOG BOX MENUS

Figure 6.2 illustrates a dialog box menu's components. Basically, a dialog box menu is a text window that displays a statement or asks a question, or both. In response, the operator must choose from a relatively short list of menu items.

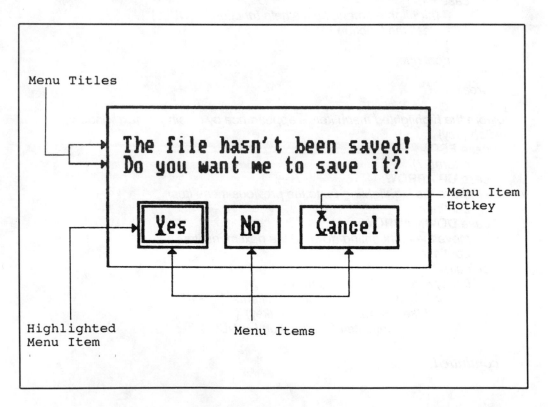

Figure 6.2   A dialog box menu

Following are more complete descriptions of a dialog box menu's components:

- **Titles:** A dialog box menu always has one or more titles. These titles are used to either display a statement or ask a question, or both.

- **Menu Items:** In addition to the titles, a dialog box menu will always have one or more menu items.

- **Highlighted Menu Item:** As Figure 6.2 illustrates, one of the dialog box menu's items will be highlighted. The highlighting can be moved from one menu item to the next by pressing the **LEFT ARROW** or the **RIGHT ARROW** key. The highlighted menu item can be selected by pressing the **ENTER** key. Furthermore, help, if it's available, can be requested by pressing the **F1** key.

- **Hotkeys:** Each of the dialog box menu items has an associated hotkey. Although Figure 6.2 shows the hotkeys as underlined characters (i.e. "Y" for Yes, "N" for No, and "C" for Cancel), a menu item's hotkey character will actually be displayed in a color different from the one used for the remainder of the menu item's characters. A dialog box menu item is selected simply by pressing its corresponding hotkey.

SOURCE LISTING: dialog.cpp

Listing 6.3, **dialog.cpp**, presents the functions for a class of dialog box menu objects.

Listing 6.3: dialog.cpp

```
/*****************************************************************************
* dialog.cpp - For the WINDOWS Toolbox
*              Dialog Box Menu Routine
*****************************************************************************/
#include <stdlib.h>
#include <string.h>
#include <stdarg.h>
#include <bios.h>
#include <ctype.h>
#include "windows.hpp"
```

continued...

```
dialog::dialog(int r, int c, boolean e)
{
    row = r;
    col = c;
    ESC_flag = e;
}

dialog::dialog(dialog &arg)
{
    row = arg.row;
    col = arg.col;
    ESC_flag = arg.ESC_flag;
}

int dialog::get(int nmenus, MENU *menu, int ntitles, ...)
{
    int i, j, key, row1, col1, row2, col2, mlen = 0, chlen, select, *tabs;
    char **titles;
    window w;
    va_list arg_marker;

    titles = new char *[ntitles];
    tabs = new int[nmenus];
    va_start(arg_marker, ntitles);
    for (i = 0; i < ntitles; i++) {
        titles[i] = va_arg(arg_marker, char *);
        mlen = max(mlen, strlen(titles[i]));
    }
    chlen = nmenus - 1;
    for (i = 0; i < nmenus; i++)
        chlen += strlen(menu[i].string) + 4;
    mlen = max(mlen, chlen);
    row1 = row - (ntitles + 7) / 2;
    row2 = row1 + ntitles + 6;
    col1 = col - (mlen + 4) / 2;
    col2 = col1 + mlen + 3;
    w = window(row1, col1, row2, col2, _menu_att, _SINGLE_LINE);
    w.open();
    for (i = 0; i < ntitles; i++)
        printcenter(row1 + i + 2, col, titles[i]);
    j = col - chlen / 2;
    for (i = 0; i < nmenus; i++) {
        tabs[i] = j;
        if (!i)
            drawbox(row2 - 3, j, row2 - 1,
                j + strlen(menu[i].string) + 3,
                _DOUBLE_LINE, _menu_att);
        else
            drawbox(row2 - 3, j, row2 - 1,
                j + strlen(menu[i].string) + 3,
                _SINGLE_LINE, _menu_att);
```

continued...

```
            hotstring(row2 - 2, j + 2, menu[i].hotkey, menu[i].string);
            j += strlen(menu[i].string) + 5;
}
select = 0;
while (TRUE) {
      while (TRUE) {
            do {
                  mouse.read();
            } while (!_bios_keybrd(1) && !mouse.lbutton()) ;
            if (mouse.lbutton()) {
                  do {
                        mouse.read();
                  } while (mouse.lbutton());
                  if (mouse.row() >= row2 - 3 && mouse.row() <= row2 - 1 &&
                        mouse.col() >= col1 && mouse.col() <= col2) {
                        for (i = 0; i < nmenus; i++) {
                              if (mouse.col() >= tabs[i] && mouse.col() <=
                                    tabs[i] + strlen(menu[i].string) + 3)
                                          break;
                        }
                        if (i < nmenus) {
                              key = menu[i].string[menu[i].hotkey];
                              break;
                        }
                        continue;
                  }
                  else {
                        if (ESC_flag && (mouse.row() < row1 || mouse.row() > row2 ||
                              mouse.col() < col1 || mouse.col() > col2)) {
                              key = 27;
                              break;
                        }
                  }
            }
            else {
                  key = waitkey();
                  switch (key) {
                        case 13:
                              key = menu[select].string[menu[select].hotkey];
                              break;
                        case 27:
                              if (!ESC_flag)
                                    continue;
                              break;
                        case 315:
                              if (menu[select].help != NULL)
                                    (*menu[select].help)();
                              continue;
                  }
                  break;
            }
      }
```

continued...

```
switch (key) {
    case 27:
        return(27);
    case 331:
        if (nmenus != 1) {
            drawbox(row2 - 3, tabs[select], row2 - 1,
                tabs[select] + strlen(menu[select].string) + 3,
                _SINGLE_LINE, _menu_att);
            select = (--select + nmenus) % nmenus;
            drawbox(row2 - 3, tabs[select], row2 - 1,
                tabs[select] + strlen(menu[select].string) + 3,
                _DOUBLE_LINE, _menu_att);
        }
        continue;
    case 333:
        if (nmenus != 1) {
            drawbox(row2 - 3, tabs[select], row2 - 1,
                tabs[select] + strlen(menu[select].string) + 3,
                _SINGLE_LINE, _menu_att);
            select = (--select + nmenus) % nmenus;
            drawbox(row2 - 3, tabs[select], row2 - 1,
                tabs[select] + strlen(menu[select].string) + 3,
                _DOUBLE_LINE, _menu_att);
        }
        continue;
    default:
        if (key > 31 && key < 128) {
            for (i = 0; i < nmenus; i++) {
                if (toupper(key) == toupper(menu[i].string[menu[i].hotkey])) {
                    w.close();
                    delete titles;
                    delete tabs;
                    if (menu[i].function != NULL) {
                        (*menu[i].function)();
                        return(0);
                    }
                    return(toupper(key));
                }
            }
        }
    }
}
```

Function Description: dialog::get

The **dialog::get** function executes dialog box menus. Its implementation is illustrated by the following pseudocode:

```
allocate memory for an array of title string pointers
allocate memory for an array of menu item tab positions
for (i = 0; i < number of titles; i + +) {
    save a title pointer
}
figure the menu's width
figure the menu's top row
figure the menu's bottom row
figure the menu's left column
figure the menu's right column
open up a text window for the menu
for (i = 0; i < number of titles; i + +) {
        display a title
}
for (i = 0; i < number of menu items; i + +) {
    save the menu item's tab position
    if (first menu item) {
        draw a highlight box
    }
    else {
        draw a regular box
    }
    display the menu item
    figure the next tab position
}
highlighted menu item = first menu item
while (TRUE) {
    while (TRUE) {
        do {
            read the mouse values
        } while (key not pressed && left mouse button not pressed) ;
        if (left mouse button pressed) {
            do {
                read the mouse values
            } while (left mouse button not released) ;
            if (mouse pointer is inside the menu) {
                for (i = 0; i < number of menu items; i + +) {
                    if (mouse pointer is within the menu item's box) {
                        break
```

continued...

```
                        }
                        if (mouse pointer was within a menu item's box) {
                            key = pointed to menu item's hotkey character
                            break
                        }
                        continue
                    }
                    else {
                        if (ESC flag && mouse pointer is outside the menu) {
                            key = ESC
                            break
                        }
                    }
                }
                else {
                    get a key
                    switch (key) {
                        case ENTER:
                            key = highlighted menu item's hotkey character
                            break
                        case ESC:
                            if (ESC flag) {
                                continue
                            }
                            break
                        case F1:
                            if (highlighted menu item's help function ! = NULL) {
                                call the function
                            }
                            continue
                    }
                    break
                }
            }
        }
        switch (key) {
            case ESC:
                return(27)
            case LEFT ARROW:
                move highlight left to the previous menu item
                continue
            case RIGHT ARROW:
                move highlight right to the next menu item
                continue

        continued...
```

```
default:
    if (key is a printable character) {
        for (i = 0; i < number of menu items; i+ +) {
        if (key = = menu item[i]'s hotkey) {
            erase the menu by closing its text window
            deallocate the array of title pointers
            deallocate the array of tab positions
            if (menu item[i]'s function ! = NULL) {
                call the function
                return(0)
            }
            return(menu item[i]'s hotkey character)
        }
    }
  }
}
}
```

PULL-DOWN MENUS

Pull-down menus are the menu system of choice among today's programmers and operators. Although a lot goes into creating a pull-down menu system, all pull-down menu systems are composed of two basic components: the pull-down menu bar and its associated pull-down menus.

Figure 6.3 illustrates a pull-down menu bar's components.

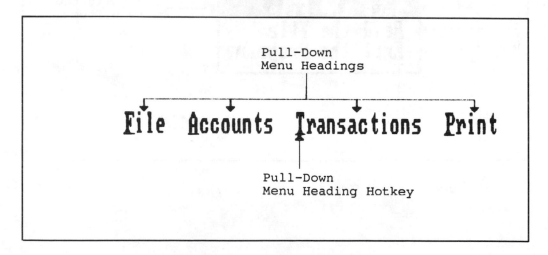

Figure 6.3   A pull-down menu bar

Following are more complete descriptions of these components:

- **Pull-down Menu Headings:** A pull-down menu bar is made up of one or more pull-down menu headings. Essentially, a pull-down menu heading categorizes its corresponding pull-down menu's items.

- **Hotkeys:** Each of the pull-down menu headings has an associated hotkey. Although Figure 6.3 shows the hotkeys as underlined characters (i.e., "F" for File, "A" for Accounts, "T" for Transactions, and "P" for Print), a pull-down menu heading's hotkey character will actually be displayed in a color different from the one used for the remainder of the pull-down menu heading's characters. A menu down is pulled down simply by pressing its corresponding hotkey.

When a pull-down menu is pulled down, its appearance is similar to that of a pop-up menu. Figure 6.4 illustrates a pull-down menu's components.

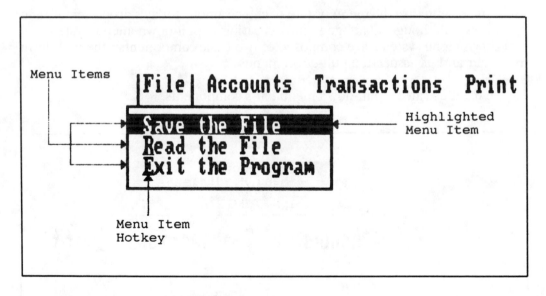

Figure 6.4   A pull-down menu

Following are more complete descriptions of these components:

- **Menu Items:** A pull-down menu is composed of one or more menu items.

- **Highlighted Menu Item:** In Figure 6.4, one of the pull-down menu's items is highlighted. The highlighting can be moved from one menu item to the next by pressing either the **UP ARROW** or the **DOWN ARROW** key. The highlighted menu item can be selected by pressing the **ENTER** key. Furthermore, help, if it's available, can be requested by pressing the **F1** key.

- **Hotkeys:** Each of the pull-down menu items has an associated hotkey. Although Figure 6.4 illustrates the hotkeys as an underlined character (i.e., "S" for Save, "R" for Read, and "E" for Exit), a pull-down menu item's hotkey character will actually be displayed in a color different from the one used for the remainder of the pull-down menu item's characters. A menu item can be pulled-down simply by pressing its corresponding hotkey.

SOURCE LISTING: pulldown.cpp

Listing 6.4, **pulldown.cpp**, presents the functions for a class of pull-down menu objects.

Listing 6.4: pulldown.cpp

```
/****************************************************************************
* pulldown.cpp - For the WINDOWS Toolbox
*                  Pull-down Menu Routine
****************************************************************************/
#include <stdio.h>
#include <stdlib.h>
#include <string.h>
#include "windows.hpp"

pulldown::pulldown(int r, int n, MENU_HEAD *m, void(*m_h)(void))
{
    row = r;
    number = n;
    menus = m;
```

continued...

```
    menu_help = m_h;
    tabs = NULL;
    hotkeys = NULL;
}

pulldown::pulldown(pulldown &arg)
{
    row = arg.row;
    number = arg.number;
    menus = arg.menus;
    menu_help = arg.menu_help;
    tabs = arg.tabs;
    hotkeys = arg.hotkeys;
}

void pulldown::display(void)
{
    int i, col, crow, ccol, cstart, cend;

    getcurpos(&crow, &ccol, &cstart, &cend);
    if (cstart < 32)
        cursoroff();
    if (tabs != NULL)
        delete tabs;
    tabs = new int[number];
    if (hotkeys != NULL)
        delete hotkeys;
    hotkeys = new char[number + 1];
    clearscreen(row, 1, row, 80, _menu_att);
    col = 3;
    for (i = 0; i < number; i++) {
        tabs[i] = col;
        hotkeys[i] = toupper(menus[i].heading[menus[i].hotkey]);
        hotstring(row, col, menus[i].hotkey, menus[i].heading);
        col += strlen(menus[i].heading) + 2;
    }
    hotkeys[number] = '0';
    setcurpos(crow, ccol);
    if (cstart < 32)
        cursoron();
}

int pulldown::get(int ikey)
{
    int i, key, col, menu, rcol, select, crow, ccol, cstart, cend;
    char *match;
    MENU *mptr;
    window w1, w2;
    static char alts[27] = "QWERTYUIOPASDFGHJKLZXCVBNM";
```

continued...

```
getcurpos(&crow, &ccol, &cstart, &cend);
if (!ikey) {
    while (TRUE) {
        do {
            mouse.read();
        } while (!_bios_keybrd(1) && !mouse.lbutton()) ;
        if (mouse.lbutton()) {
            do {
                mouse.read();
            } while (mouse.lbutton()) ;
            if (mouse.row() != row)
                continue;
            for (i = 0; i < number; i++) {
                if (mouse.col() >= tabs[i] &&
                    mouse.col() < tabs[i] + strlen(menus[i].heading)) {
                        key = i + 512;
                        break;
                }
            }
            if (i < number)
                break;
        }
        else {
            key = waitkey();
            break;
        }
    }
}
else
    key = ikey;
if (menu_help != NULL && key == 315) {
    if (cstart < 32)
        cursoroff();
    (*menu_help)();
    setcurpos(crow, ccol);
    if (cstart < 32)
        cursoron();
    return(0);
}
if (key >= 272 && key <= 281)
    menu = alts[key - 272];
else {
    if (key >= 286 && key <= 294)
        menu = alts[key - 276];
    else {
        if (key >= 300 && key <= 306)
            menu = alts[key - 281];
        else {
            if (key < 512)
                return(key);
```

continued...

```
            }
        }
    }
    if (key >= 512)
        menu = key - 512;
    else {
        if (!(match = strchr(hotkeys, menu)))
            return(key);
        else
            menu = match - hotkeys;
    }
    if (cstart < 32)
        cursoroff();
    while (TRUE) {
        mptr = menus[menu].mptr;
        if (menus[menu].number == 1) {
            if (mptr[0].function!= NULL)
                (mptr[0].function)();
            setcurpos(crow, ccol);
            if (cstart < 32)
                cursoron();
            return(0);
        }
        mptr = menus[menu].mptr;
        col = tabs[menu];
        rcol = strlen(menus[menu].heading);
        for (i = 0; i < menus[menu].number; i++)
            rcol = max(rcol, strlen(mptr[i].string));
        rcol += col + 1;
        w1 = window(row, col - 2, row + 2 + menus[menu].number,
            rcol, 0);
        w1.open();
        window(row + 1, col - 2, row + 2 + menus[menu].number,
            rcol, _menu_att, _SINGLE_LINE, _menu_att).draw();
        printone(row, col - 1, 0xb3);
        printone(row, col + strlen(menus[menu].heading), 0xb3);
        printone(row + 1, col - 1, 0xc1);
        printone(row + 1, col + strlen(menus[menu].heading), 0xc1);
        for (i = 0; i < menus[menu].number; i++)
            hotstring(row + 2 + i, col, mptr[i].hotkey, mptr[i].string);
        select = 0;
        while (TRUE) {
            w2 = window(row + 2 + select, col - 1,
                row + 2 + select, rcol - 1, 0);
            w2.open();
            setattrib(row + 2 + select, col - 1, row + 2 + select,
                rcol - 1, _menu_highlight);
            while (TRUE) {
                do {
                    mouse.read();
                } while (!_bios_keybrd(1) && !mouse.lbutton()) ;
                if (mouse.lbutton()) {
```

continued...

```
        do {
            mouse.read();
        } while (mouse.lbutton()) ;
        if (mouse.row() == row) {
            for (i = 0; i < number; i++) {
                if (mouse.col() >= tabs[i] &&
                    mouse.col() <= tabs[i] + strlen(menus[i].heading)) {
                        key = i + 512;
                        break;
                }
            }
            if (i != number)
                break;
        }
        else {
            if (mouse.row() > row + 1 && mouse.row() < row + 2 +
                menus[menu].number &&
                mouse.col() > col - 2 && mouse.col() < rcol) {
                    key = mptr[mouse.row() - row - 2].string[mptr
                    [mouse.row() - row - 2].hotkey];
                    break;
            }
            if (mouse.row() < row + 1 || mouse.row() > row + 2 +
                menus[menu].number ||
                mouse.col() > col - 2 || mouse.col() < rcol) {
                    key = 27;
                    break;
            }
        }
    }
    else {
        key = waitkey();
        switch (key) {
            case 13:
                key = mptr[select].string[mptr[select].hotkey];
                break;
            case 315:
                if (mptr[select].help != NULL)
                    (*mptr[select].help)();
                continue;
        }
        break;
    }
}
w2.close();
if (key >= 512) {
    menu = key - 512;
    w1.close();
    break;
```

continued...

```
        }
        else {
            switch (key) {
                case 27:
                    w1.close();
                    setcurpos(crow, ccol);
                    if (cstart < 32)
                        cursoron();
                    return(0);
                case 328:
                    select = (--select + menus[menu].number) %
                        menus[menu].number;
                    continue;
                case 331:
                    w1.close();
                    do {
                        menu = (--menu + number) % number;
                    } while (menus[menu].number == 1);
                    break;
                case 333:
                    w1.close();
                    do {
                        menu = ++menu % number;
                    } while (menus[menu].number == 1);
                    break;
                case 336:
                    select = ++select % menus[menu].number;
                    continue;
                default:
                    if (key > 31 && key < 128) {
                        for (i = 0; i < menus[menu].number; i++) {
                            if (toupper(key) == toupper(mptr[i].string[mptr
                                [i].hotkey])) {
                                w1.close();
                                if (mptr[i].function != NULL)
                                    (*mptr[i].function)();
                                setcurpos(crow, ccol);
                                if (cstart < 32)
                                    cursoron();
                                return(0);
                            }
                        }
                    }
                    continue;
            }
        }
        break;
    }
}
}
```

Function Description: pulldown::display

The **pulldown::display** function displays pull-down menu bars. Its implementation is illustrated by the following pseudocode:

```
save the cursor values
if (cursor is on) {
    turn off the cursor
}
if (array of tab positions has already been allocated) {
    deallocate the array of tab positions
}
allocate memory for an array of tab positions
if (string of hotkeys has already been allocated) {
    deallocate the string of hotkeys
}
allocate memory for a string of hotkeys
clear the menu bar's row
for (i = 0; i < number of headings; i+ +) {
    save the heading's tab position
    save the heading's hotkey character
    display the heading
    figure the next tab position
}
flag the end of the string of hotkeys
restore the cursor position
if (cursor was on) {
    turn on the cursor
}
```

Function Description: pulldown::get

The **pulldown::get** function executes a pull-down menu system. Its implementation is illustrated by the following pseudocode:

```
save the cursor values
if (an initial key wasn't passed) {
    while (TRUE) {
        do {
            read the mouse values

        continued...
```

```
            } while (key not pressed && left mouse button not pressed) ;
            if (left mouse button pressed) {
                do {
                    read the mouse values
                } while (left mouse button not released) ;
                if (mouse pointer isn't in the menu bar row) {
                    continue
                }
                for (i = 0; i < number of headings; i+ +) {
                    if (mouse pointer is pointing to menu heading[I]) {
                        key = i + 512
                        break
                    }
                }
                if (menu heading was selected) {
                    break
                }
            }
            else {
                get a key
                break
            }
        }
    }
    else {
     key = initial key
    }
    if (overall help function ! = NULL and key = = F1) {
        if (cursor is on) {
            turn off the cursor
        }
        call the help function
        restore the cursor position
        if (cursor was on) {
            turn on the cursor
        }
        return(0)
    }
    if (key isn't an ALT key && mouse wasn't used) {
        return(key)
    }
    if (heading was selected with the mouse) {
        menu = mouse menu

        continued...
```

```
}
else {
    if (key isn't a heading hotkey) {
        return(key)
    }
    else {
        menu = hotkey menu
    }
}
if (cursor is on) {
    turn off the cursor
}
while (TRUE) {
    if (number of menu items = = 1) {
        if (menu item[0]'s function ! = NULL) {
            call the function
        }
        restore the cursor position
        if (cursor was on) {
            turn on the cursor
        }
        return(0)
    }
    figure the menu's width
    open a text window for the menu
    draw the menu's window
    draw the rest of the menu's frame
    for (i = 0; i < number of menu items; i + +) {
        display a menu item
    }
    highlighted menu item = first menu item
    while (TRUE) {
        open a text window to save the highlighted menu item
        highlight the highlighted menu item
        while (TRUE) {
            do {
                read the mouse values
            } while (key not pressed && left mouse button not pressed);
            if (left mouse button pressed) {
                do {
                    read the mouse values
                } while (left mouse button not released) ;
                if (mouse pointer is in the menu bar row) {
```

continued...

```
        for (i = 0; i < number of headings; i + +) {
            if (mouse pointer is pointing to menu heading[i]) {
                key = i + 512
                break
            }
            if (menu heading was selected) {
                break
            }
        }
        else {
            if (mouse pointer is inside the menu) {
                key = pointed to menu item's hotkey character
                break
            }
            if (mouse pointer is outside the menu) {
                key = ESC
                break
            }
        }
    }
    else {
        get a key
        switch (key) {
            case ENTER:
                key = highlighted menu item's hotkey character
                break;
            case F1:
                if (highlighted menu item's help function ! = NULL) {
                    call the function
                    continue
                }
        }
        break
    }
}
restore the highlighted menu item's appearance by closing
    its text window
if (a new menu was selected by the mouse) {
    menu = mouse menu
    erase the pull-down menu by closing its text window
    break
```

continued...

```
        }
        else {
            switch (key) {
                case ESC:
                    erase the pull-down menu by closing its text window
                    restore the cursor position
                    if (cursor was on) {
                        turn on the cursor
                    }
                    return(0)
                case UP ARROW:
                    move the highlighting up to the previous menu item
                    continue
                case LEFT ARROW:
                    erase the pull-down menu by closing its text window
                    heading hotkey = previous heading's hotkey
                    break
                case RIGHT ARROW:
                    erase the pull-down menu by closing its text window
                    heading hotkey = next heading's hotkey
                    break
                case DOWN ARROW:
                    move the highlighting down to the next menu item
                    continue
                default:
                    if (key is a printable character) {
                        for (i = 0; i < number of menu items; i++) {
                            If (key == menu item[i]'s hotkey) {
                                erase the pull-down menu by closing its text
                                    window
                                if (menu item[i]'s function != NULL) {
                                    call the function
                                }
                                restore the cursor position
                                if (cursor was on) {
                                 turn on the cursor
                                }
                                return(0)
                            }
                        }
                    }
                    continue
            }
        }
        break
    }
}
```

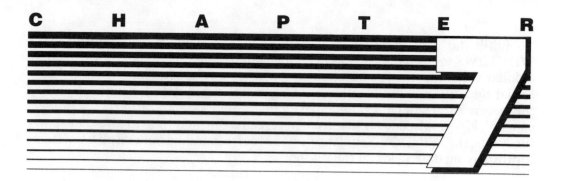

C H A P T E R

7

THE FORMATTED INPUT FUNCTIONS

Although the C++ **scanf** function may have been an adequate data entry method during the teletype days, it just doesn't cut it in today's world of windowing user interfaces. Indeed, today's windowing user interfaces require data entry functions that restrict data entry to a specific portion of the display screen. Furthermore, a good set of data entry functions should perform a minimal amount of editing and error checking on the entered data. This chapter presents routines for displaying and retrieving dates, dollar values, numeric values, telephone numbers, Social Security numbers, and strings.

To fulfill the data entry requirements of today's modern user interface, the WINDOWS toolbox provides six basic formatted input functions: a date function, a dollar value function, a numeric data function, a telephone number function, a Social Security number function, and a general string data function. By using these formatted input functions as basic building blocks, application programmers can quickly build complex data entry screens. In addition to the data entry functions, the WINDOWS toolbox provides corresponding data display functions for displaying data fields on the display screen.

SOURCE LISTING: idate.cpp

Listing 7.1, **idate.cpp**, presents functions for displaying dates, retrieving dates, and building date strings.

Listing 7.1: idate.cpp

```
/******************************************************************************
* idate.cpp - For the Windows Toolbox
*               Formatted Date Routines
******************************************************************************/
#include <stdio.h>
#include <stdlib.h>
#include "windows.hpp"

char *date_string(char *string, date &date)
{
        sprintf(string, "%02d/%02d/%02d", date.month % 100, date.day % 100,
                date.year % 100);
        return(string);
}

static int date_func(boolean flag, int row, int col, date &date)
{
        int cpos = 0, key;
        char field[9];

        date_string(field, date);
        while (TRUE) {
                printstring(row, col, field);
                if (!flag)
                        return(0);
                setcurpos(row, col + cpos);
                cursoron();
                key = waitkey();
```

continued...

```
cursoroff();
switch (key) {
        case 47:
                continue;
        case 327:
                cpos = 0;
                continue;
        case 8:
        case 331:
                switch (cpos) {
                        case 1:
                        case 4:
                        case 7:
                                cpos--;
                                break;
                        case 3:
                        case 6:
                                cpos -= 2;
                }
                continue;
        case 333:
                switch (cpos) {
                        case 0:
                        case 3:
                        case 6:
                                cpos++;
                                break;
                        case 1:
                        case 4:
                                cpos += 2;
                }
                continue;
        case 335:
                cpos = 7;
                continue;
        default:
                if (key >= 48 && key <= 57) {
                        field[cpos] = key;
                        switch (cpos) {
                                case 0:
                                case 3:
                                case 6:
                                        cpos++;
                                        break;
                                case 1:
                                case 4:
                                        cpos += 2;
                        }
                        continue;
```

continued...

```
                              }
                              date.month = atoi(field);
                              date.day = atoi(field + 3);
                              date.year = atoi(field + 6);
                              return(key);
                    }
          }
}

void display_date(int row, int col, date &date)
{
        date_func(FALSE, row, col, date);
}

int input_date(int row, int col, date &date)
{
        return(date_func(TRUE, row, col, date));
}
```

Function Description: date_string

The **date_string** function builds date strings. Its implementation is illustrated by the following pseudocode:

build the date string
return(a pointer to the string)

Function Description: date_func

The **date _func** function is used internally by the **display_date** and **input _date** functions to display and retrieve dates. Its implementation is illustrated by the following pseudocode:

field = date string
while (TRUE) {
    display field
    *if (called by **display_date**) {*
        return(0)
    }

        continued...

```
move the cursor to the current character position
turn on the cursor
get a key
turn off the cursor
switch (key) {
    case /:
        continue
    case HOME:
        current character position = 0
        continue
    case BACKSPACE:
    case LEFT ARROW:
        switch (current character position) {
            case 1:
            case 4:
            case 7:
                current character position--
                break
            case 3:
            case 6:
                current character position -= 2
        }
        continue
    case RIGHT ARROW:
        switch (current character position) {
            case 0:
            case 3:
            case 6:
                current character position++
                break
            case 1:
            case 4:
                current character position += 2
        }
        continue
    case END:
        current character position = 7
        continue
    default:
        if (key is numeric) {
            field[current character position] = key
            switch (current character position) {
                case 0:
                case 3:
```

continued...
```
```

```
            case 6:
                current character position + +
                break
            case 1:
            case 4:
                current character position  + = 2
        }
        continue
    }
    save the date's month
    save the date's day
    save the date's year
    return(key)
    }
}
```

Function Description: display_date

The **display_date** function displays dates. Its implementation is illustrated by the following pseudocode:

display the date

Function Description: input_date

The **input_date** function retrieves dates. Its implementation is illustrated by the following pseudocode:

retrieve the date
return(last key pressed)

SOURCE LISTING: idollar.cpp

Listing 7.2, **idollar.cpp**, presents functions for displaying and retrieving dollar values.

Listing 7.2: idollar.cpp

```cpp
/******************************************************************************
* idollar.cpp - For the WINDOWS Toolbox
*                Formatted Dollar Routines
******************************************************************************/
#include <stdio.h>
#include <stdlib.h>
#include <string.h>
#include "windows.hpp"

static int dollar_func(boolean flag, int row, int col, int length,
        double &value)
{
        int i, d_cnt = 2, key;
        boolean d_flag = TRUE, s_flag = FALSE;
        char field[81];

        if (value > -.01 && value < .01)
                value = 0;
        if (value < 0)
                s_flag = TRUE;
        sprintf(field, "%*.2f", length, value);
        if (field[length - 1] == '0' && field[length - 2] == '0')
                d_flag = FALSE;
        while (TRUE) {
                sprintf(field, "%*.2f", length, value);
                if (value == 0 && s_flag)
                        field[length - 5] = '-';
                else {
                        if (strlen(field) > length) {
                                for (i = 0; i < length; i++)
                                        field[i] = '*';
                                field[length] = 0;
                        }
                }
                printstring(row, col, field);
                if (!flag)
                        return(0);
                if (d_flag)
                        if (d_cnt)
                                setcurpos(row, col + length - 1);
                        else
                                setcurpos(row, col + length - 2);
                else
                        setcurpos(row, col + length - 4);
                cursoron();
                key = waitkey();
                cursoroff();
```

continued...

```
switch (key) {
        case 8:
                if (d_flag) {
                        switch (d_cnt) {
                                case 0:
                                        d_flag = FALSE;
                                        break;
                                default:
                                        field[length + d_cnt - 3] =
                                        '0';
                                        value = atof(field);
                                        d_cnt--;
                        }
                }
                else {
                        field[length - 4] = '0';
                        value = atof(field);
                        value /= 10;
                        sprintf(field, "%*.2f", length, value);
                        value = atof(field);
                }
                if (!value)
                        s_flag = FALSE;
                continue;
        case 46:
                if (!d_flag) {
                        d_flag = TRUE;
                        d_cnt = 0;
                }
                continue;
        case 45:
                value = -value;
                s_flag = !s_flag;
                continue;
        case 327:
                value = 0;
                d_flag = s_flag = FALSE;
                continue;
        default:
                if (key >= 48 && key <= 57) {
                        if (d_flag) {
                                switch (d_cnt) {
                                        case 0:
                                                field[length - 2] =
                                                key;
                                                value = atof(field);
                                                d_cnt++;
                                                break;
```

continued...

```
                                        case 1:
                                                field[length - 1] =
                                                key;
                                                value = atof(field);
                                                d_cnt++;
                                }
                        }
                        else {
                                if (field[1] == ' ' || field[1] ==
                                '-') {
                                        strncpy(field, field + 1,
                                        length - 4);
                                        field[length - 4] = key;
                                        value = atof(field);
                                }
                        }
                        if (value >= 0 && s_flag)
                                value = -value;
                }
                else
                        return(key);
        }
    }
}

void display_dollar(int row, int col, int length, double &value)
{
        dollar_func(FALSE, row, col, length, value);
}

int input_dollar(int row, int col, int length, double &value)
{
        return(dollar_func(TRUE, row, col, length, value));
}
```

Function Description: dollar_func

The **dollar_func** function is used internally by the **display_dollar** and **input_dollar** functions to display and retrieve dollar values. Its implementation is illustrated by the following pseudocode:

```
if (dollar value > -.01 && dollar value < .01) {
    dollar value = 0
}
if (dollar value is negative) {
    sign flag = TRUE
}
field = dollar value string
if (last two characters == "00") {
    decimal flag = FALSE
}
while (TRUE) {
    field = dollar value string
    if (dollar value == 0 && dollar value is negative) {
        field = "-0.00"
    }
    else {
        if (field is too long) {
            set field to all "*"
        }
    }
    display the dollar value
    if (called by display_dollar) {
        return(0)
    }
    position the cursor
    turn on the cursor
    get a key
    turn off the cursor
    switch (key) {
        case BACKSPACE:
            if (decimal flag) {
                switch (decimal count) {
                    case 0:
                        decimal flag = FALSE
                        break
```

continued...

```
        default:
            last decimal character = '0'
            decimal value = atof(field)
            decimal count--
        }
    }
    else {
        one's place digit = '0'
        dollar value = atof(field) / 10
        round the value
    }
    if (dollar value = = 0) {
        sign flag = FALSE
    }
    continue
case .:
    if (!decimal flag) {
        decimal flag = TRUE
        decimal count = 0
    }
    continue
case -:
    dollar value = -dollar value
    sign flag = !sign flag
    continue
case HOME:
    dollar value = 0
    decimal flag = FALSE
    sign flag = FALSE
    continue
default:
    if (key is numeric) {
        if (decimal flag) {
            switch (decimal count) {
                case 0:
                    save the tenth's place digit
                    dollar value = atof(field)
                    decimal count + +
                    break
                case 1:
                    save the hundredth's place digit
                    dollar value = atof(field)
                    decimal count + +
            }
        }
```

continued...

```
        else {
            if (data entry field isn't full) {
                save the key as the new one's place digit
                dollar value = atof(field)
            }
        }
        if (dollar value is positive && sign flag == FALSE) {
            dollar value = -dollar value
        }
        else {
            return(key)
        }
    }
}
}
```

Function Description: display_dollar

The **display_dollar** function displays dollar values. Its implementation is illustrated by the following pseudocode:

display the dollar value

Function Description: input_dollar

The **input_dollar** function retrieves dollar values. Its implementation is illustrated by the following pseudocode:

retrieve the dollar value
return(last key pressed)

SOURCE LISTING: inumber.cpp

Listing 7.3, **inumber.cpp**, presents functions for displaying and retrieving numeric values.

Listing 7.3: inumber.cpp

```
/****************************************************************************
* inumber.cpp - For the WINDOWS Toolbox
*                Formatted Number Routines
****************************************************************************/
#include <stdio.h>
#include <stdlib.h>
#include <string.h>
#include "windows.hpp"

static int number_func(boolean flag, int row, int col, int length,
        unsigned long &value)
{
        int i, key;
        char field[81];

        while (TRUE) {
                if (value) {
                        sprintf(field, "%*lu", length, value);
                        if (strlen(field) > length) {
                                for (i = 0; i < length; i++)
                                        field[i] = '*';
                                field[length] = '\0';
                        }
                }
                else
                        sprintf(field, "%*s", length, "");
                printstring(row, col, field);
                if (!flag)
                        return(0);
                setcurpos(row, col + length - 1);
                cursoron();
                key = waitkey();
                cursoroff();
                switch (key) {
                        case 8:
                                field[length - 1] = '0';
                                value = atol(field) / 10;
                                continue;
                        case 327:
                                value = 0;
                                continue;
```

continued...

```
                          default:
                                  if (key >= 48 && key <= 57) {
                                          if (field[0] == ' ')
                                                  value = value * 10 + (key - 48);
                                          continue;
                                  }
                                  return(key);
                  }
          }
}

void display_number(int row, int col, int length, unsigned long &value)
{
          number_func(FALSE, row, col, length, value);
}

int input_number(int row, int col, int length, unsigned long &value)
{
          return(number_func(TRUE, row, col, length, value));
}
```

Function Description: number_func

The **number_func** function is used internally by the **display_number** and **input_number** functions to display and retrieve numeric values. Its implementation is illustrated by the following pseudocode:

```
while (TRUE) {
    if (numeric value ! = 0) {
        field = numeric value string
        if (field is too long) {
            set field to all '*'
        }
    }
    else {
        field = all spaces
    }
    display the numeric value string
    if (called by display_number) {
        return(0)
    }
    move the cursor to the last character position
    turn on the cursor
```

continued...

```
get a key
turn off the cursor
switch (key) {
    case BACKSPACE:
        set the one's place character to '0'
        numeric value = atol(field) / 10
        continue
    case HOME:
        numeric value = 0
        continue
    default:
        if (key is numeric) {
            if (data entry field isn't full) {
                numeric value = numeric value * 10 + (key - '0')
            }
            continue
        }
        return(key)
    }
}
```

Function Description: display_number

The **display_number** function displays numeric values. Its implementation is illustrated by the following pseudocode:

display the numeric value

Function Description: input_number

The **input_number** function retrieves numeric values. Its implementation is illustrated by the following pseudocode:

retrieve the numeric value
return(last key pressed)

SOURCE LISTING: iphone.cpp

Listing 7.4, **iphone.cpp**, presents functions for displaying phone numbers, retrieving phone numbers, and building phone number strings.

Listing 7.4: iphone.cpp

```
/****************************************************************************
* iphone.cpp - For the WINDOWS Toolbox
*              Formatted Phone Number Routines
****************************************************************************/
#include <stdio.h>
#include <stdlib.h>
#include <string.h>
#include "windows.hpp"

char *phone_string(char *string, phone &pn)
{
        sprintf(string, "(%03d) %03d-%04d", pn.area % 1000, pn.exchange % 1000,
                pn.no % 10000);
        return(string);
}

static int phone_func(boolean flag, int row, int col, phone &pn)
{
        int cpos = 1, key;
        char field[15];

        phone_string(field, pn);
        while (TRUE) {
                printstring(row, col, field);
                if (!flag)
                        return(0);
                setcurpos(row, col + cpos);
                cursoron();
                key = waitkey();
                cursoroff();
                switch (key) {
                        case 327:
                                cpos = 1;
                                continue;
                        case 8:
                        case 331:
                                switch (cpos) {
                                        case 2:
                                        case 3:
                                        case 7:
                                        case 8:
```

continued...

```
                                  case 11:
                                  case 12:
                                  case 13:
                                          cpos--;
                                          continue;
                                  case 6:
                                          cpos = 3;
                                          continue;
                                  case 10:
                                          cpos = 8;
                          };
                          continue;
                  case 333:
                          switch (cpos) {
                                  case 1:
                                  case 2:
                                  case 6:
                                  case 7:
                                  case 10:
                                  case 11:
                                  case 12:
                                          cpos++;
                                          continue;
                                  case 3:
                                          cpos = 6;
                                          continue;
                                  case 8:
                                          cpos = 10;
                          }
                          continue;
                  case 335:
                          cpos = 13;
                          continue;
                  default:
                          if (key >= 48 && key <= 57) {
                                  field[cpos] = key;
                                  switch (cpos) {
                                          case 1:
                                          case 2:
                                          case 6:
                                          case 7:
                                          case 10:
                                          case 11:
                                          case 12:
                                                  cpos++;
                                                  continue;
                                          case 3:
                                                  cpos = 6;
                                                  continue;
                                          case 8:
                                                  cpos = 10;
                                  }
```

continued...

```
                                continue;
                    }
                    pn.area = atoi(field + 1);
                    pn.exchange = atoi(field + 6);
                    pn.no = atoi(field + 10);
                    return(key);
               }
          }
}

void display_phone(int row, int col, phone &pn)
{
          phone_func(FALSE, row, col, pn);
}

int input_phone(int row, int col, phone &pn)
{
          return(phone_func(TRUE, row, col, pn));
}
```

Function Description: phone_string

The **phone_string** function builds phone number strings. Its implementation is illustrated by the following pseudocode:

build the phone number string
return(a pointer to the string)

Function Description: phone_func

The **phone_func** function is used internally by the **display_phone** and **input_phone** functions to display and retrieve phone numbers. Its implementation is illustrated by the following pseudocode:

field = phone number string
while (TRUE) {
*   display field*
*   if (called by* **display_phone***) {*
*   return(0)*
*   }*

*   continued...*

move the cursor to the current character position
turn on the cursor
get a key
turn off the cursor
switch (key) {
    case **HOME***:*
        current character position = 1
        continue
    case **BACKSPACE***:*
    case **LEFT ARROW***:*
        switch (current character position) {
            case 2:
            case 3:
            case 7:
            case 8:
            case 11:
            case 12:
            case 13:
                current character position--
                continue
            case 6:
                current character position = 3
                continue
            case 10:
                current character position = 8
        }
        continue
    case **RIGHT ARROW***:*
        switch (current character position) {
            case 1:
            case 2:
            case 6:
            case 7:
            case 10:
            case 11:
            case 12:
                current character position+ +
                continue
            case 3:
                current character position − 6
                continue
            case 8:
                current character position = 10
        }
        continue

continued...

```
    case END:
        current character position = 13
        continue
    default:
        if (key is numeric) {
            field[current character position] = key
            switch (current character position) {
                case 1:
                case 2:
                case 6:
                case 7:
                case 10:
                case 11:
                case 12:
                    current character position + +
                    continue
                case 3:
                    current character position = 6
                    continue
                case 8:
                    current character position = 10
            }
            continue
        }
        save the phone number's area code
        save the phone number's exchange
        save the phone number's number
        return(key)
    }
}
```

Function Description: display_phone

The **display_phone** function displays phone numbers. Its implementation is illustrated by the following pseudocode:

display the phone number

Function Description: input_phone

The **input_phone** function retrieves phone numbers. Its implementation is illustrated by the following pseudocode:

retrieve the phone number
return(last key pressed)

SOURCE LISTING: issn.cpp

Listing 7.5, **issn.cpp**, presents routines for displaying Social Security numbers, retrieving Social Security numbers, and building Social Security number strings.

Listing 7.5: issn.cpp

```
/*****************************************************************************
* issn.cpp - For the WINDOWS Toolbox
*            Formatted Social Security Number Routines
*****************************************************************************/
#include <stdio.h>
#include <stdlib.h>
#include <string.h>
#include "windows.hpp"

char *ssn_string(char *string, ssn &ssn)
{
        sprintf(string, "%03d-%02d-%04d", ssn.no1 % 1000, ssn.no2 %100,
        ssn.no3 % 10000);
        return(string);
}

static int ssn_func(boolean flag, int row, int col, ssn &ssn)
{
        int cpos = 0, key;
        char field[12];

        ssn_string(field, ssn);
        while (TRUE) {
                printstring(row, col, field);
                if (!flag)
                        return(0);
                setcurpos(row, col + cpos);
                cursoron();
                key = waitkey();
```

continued...

```
        cursoroff();
        switch (key) {
                case 45:
                        continue;
                case 327:
                        cpos = 0;
                        continue;
                case 8:
                case 331:
                        switch (cpos) {
                                case 1:
                                case 2:
                                case 5:
                                case 8:
                                case 9:
                                case 10:
                                        cpos--;
                                        continue;
                                case 4:
                                case 7:
                                        cpos -= 2;
                        }
                        continue;
                case 333:
                        switch (cpos) {
                                case 0:
                                case 1:
                                case 4:
                                case 7:
                                case 8:
                                case 9:
                                        cpos++;
                                        continue;
                                case 2:
                                case 5:
                                        cpos += 2;
                        }
                        continue;
                case 335:
                        cpos = 10;
                        continue;
                default:
                        if (key >= 48 && key <= 57) {
                                field[cpos] = key;
                                switch (cpos) {
                                        case 0:
                                        case 1:
                                        case 4:
                                        case 7:
                                        case 8:
```

continued...

```
                                        case 9:
                                                cpos++;
                                                continue;
                                        case 2:
                                        case 5:
                                                cpos += 2;
                                }
                                continue;
                        }
                        ssn.no1 = atoi(field);
                        ssn.no2 = atoi(field + 4);
                        ssn.no3 = atoi(field + 7);
                        return(key);
                }
        }
}

void display_ssn(int row, int col, ssn &ssn)
{
        ssn_func(FALSE, row, col, ssn);
}

int input_ssn(int row, int col, ssn &ssn)
{
        return(ssn_func(TRUE, row, col, ssn));
}
```

Function Description: ssn_string

The **ssn_string** function builds Social Security number strings. Its implementation is illustrated by the following pseudocode:

build the Social Security number string
return(a pointer to the string)

Function Description: ssn_func

The **ssn_func** function is used internally be the **display_ssn** and **input_ssn** functions to display and retrieve Social Security numbers. Its implementation is illustrated by the following pseudocode:

```
field = Social Security number string
while (TRUE) {
    display field
    if (called by display_ssn) {
        return(0)
    }
    move the cursor to the current character position
    turn on the cursor
    get a key
    turn off the cursor
    switch (key) {
        case -:
            continue
        case HOME:
            current character position = 0
            continue
        case BACKSPACE:
        case LEFT ARROW:
            switch (current character position) {
                case 1:
                case 2:
                case 5:
                case 8:
                case 9:
                case 10:
                    current character position--
                    continue
                case 4:
                case 7:
                    current character position -= 2
            }
            continue
        case RIGHT ARROW:
            switch (current character position) {
                case 0:
                case 1:
                case 4:
```

continued...

```
            case 7:
            case 8:
            case 9:
                current character position + +
                continue
            case 2:
            case 5:
                current character position  + = 2
        }
        continue
    case END:
        current character position = 10
        continue
    default:
        if (key is numeric) {
            field[current character position] = key
            switch (key) {
                case 0:
                case 1:
                case 4:
                case 7:
                case 8:
                case 9:
                    current character position + +
                    continue
                case 2:
                case 5:
                    current character position  + = 2
            }
            continue
        }
        save the Social Security number's first three digits
        save the Social Security number's middle two digits
        save the Social Security number's last four digits
        return(key)
    }
}
```

Function Description: display_ssn

The **display_ssn** function displays Social Security numbers. Its implementation is illustrated by the following pseudocode:

display the Social Security number

Function Description: input_ssn

The **input_ssn** function retrieves Social Security numbers. Its implementation is illustrated by the following pseudocode:

retrieve the Social Security number
return(last key pressed)

SOURCE LISTING: istring.cpp

Listing 7.6, **istring.cpp**, presents functions for displaying and retrieving strings.

Listing 7.6: istring.cpp

```
/**************************************************************************
* istring.cpp - For the WINDOWS Toolbox
*               Formatted String Input Routines
**************************************************************************/
#include <stdio.h>
#include <stdlib.h>
#include <string.h>
#include "windows.hpp"

static int string_func(boolean flag, int row, int col, int length,
       char *string)
{
       int i, key;
       char field[81];

       if (strlen(string) > length)
               string[length] = '\0';
```

continued...

```
        while (TRUE) {
                sprintf(field, "%-*s", length, string);
                printstring(row, col, field);
                if (!flag)
                        return(0);
                setcurpos(row, col + strlen(string) - (strlen(string) == length));
                cursoron();
                key = waitkey();
                cursoroff();
                switch (key) {
                        case 8:
                                if (strlen(string))
                                        string[strlen(string) - 1] = '\0';
                                continue;
                        case 327:
                                string[0] = '\0';
                                continue;
                        default:
                                if (key > 31 && key < 128) {
                                        if (strlen(string) != length) {
                                                string[strlen(string) + 1] = '\0';
                                                string[strlen(string)] = key;
                                        }
                                        continue;
                                }
                                return(key);
                }
        }
}

void display_string(int row, int col, int length, char *string)
{
        string_func(FALSE, row, col, length, string);
}

int input_string(int row, int col, int length, char *string)
{
        return(string_func(TRUE, row, col, length, string));
}
```

Function Description: string_func

The **string_func** is used internally by the **display_string** and **input_string** functions to display and retrieve strings. Its implementation is illustrated by the following pseudocode:

```
if (string length > length of data entry field) {
    truncate the string
}
while (TRUE) {
    field = formatted string
    display field
    if (called by display_string) {
        return(0)
    }
    move the cursor to the end of the string
    turn on the cursor
    get a key
    turn off the cursor
    switch (key) {
        case BACKSPACE:
            erase the last character
            continue
        case HOME:
            string = ""
            continue
        default:
            if (key is a printable character) {
                if (data entry field isn't full) {
                    field[length(string)] = key
                }
                continue
            }
            return(key)
    }
}
```

Function Description: display_string

The **display_string** function displays strings. Its implementation is illustrated by the following pseudocode:

display the string

Function Description: input_string

The **input_string** function retrieves strings. Its implementation is illustrated by the following pseudocode:

retrieve the string
return(last key pressed)

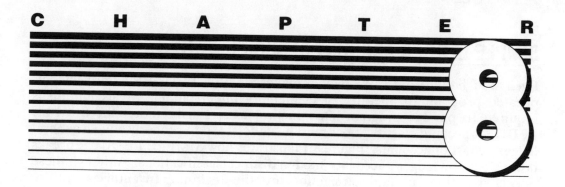

CHAPTER 8

SIMPLE LEDGER

The previous seven chapters have been devoted to constructing the WINDOWS toolbox. To illustrate how the WINDOWS toolbox is used in an actual application program's implementation, this chapter presents a sample WINDOWS application program called SIMPLE LEDGER. As its name implies, SIMPLE LEDGER is a rudimentary general ledger accounting system. Although its features are quite basic, SIMPLE LEDGER can be used to successfully maintain a general ledger for almost any small business.

SIMPLE LEDGER ACCOUNT CLASSIFICATIONS

Even though the WINDOWS toolbox makes SIMPLE LEDGER a fairly uncomplicated program to operate, an elementary understanding of accounting is required to put the program into practical use. Furthermore, the SIMPLE LEDGER account classifications must be understood to properly build a general ledger's chart of accounts. Figure 8.1 illustrates how SIMPLE LEDGER breaks down a general ledger's accounts into ten distinct classifications. Although these ten classifications are fairly straightforward, the **Beginning Inventories** and **Ending Inventories** classifications require some clarification.

Number Range	Account Type	Examples
10000 - 17999	Current Asset	Cash, Accounts Receivable, Marketable Securities, etc.
18000 - 18999	Beginning Inventory	Merchandise Inventory, Raw Materials, Unfinished Goods, Finished Goods, etc.
19000 - 19999	Ending Inventory	Merchandise Inventory, Raw Materials, Unfinished Goods, Finished Goods, etc.
20000 - 29999	Plant Asset	Land, Buildings, Equipment, etc.
30000 - 39999	Current Liability	Accounts Payable, Notes Payable, etc.
40000 - 49999	Long-Term Liability	Notes Payable, Mortgage Payable, etc.
50000 - 59999	Capital	Capital, Common Stock, Treasury Stock, Preferred Stock, etc.
60000 - 69999	Revenue	Sales, Sales Discounts, Sales Allowances, etc.
70000 - 79999	Purchases	Purchases, Purchases Discounts, etc.
80000 - 89999	Expense	Wages, Salaries, Utilities, Travel, etc.
90000 - 99999	Other Revenue or Expense	Interest, Income Taxes, Cash Short and Over, etc.

Figure 8.1   SIMPLE LEDGER account classifications

To correctly determine the cost of goods sold on an income statement, SIMPLE LEDGER needs to know both the starting values and the ending values for a business's inventories. Accordingly, SIMPLE LEDGER requires the operator to maintain two separate accounts for each of the business's inventories. Although this duplication of inventory accounts may seem to be an unacceptable accounting practice, SIMPLE LEDGER knows which inventory figure is appropriate for a particular financial report; therefore, the equality of debits and credits is never corrupted by SIMPLE LEDGER's use of duplicate inventory accounts.

SOURCE LISTING: ledger.cpp

Listing 8.1, **ledger.cpp**, is the source code for SIMPLE LEDGER. This demonstration program illustrates many of the functions that are found in the WINDOWS toolbox: pull-down menus for program navigation, extensive use of dynamic text windows for screen displays, dialog box menus for operator prompts, and considerable use of formatted data entry routines.

Listing 8.1: ledger.cpp

```
/*****************************************************************************
* ledger.cpp - For the WINDOWS Toolbox
*               SIMPLE LEDGER - A Demonstration Program
*****************************************************************************/
#include <stdio.h>
#include <stdlib.h>
#include <string.h>
#include <ctype.h>
#include <time.h>
#include <io.h>
#include "windows.hpp"

#define print_cr() report_line[0] = '\0';\
                   print_line()

typedef struct {
   unsigned long number;
   char name[31];
   double balance;
} ACCOUNT;
```

continued...

```
typedef struct {
    unsigned long acct_no;
    char date[9], description[31];
    double amount;
} TRANSACTION;

void ol_func(void);
void cl_func(void);
void ep_func(void);
void ea_func(void);
void edit_accounts(void);
void et_func(void);
void edit_trans(void);
void ca_func(void);
void tb_func(void);
void glar_func(void);
void fs_func(void);
void setbit(char *, int);
void resetbit(char *, int);
int testbit(char *, int);
int nextbit(char *, int);
int compare(ACCOUNT *, ACCOUNT *);
void savenums(void);
void saveaccts(void);
void savetrans(void);
void start_report(void);
void print_heading(void);
void print_line(void);
double print_accounts(unsigned long, unsigned long, int);
void display_error(char *);

static MENU file[3] = {
    {"Open a Ledger", 0, ol_func, NULL},
    {"Close a Ledger", 0, cl_func, NULL},
    {"Exit the Program", 0, ep_func, NULL} };

static MENU print[4] = {
    {"Print a Chart of Accounts", 8, ca_func, NULL},
    {"Print a Trial Balance", 8, tb_func, NULL},
    {"Print a General Ledger Activity Report", 8, glar_func, NULL},
    {"Print the Financial Statements", 10, fs_func, NULL} };

static MENU accts[1] = {"", 0, ea_func, NULL};

static MENU trans[1] = {"", 0, et_func, NULL};

static MENU_HEAD heads[4] = {
    {"File", 0, 3, file},
    {"Print", 0, 4, print},
    {"Accounts", 0, 1, accts},
    {"Transactions", 0, 1, trans} };
```

continued...

```
static char company_name[31], report_title[81], report_line[81];
static int num_accts, num_trans, gen_att = 0x70;
static int report_page, report_lines;
static ACCOUNT account[100];
static TRANSACTION transaction[200];
static char cnname[13], aname[13], tname[13];
window rwindow;
FILE *cname, *accounts, *transactions;

main(int argc, char *argv[])
{
    int number;
    boolean mono = FALSE;
    pulldown menu(1, 4, heads);

    save_initial_video();
    mouse.on();
    if (argc == 2) {
        if (toupper(argv[1][0]) == 'B')
            mono = TRUE;
    }
    if (!mono) {
        _menu_att = 0x30;
        _menu_hotkey = 0x34;
        _menu_highlight = 0x47;
        gen_att - 0x17;
    }
    menu.display();
    clearscreen(25, 1, 25, 80, _menu_att);
    while (TRUE) {
        printcenter(25, 40, company_name);
        switch (menu.get(0)) {
            case 0:
                rwindow.close();
                fflush(stdprn);
        }
    }
}

void ol_func(void)
{
    char string[9], title[31];
    window w;
    static MENU menu[3] = {
        {"Open a New Ledger", 0, NULL, NULL},
        {"New Ledger Name", 0, NULL, NULL},
        {"Cancel", 0, NULL, NULL} };

    cl_func();
    while (TRUE) {
```

continued...

```
w = window(11, 27, 15, 53, gen_att, _SINGLE_LINE);
w.open();
printstring(13, 29, "Open Ledger:");
drawbox(12, 42, 14, 51, _SINGLE_LINE, gen_att);
string[0] = '\0';
while (TRUE) {
    switch(input_string(13, 43, 8, string)) {
        case 13:
            if (string[0])
                break;
            else
                continue;
        case 27:
            return;
        default:
            continue;
    }
    break;
}
w.close();
sprintf(cnname, "%s.l1", string);
sprintf(aname, "%s.l2", string);
sprintf(tname, "%s.l3", string);
if (filesize(cnname) != -1)
    break;
sprintf(title, "Couldn't Find Ledger: %s", string);
switch (dialog(13, 40, FALSE).get(3, menu, 1, title)) {
    case 'C':
        return;
    case 'N':
        continue;
}
w = window(11, 15, 15, 64, gen_att, _SINGLE_LINE);
w.open();
printstring(13, 17, "Company Name:");
drawbox(12, 31, 14, 62, _SINGLE_LINE, gen_att);
company_name[0] = '\0';
while (TRUE) {
    switch(input_string(13, 32, 30, company_name)) {
        case 13:
            if (company_name[0])
                break;
            else
                continue;
        case 27:
            return;
        default:
            continue;
    }
    break;
```

continued...

```
        }
        w.close();
        w = window(12, 27, 14, 52, gen_att, _SINGLE_LINE, gen_att);
        w.open();
        printstring(13, 29, "Initializing the Files");
        if (!((cname = fopen(cnname, "w+b")) != NULL &&
            fwrite(company_name, 1, 31, cname) == 31 &&
            fwrite(&num_accts, sizeof(int), 1, cname) == 1 &&
            fwrite(&num_trans, sizeof(int), 1, cname) == 1)) {
                if (cname != NULL)
                    fclose(cname);
                cname = NULL;
                company_name[0] = '\0';
                w.close();
                display_error("Couldn't Successfully Open the Ledger");
                return;
        }
        if (!((accounts = fopen(aname, "w+b")) != NULL &&
            fwrite(account, sizeof(ACCOUNT), 100, accounts) == 100)) {
                fclose(cname);
                if (accounts != NULL)
                    fclose(accounts);
                cname = NULL;
                company_name[0] = '\0';
                w.close();
                display_error("Couldn't Successfully Open the Ledger");
                return;
        }
        if (!((transactions = fopen(tname, "w+b")) != NULL &&
            fwrite(transaction, sizeof(TRANSACTION), 200,
                transactions) == 200)) {
                fclose(cname);
                fclose(accounts);
                if (transactions != NULL)
                    fclose(transactions);
                cname = NULL;
                company_name[0] = '\0';
                w.close();
                display_error("Couldn't Successfully Open the Ledger");
                return;
        }
        return;
}
w = window(12, 29, 14, 50, gen_att, _SINGLE_LINE);
w.open();
printstring(13, 31, "Opening the Ledger");
if (!(((cname = fopen(cnname, "r+b")) != NULL &&
    fread(company_name, 1, 31, cname) == 31 &&
    fread(&num_accts, sizeof(int), 1, cname) == 1 &&
    fread(&num_trans, sizeof(int), 1, cname) == 1)) {
```

continued...

```
                    fclose(cname);
                    cname = NULL;
                    company_name[0] = '\0';
                    num_trans = 0;
                    w.close();
                    display_error("Couldn't Successfully Open the Ledger");
                    return;
        }
    if (!((accounts = fopen(aname, "r+b")) != NULL &&
            fread(account, sizeof(ACCOUNT), num_accts,
                accounts) == num_accts)) {
                    fclose(cname);
                    if (accounts != NULL)
                        fclose(accounts);
                    cname = NULL;
                    company_name[0] = '\0';
                    num_trans = 0;
                    w.close();
                    display_error("Couldn't Successfully Open the Ledger");
                    return;
        }
    if (!((transactions = fopen(tname, "r+b")) != NULL &&
            fread(transaction, sizeof(TRANSACTION), num_trans,
                transactions) == num_trans)) {
                    fclose(cname);
                    fclose(accounts);
                    if (transactions != NULL)
                        fclose(transactions);
                    cname = NULL;
                    company_name[0] = '\0';
                    num_trans = 0;
                    w.close();
                    display_error("Couldn't Successfully Open the Ledger");
        }
}

void cl_func(void)
{
    int i;

    if (cname != NULL) {
        fclose(cname);
        fclose(accounts);
        fclose(transactions);
        cname = accounts = transactions = NULL;
        company_name[0] = '\0';
        clearscreen(25, 1, 25, 80, _menu_att);
        num_accts = num_trans = 0;
    }
}
```

continued...

```
void ep_func(void)
{
    cl_func();
    exit(0);
}

void ea_func(void)
{
    int number;

    number = num_accts;
    edit_accounts();
    if (num_accts || number) {
        savenums();
        saveaccts();
    }
}

void edit_accounts(void)
{
    int i, field, current_account = 0, key;
    ACCOUNT acct;
    window w1, w2;

    if (cname == NULL)
        return;
    w1 = window(7, 14, 19, 65, gen_att, _SINGLE_LINE);
    w1.open();
    printstring(9, 16, "Account Number");
    drawbox(8, 32, 10, 30, _SINGLE_LINE, gen_att);
    printstring(12, 16, "Account Name");
    drawbox(11, 32, 13, 63, _SINGLE_LINE, gen_att);
    printstring(15, 16, "Account Balance");
    drawbox(14, 32, 16, 43, _SINGLE_LINE, gen_att);
    while (TRUE) {
        clearscreen(18, 15, 18, 64, gen_att);
        if (num_accts) {
            printcenter(18, 40, "ESC - Cancel  A - Add  E - Edit  D - Delete");
            display_number(9, 33, 5, account[current_account].number);
            display_string(12, 33, 30, account[current_account].name);
            display_dollar(15, 33, 10, account[current_account].balance);
        }
        else {
            printcenter(18, 40, "ESC - Cancel  A - Add");
            clearscreen(9, 33, 9, 37, gen_att);
            clearscreen(12, 33, 12, 62, gen_att);
            clearscreen(15, 33, 15, 42, gen_att);
        }
```

continued...

```
while (TRUE) {
    key = waitkey();
    if (key == 27) {
        return;
    }
    if (key == 328) {
        if (current_account) {
            current_account--;
            break;
        }
        continue;
    }
    if (key == 336) {
        if (current_account + 1 < num_accts) {
            current_account++;
            break;
        }
        continue;
    }
    if (key < 32 || key > 127)
        continue;
    switch (toupper(key)) {
        case 'A':
            if (num_accts == 100)
                continue;
            acct.number = acct.balance = 0;
            acct.name[0] = '\0';
            clearscreen(18, 15, 18, 64, gen_att);
            printcenter(18, 40, "ESC - Cancel");
            clearscreen(12, 33, 12, 62, gen_att);
            clearscreen(15, 33, 15, 42, gen_att);
            while (TRUE) {
                while (acct.number < 10000 || acct.number > 99999) {
                    if (input_number(9, 33, 5, acct.number)
                        == 27) {
                        return;
                    }
                }
                for (i = 0; i < num_accts; i++) {
                    if (account[i].number == acct.number) {
                        w2 = window(20, 14, 20, 65, _menu_highlight);
                        w2.open();
                        putchar(7);
                        printcenter(20, 40,
                            "Account already exists!");
                        waitkey();
                        w2.close();
                        break;
                    }
                }
```

continued...

```
                        if (i == num_accts)
                                break;
                        acct.number = 0;
                }
                field = 1;
                clearscreen(18, 15, 18, 64, gen_att);
                printcenter(18, 40, "ESC - Cancel  F10 - Process");
                while (TRUE) {
                        if (field == 1)
                                key = input_string(12, 33, 30, acct.name);
                        else
                                key = input_dollar(15, 33, 10, acct.balance);
                        switch (key) {
                                case 27:
                                        return;
                                case 13:
                                case 336:
                                        if (field == 1)
                                                field = 2;
                                        continue;
                                case 324:
                                        account[num_accts].number = acct.number;
                                        strcpy(account[num_accts].name, acct.name);
                                        account[num_accts++].balance = acct.balance;
                                        qsort(account, num_accts, sizeof(ACCOUNT),
                                                compare);
                                        for (i = 0; i < num_accts; i++) {
                                                if (account[i].number == acct.number) {
                                                        current_account = i;
                                                        break;
                                                }
                                        }
                                        break;
                                case 328:
                                        if (field == 2)
                                                field = 1;
                                        continue;
                                default:
                                        continue;
                        }
                        break;
                }
                break;
        case 'D':
                if (!num_accts)
                        break;
                if (!--num_accts)
                        break;
```

continued...

```
                    for (i = current_account; i < num_accts; i++) {
                        account[i].number = account[i + 1].number;
                        strcpy(account[i].name, account[i + 1].name);
                        account[i].balance = account[i + 1].balance;
                    }
                    if (current_account == num_accts)
                        current_account--;
                    break;
                case 'E':
                    strcpy(acct.name, account[current_account].name);
                    acct.balance = account[current_account].balance;
                    field = 1;
                    clearscreen(18, 15, 18, 64, gen_att);
                    printcenter(18, 40, "ESC - Cancel  F10 - Process");
                    while (TRUE) {
                        if (field == 1)
                            key = input_string(12, 33, 30, acct.name);
                        else
                            key = input_dollar(15, 33, 10, acct.balance);
                        switch (key) {
                            case 27:
                                return;
                            case 13:
                            case 336:
                                if (field == 1)
                                    field = 2;
                                continue;
                            case 324:
                                strcpy(account[current_account].name,
                                    acct.name);
                                account[current_account].balance =
                                    acct.balance;
                                break;
                            case 328:
                                if (field == 2)
                                    field = 1;
                                continue;
                            default:
                                continue;
                        }
                        break;
                    }
                    break;
                default:
                    continue;
            }
            break;
        }
    }
}
```

continued...

```
void et_func(void)
{
    int number;

    number = num_trans;
    edit_trans();
    if (num_trans || number) {
        savenums();
        savetrans();
    }
}

void edit_trans(void)
{
    int i, field, current_trans = 0, key;
    double total = 0;
    ACCOUNT acct, *acct_ptr;
    TRANSACTION trans;
    window w1, w2;

    if (!num_accts)
        return;
    for (i = 0; i < num_trans; i++)
        total += transaction[i].amount;
    w1 = window(4, 14, 22, 65, gen_att, _SINGLE_LINE);
    w1.open();
    printstring(6, 16, "Account Number");
    drawbox(5, 32, 7, 38, _SINGLE_LINE, gen_att);
    printstring(9, 16, "Account Name");
    drawbox(8, 32, 10, 63, _SINGLE_LINE, gen_att);
    printstring(12, 16, "Date");
    drawbox(11, 32, 13, 41, _SINGLE_LINE, gen_att);
    printstring(15, 16, "Description");
    drawbox(14, 32, 16, 63, _SINGLE_LINE, gen_att);
    printstring(18, 16, "Amount");
    drawbox(17, 32, 19, 43, _SINGLE_LINE, gen_att);
    drawbox(17, 52, 19, 63, _SINGLE_LINE, gen_att);
    while (TRUE) {
        clearscreen(21, 15, 21, 64, gen_att);
        if (num_trans) {
            printcenter(21, 40, "ESC - Cancel  A - Add  E - Edit  D - Delete");
            acct.number = transaction[current_trans].acct_no;
            display_number(6, 33, 5, acct.number);
            acct_ptr = bsearch(&acct, account, num_accts,
                sizeof(ACCOUNT), compare);
            display_string(9, 33, 30, acct_ptr->name);
            display_string(12, 33, 8, transaction[current_trans].date);
            display_string(15, 33, 30,
                transaction[current_trans].description);
            display_dollar(18, 33, 10,
                transaction[current_trans].amount);
```

continued...

```
                display_dollar(18, 53, 10, total);
        }
        else {
                printcenter(21, 40, "ESC - Cancel  A - Add");
                clearscreen(6, 33, 6, 37, gen_att);
                clearscreen(9, 33, 9, 62, gen_att);
                clearscreen(12, 33, 12, 40, gen_att);
                clearscreen(15, 33, 15, 62, gen_att);
                clearscreen(18, 33, 18, 42, gen_att);
                clearscreen(18, 53, 18, 62, gen_att);
        }
        while (TRUE) {
                key = waitkey();
                if (key == 27) {
                        return;
                }
                if (key == 328) {
                        if (current_trans) {
                                current_trans--;
                                break;
                        }
                        continue;
                }
                if (key == 336) {
                        if (current_trans + 1 < num_trans) {
                                current_trans++;
                                break;
                        }
                        continue;
                }
                if (key < 32 || key > 127)
                        continue;
                switch (toupper(key)) {
                        case 'A':
                                if (num_trans == 200)
                                        continue;
                                trans.acct_no = trans.amount = 0;
                                if (num_trans) {
                                        strcpy(trans.date, transaction[num_trans - 1].date);
                                        strcpy(trans.description,
                                                transaction[num_trans - 1].description);
                                }
                                else
                                        trans.date[0] = trans.description[0] = '\0';
                                clearscreen(21, 15, 21, 64, gen_att);
                                printcenter(21, 40, "ESC - Cancel");
                                clearscreen(6, 33, 6, 37, gen_att);
                                clearscreen(9, 33, 9, 62, gen_att);
                                display_string(12, 33, 8, trans.date);
                                display_string(15, 33, 30, trans.description);
                                clearscreen(18, 33, 18, 42, gen_att);
                                while (TRUE) {
```

continued...

```
            while (trans.acct_no < 10000 ||
                trans.acct_no > 99999) {
                if (input_number(6, 33, 5, trans.acct_no) == 27) {
                        return;
                }
            }
            acct.number = trans.acct_no;
            if ((acct_ptr = bsearch(&acct, account, num_accts,
                sizeof(ACCOUNT), compare)) == NULL) {
                w2 = window(23, 14, 23, 65, _menu_highlight);
                w2.open();
                putchar(7);
                printcenter(23, 40,
                    "That account number doesn't exist");
                waitkey();
                w2.close();
                trans.acct_no = 0;
            }
            else
                break;
    }
    display_string(9, 33, 30, acct_ptr->name);
    field = 3;
    clearscreen(21, 15, 21, 64, gen_att);
    printcenter(21, 40, "ESC - Cancel   F10 - Process");
    while (TRUE) {
        switch (field) {
            case 1:
                key = input_string(12, 33, 8, trans.date);
                break;
            case 2:
                key = input_string(15, 33, 30,
                    trans.description);
                break;
            case 3:
                key = input_dollar(18, 33, 10, trans.amount);
        }
        switch (key) {
            case 27:
                return;
            case 13:
            case 336:
                if (field == 1 || field == 2)
                    field++;
                continue;
            case 324:
                transaction[num_trans].acct_no =
                    trans.acct_no;
                strcpy(transaction[num_trans].date,
                    trans.date);
                strcpy(transaction[num_trans].description,
                    trans.description);
```

continued...

```
                                transaction[num_trans].amount =
                                        trans.amount;
                                total += trans.amount;
                                current_trans = num_trans;
                                num_trans++;
                                break;
                        case 328:
                                if (field == 2 || field == 3)
                                        field--;
                                continue;
                        default:
                                continue;
                    }
                    break;
            }
            break;
        case 'D':
            if (!num_trans)
                    break;
            if (!--num_trans) {
                    total = 0;
                    break;
            }
            total -= transaction[current_trans].amount;
            for (i = current_trans; i < num_trans; i++) {
                    transaction[i].acct_no = transaction[i + 1].acct_no;
                    strcpy(transaction[i].date, transaction[i + 1].date);
                    strcpy(transaction[i].description,
                            transaction[i + 1].description);
                    transaction[i].amount = transaction[i + 1].amount;
            }
            if (current_trans == num_trans)
                    current_trans--;
            break;
        case 'E':
            strcpy(trans.date, transaction[current_trans].date);
            strcpy(trans.description,
                    transaction[current_trans].description);
            trans.amount = transaction[current_trans].amount;
            field = 1;
            clearscreen(21, 15, 21, 64, gen_att);
            printcenter(21, 40, "ESC - Cancel  F10 - Process");
            while (TRUE) {
                    switch (field) {
                            case 1:
                                    key = input_string(12, 33, 8, trans.date);
                                    break;
                            case 2:
                                    key = input_string(15, 33, 30,
                                            trans.description);
                                    break;
```

continued...

```
                                case 3:
                                    key = input_dollar(18, 33, 10, trans.amount);
                            }
                            switch (key) {
                                case 27:
                                    return;
                                case 13:
                                case 336:
                                    if (field == 1 || field == 2)
                                        field++;
                                    continue;
                                case 324:
                                    strcpy(transaction[current_trans].date,
                                        trans.date);
                                    strcpy(transaction[current_trans].description,
                                        trans.description);
                                    total += -transaction[current_trans].amount +
                                        trans.amount;
                                    transaction[current_trans].amount =
                                        trans.amount;
                                    break;
                                case 328:
                                    if (field == 2 || field == 3)
                                        field--;
                                    continue;
                                default:
                                    continue;
                            }
                            break;
                        }
                        break;
                default:
                    continue;
            }
            break;
        }

    }
}

void ca_func(void)
{
    int i;

    if (!num_accts)
        return;
    sprintf(report_title, "Chart of Accounts");
    start_report();
    for (i = 0; i < num_accts; i++) {
        sprintf(report_line, "%5lu %-30s %10.2f ", account[i].number,
            account[i].name, account[i].balance);
```

continued...

```
        while (TRUE) {
            if (account[i].number < 18000) {
                strcat(report_line, " Current Asset");
                break;
            }
            if (account[i].number < 19000) {
                strcat(report_line, " Beginning Inventory");
                break;
            }
            if (account[i].number < 20000) {
                strcat(report_line, " Ending Inventory");
                break;
            }
            if (account[i].number < 30000) {
                strcat(report_line, " Plant Asset");
                break;
            }
            if (account[i].number < 40000) {
                strcat(report_line, " Current Liability");
                break;
            }
            if (account[i].number < 50000) {
                strcat(report_line, " Long-Term Liability");
                break;
            }
            if (account[i].number < 60000) {
                strcat(report_line, " Capital");
                break;
            }
            if (account[i].number < 70000) {
                strcat(report_line, " Revenue");
                break;
            }
            if (account[i].number < 80000) {
                strcat(report_line, " Purchase");
                break;
            }
            if (account[i].number < 90000) {
                strcat(report_line, " Expense");
                break;
            }
            strcat(report_line, " Other Revenue or Expense");
            break;
        }
        print_line();
    }
    fprintf(stdprn, "%c", 12);;
}
```

continued...

```
void tb_func(void)
{
    int i;
    double debits = 0, credits = 0;

    if (!num_accts)
        return;
    sprintf(report_title, "Trial Balance");
    start_report();
    for (i = 0; i < num_accts; i++) {
        if (account[i].number < 19000 || account[i].number > 19999) {
            if (account[i].balance >= 0) {
                debits += account[i].balance;
                sprintf(report_line, "%5lu %-30s %10.2f", account[i].number,
                    account[i].name, account[i].balance);
                print_line();
            }
        }
    }
    for (i = 0; i < num_accts; i++) {
        if (account[i].number < 19000 || account[i].number > 19999) {
            if (account[i].balance < 0) {
                credits += account[i].balance;
                sprintf(report_line, "%5lu %-30s %21.2f", account[i].number,
                    account[i].name, -account[i].balance);
                print_line();
            }
        }
    }
    sprintf(report_line, "%37s---------- ----------", "");
    print_line();
    sprintf(report_line, "%37s%10.2f %10.2f", "", debits, -credits);
    print_line();
    sprintf(report_line, "%37s========== ==========", "");
    print_line();
    fprintf(stdprn, "%c", 12);;
}

void glar_func(void)
{
    int i, j, k;
    ACCOUNT acct, *acct_ptr;
    static double acct_bal[100];

    if (!num_accts || !num_trans)
        return;
    sprintf(report_title, "Journal Entries");
    start_report();
    for (i = 0; i < num_trans; i++) {
        acct.number = transaction[i].acct_no;
        acct_ptr = bsearch(&acct, account, num_accts, sizeof(ACCOUNT),
            compare);
```

continued...

```
        if (transaction[i].amount >= 0)
            sprintf(report_line, "%8s %5lu %-30s %10.2f", transaction[i].date,
                transaction[i].acct_no, acct_ptr->name,
                transaction[i].amount);
        else
            sprintf(report_line, "%8s %5lu %-30s %21.2f", transaction[i].date,
                transaction[i].acct_no, acct_ptr->name,
                -transaction[i].amount);
        print_line();
}
fprintf(stdprn, "%c", 12);;
rwindow.close();
sprintf(report_title, "Account Activity Report");
start_report();
for (i = 0; i < num_accts; i++) {
    acct_bal[i] = account[i].balance;
    for (j = 0; j < num_trans; j++) {
        if (account[i].number == transaction[j].acct_no) {
            sprintf(report_line, "Account Number: %5lu",
                account[i].number);
            print_line();
            sprintf(report_line, "Account Name  : %s", account[i].name);
            print_line();
            for (k = 0; k < 61; k++)
                fprintf(stdprn, "=");
            print_cr();
            sprintf(report_line, "%-8s %-30s %10s %10s", "Date",
                "Description", "Amount", "Balance");
            print_line();
            for (k = 0; k < 61; k++)
                fprintf(stdprn, "-");
            print_cr();
            sprintf(report_line, "%8s %-30s %21.2f", "",
                "Beginning Balance", acct_bal[i]);
            print_line();
            for (k = j; k < num_trans; k++) {
                if (account[i].number == transaction[k].acct_no) {
                    acct_bal[i] += transaction[k].amount;
                    sprintf(report_line, "%8s %-30s %10.2f %10.2f",
                        transaction[k].date, transaction[k].description,
                        transaction[k].amount, acct_bal[i]);
                    print_line();
                }
            }
            sprintf(report_line, "%8s %-30s %21.2f", "",
                "Ending Balance", acct_bal[i]);
            print_line();
            for (k = 0; k < 61; k++)
                fprintf(stdprn, "=");
            print_cr();
            print_cr();
            break;
```

continued...

```
                }
            }
        }
        fprintf(stdprn, "%c", 12);;
        for (i = 0; i < num_accts; i++)
            account[i].balance = acct_bal[i];
        num_trans = 0;
        savenums();
        saveaccts();
}

void fs_func(void)
{
        double reg1, reg2, net_income;

        if (!num_accts)
            return;
        sprintf(report_title, "Income Statement");
        start_report();
        sprintf(report_line, "Revenues:");
        print_line();
        reg1 = print_accounts(60000, 69999, -1);
        sprintf(report_line, "%-30s %21.2f", "Total Revenues", reg1);
        print_line();
        print_cr();
        sprintf(report_line, "Cost of Goods Sold:");
        print_line();
        print_cr();
        sprintf(report_line, "Beginning Inventories:");
        print_line();
        reg2 = print_accounts(18000, 18999, 1);
        sprintf(report_line, "%-30s %10.2f", "Total Beginning Inventories", reg2);
        print_line();
        print_cr();
        sprintf(report_line, "Plus Purchases:");
        print_line();
        reg2 += print_accounts(70000, 79999, 1);
        sprintf(report_line, "%-30s %10.2f", "Goods Available for Sale", reg2);
        print_line();
        print_cr();
        sprintf(report_line, "Less Ending Inventories:");
        print_line();
        reg2 -= print_accounts(19000, 19999, 1);
        sprintf(report_line, "%-30s %21.2f", "Total Cost of Goods Sold", reg2);
        print_line();
        sprintf(report_line, "%30s %21s", "", "----------");
        print_line();
        reg1 -= reg2;
        sprintf(report_line, "%-30s %21.2f", "Gross Profit", reg1);
        print_line();
        print_cr();
        sprintf(report_line, "Operating Expenses:");
```

continued...

```
print_line();
reg2 = print_accounts(80000, 89999, 1);
sprintf(report_line, "%-30s %21.2f", "Total Operating Expenses", reg2);
print_line();
sprintf(report_line, "%30s %21s", "", "----------");
print_line();
reg1 -= reg2;
sprintf(report_line, "%-30s %21.2f", "Income from Operations", reg1);
print_line();
print_cr();
sprintf(report_line, "Other Revenues & Expenses:");
print_line();
reg2 = print_accounts(90000, 99999, -1);
sprintf(report_line, "%-30s %21.2f", "Totl Other Revenues & Expenses",
     reg2);
print_line();
sprintf(report_line, "%30s %21s", "", "----------");
print_line();
reg1 += reg2;
sprintf(report_line, "%-30s %21.2f", "Net Income", reg1);
print_line();
sprintf(report_line, "%30s %21s", "", "==========");
print_line();
fprintf(stdprn, "%c", 12);
net_income = reg1;
rwindow.close();
sprintf(report_title, "Balance Sheet");
start_report();
sprintf(report_line, "Assets:");
print_line();
print_cr();
sprintf(report_line, "Current Assets:");
print_line();
reg1 = print_accounts(10000, 17999, 1) +
     print_accounts(19000, 19999, 1);
sprintf(report_line, "%-30s %21.2f", "Total Current Assets", reg1);
print_line();
print_cr();
sprintf(report_line, "Plant Assets:");
print_line();
reg2 = print_accounts(20000, 29999, 1);
sprintf(report_line, "%-30s %21.2f", "Total Plant Assets", reg2);
print_line();
sprintf(report_line, "%30s %21s", "", "----------");
print_line();
reg1 += reg2;
sprintf(report_line, "%-30s %21.2f", "Total Assets", reg1);
print_line();
sprintf(report_line, "%30s %21s", "", "==========");
print_line();
print_cr();
sprintf(report_line, "Liabilities:");
```

continued...

```
    print_line();
    print_cr();
    sprintf(report_line, "Current Liabilities:");
    print_line();
    reg1 = print_accounts(30000, 39999, -1);
    sprintf(report_line, "%-30s %21.2f", "Total Current Liabilities", reg1);
    print_line();
    print_cr();
    sprintf(report_line, "Long-Term Liabilities:");
    print_line();
    reg2 = print_accounts(40000, 49999, -1);
    sprintf(report_line, "%-30s %21.2f", "Total Plant Assets", reg2);
    print_line();
    sprintf(report_line, "%30s %21s", "", "----------");
    print_line();
    reg1 += reg2;
    sprintf(report_line, "%-30s %21.2f", "Total Liabilities", reg1);
    print_line();
    print_cr();
    sprintf(report_line, "Capital:");
    print_line();
    reg2 = print_accounts(50000, 59999, -1);
    sprintf(report_line, "%-30s %10.2f", "Net Income", net_income);
    print_line();
    sprintf(report_line, "%30s ----------", "");
    print_line();
    reg2 += net_income;
    sprintf(report_line, "%-30s %21.2f", "Total Capital", reg2);
    print_line();
    sprintf(report_line, "%30s %21s", "", "----------");
    print_line();
    reg1 += reg2;
    sprintf(report_line, "%-30s %21.2f", "Total Liabilities and Capital",
        reg1);
    print_line();
    sprintf(report_line, "%30s %21s", "", "==========");
    print_line();
    fprintf(stdprn, "%c", 12);
}

int compare(ACCOUNT *acct1, ACCOUNT *acct2)
{
    if (acct1->number < acct2->number)
        return(-1);
    if (acct1->number > acct2->number)
        return(1);
    return(0);
}
```

continued...

```
void savenums(void)
{
    if (!(!fseek(cname, 31, SEEK_SET) &&
        fwrite(&num_accts, sizeof(int), 1, cname) == 1 &&
        fwrite(&num_trans, sizeof(int), 1, cname) == 1)) {
        display_error("Disk write error");
    }
}

void saveaccts(void)
{
    if (!(!fseek(accounts, 0, SEEK_SET) &&
        fwrite(account, sizeof(ACCOUNT), num_accts,
        accounts) == num_accts))
        display_error("Disk write error");
}

void savetrans(void)
{
    if (!(!fseek(transactions, 0, SEEK_SET) &&
        fwrite(transaction, sizeof(TRANSACTION), num_trans,
        transactions) == num_trans))
        display_error("Disk write error");
}

void start_report(void)
{
    int col1, col2;
    char mess[81];

    sprintf(mess, "Please wait while I print the %s", report_title);
    col1 = 40 - (strlen(mess) + 4) / 2;
    col2 = col1 + strlen(mess) + 3;
    rwindow = window(12, col1, 14, col2, gen_att, _SINGLE_LINE);
    rwindow.open();
    printstring(13, col1 + 2, mess);
    report_page = 0;
    print_heading();
}

void print_heading(void)
{
    char *tstring;
    time_t ltime;

    fprintf(stdprn, "\n");
    fprintf(stdprn, "%s\n", company_name);
    fprintf(stdprn, "%s\n", report_title);
    time(&ltime);
    tstring = ctime(&ltime);
    fprintf(stdprn, "%3.3s %2.2s, %4.4s\n", tstring + 4, tstring + 8,
        tstring + 20);
```

continued...

```c
        fprintf(stdprn, "Page: %d\n", ++report_page);
        fprintf(stdprn, "\n");
        report_lines = 6;
}

void print_line(void)
{
    fprintf(stdprn, "%s\n", report_line);
    if (++report_lines == 60) {
        fprintf(stdprn, "%c", 12);;
        print_heading();
    }
}

double print_accounts(unsigned long facct, unsigned long lacct, int sign)
{
    int i;
    double total = 0;

    for (i = 0; i < num_accts; i++) {
        if (account[i].number >= facct && account[i].number <= lacct) {
            sprintf(report_line, "%-30s %10.2f", account[i].name,
                account[i].balance * sign);
            print_line();
            total += account[i].balance * sign;
        }
    }
    if (facct != 10000 && facct != 50000) {
        sprintf(report_line, "%30s ----------", "");
        print_line();
    }
    return(total);
}

void display_error(char *string)
{
    static MENU menu[1] = {"OK", 0, NULL, NULL};

    dialog(13, 40, FALSE).get(1, menu, 1, string);
}
```

Function Description: main

As with all C++ programs, the **main** function is the main program loop. Its implementation is illustrated by the following pseudocode:

```
initialize WINDOWS and save the current display screen
turn on the mouse pointer
if (parameter = = 'B') {
    monochrome flag = TRUE
}
if (!monochrome flag) {
    set the attributes for a color display
}
display the pull-down menu bar
clear the bottom display line
while (TRUE) {
    display the company name on the bottom display line
    switch (pull-down menu return key) {
        case 0:
            close the report window
            flush the printer buffer
    }
}
```

Function Description: ol_func

The **ol_func** function opens a general ledger. Its implementation is illustrated by the following pseudocode:

```
close any currently open ledger
while (TRUE) {
    open and display the data entry window
    while (TRUE) {
        switch (data entry return key) {
            case ENTER:
                if (ledger name was entered) {
                    break
                }
                else {
                    continue
```

continued...

```
            }
        case ESC:
            close the data entry window
            return to the pull-down menu system
        default:
            continue
    }
}
close the data entry window
set the filenames
if (the ledger exists) {
    break
}
switch (dialog box return key) {
    case 'C':
        return to the pull-down menu system
    case 'N':
        loop to get a new ledger name
}
open and display the data entry window
while (TRUE) {
    switch (data entry return key) {
        case ENTER:
            if (a company name was entered) {
                break
            }
            else {
                continue
            }
        case ESC:
            close the data entry window
            return to the pull-down menu system
        default:
            continue
    }
}
close the data entry window
open and display a message window
open and initialize the company data file
open and initialize the accounts file
open and initialize the transactions file
close the message window
return to the pull-down menu system
}
```

continued...

read the company data file
open and read the accounts file
open and read the transactions file
close the data entry window

Function Description: cl_func

The **cl_func** function closes an open general ledger. Its implementation is illustrated by the following pseudocode:

if (a ledger is open) {
    close the company data file
    close the accounts file
    close the transactions file
    set the streams to NULL
    company name string = ""
    erase the company name on the bottom display screen line
    number of accounts = 0
    number of transactions = 0
}

Function Description: ep_func

The **ep_func** function exits from SIMPLE LEDGER to MS-DOS. Its implementation is illustrated by the following pseudocode:

close any currently open general ledger
exit to DOS and signal no errors

Function Description: ea_func

The **ea_func** function adds, edits, and deletes general ledger accounts. Its implementation is illustrated by the following pseudocode:

save the current number of accounts
edit the accounts
if (number of accounts has changed) {
    save the new account data
}

Function Description: edit_accounts

The **edit_accounts** function is used by the **ea_func** function to add, edit, and delete general ledger accounts. Its implementation is illustrated by the following pseudocode:

```
if (a ledger isn't open) {
    return
}
open and display the data entry window
while (TRUE) {
    erase the control keys message
    if (ledger isn't empty) {
        display the new control keys message
        display the current account's number
        display the current account's name
        display the current account's balance
    }
    else {
        display the new control keys message
        erase the data entry fields
    }
    while (TRUE) {
        get a key
        if (key = = ESC) {
            return
        }
        if (key = = UP ARROW) {
            if (current account ! = first account) {
                current account--
                break
            }
            continue
        }
        if (key = = DOWN ARROW) {
            if (current account ! = last account) {
                current account + +
                break
            }
            continue
        }
        if (key isn't a printable character) {
            continue
```

continued...

```
        }
        switch (key) {
            case 'A':
                if (ledger is full) {
                    continue
                }
                account number = 0
                account balance = 0
                account name = ""
                erase the control keys message
                display the new control keys message
                get a valid account number
                get the account name and balance
                break
            case 'D':
                if (ledger is empty) {
                    break
                }
                number of accounts--
                if (there was only one account) {
                    break
                reposition the remaining accounts
                break
            case 'E':
                account name = current account name
                account balance = current account balance
                erase the control keys message
                display the control keys message
                get the new account name and balance
                save the new account name and balance
                break
            default:
                continue
        }
        break
    }
}
```

Function Description: et_func

The **et_func** function adds, edits, and deletes general ledger transactions. Its implementation is illustrated by the following pseudocode:

```
save the number of transactions
edit the transactions
if (number of transactions has changed) {
    save the new transactions data
}
```

Function Description: edit_trans

The **edit_trans** function is called by the **et_func** to add, edit, and delete general ledger transactions. Its implementation is illustrated by the following pseudo-code:

```
if (ledger is empty) {
    return
}
figure the debits/credits difference
open and display the data entry window
while (TRUE) {
    erase the control keys message
    if (number of transactions) {
        display the new control keys message
        display the current transaction's account number
        display the current transaction's account name
        display the current transaction's date
        display the current transaction's description
        display the current transaction's amount
        display the debits/credits difference
    }
    else {
        display the new control keys message
        erase the data entry fields
        erase the debits/credits difference
    }

    continued...
```

```
while (TRUE) {
    get a key
    if (key = = ESC) {
        return
    }
    if (key = = UP ARROW) {
        if (current transaction ! = first transaction) {
            current transaction--
            break
        }
        continue
    }
    if (key = = DOWN ARROW) {
        if (current transaction ! = last transaction) {
            current transaction + +
            break
        }
        continue
    }
    if (key isn't a printable character) {
        continue
    }
    switch (key) {
        case 'A':
            if (transactions file is full) {
                continue
            }
            transaction account number = 0
            transaction amount = 0
            if (transactions file isn't empty) {
                transaction date = last transaction date
                transaction description = last transaction description
            }
            else {
                transaction date = ""
                transaction description = ""
            }
            erase the control keys message
            display the new control keys message
            get the transaction account number
            get the transaction date
            get the transaction description
            get the transaction amount
            break
```

continued...

```
        case 'D':
            if (there aren't any transactions) {
                break
            }
            number of transactions--
            if (there was only one transaction) {
                break
            }
            adjust the debits/credits difference
            reposition the remaining transactions
            break
        case 'E':
            transaction date = current transaction date
            transaction description = current transaction description
            transaction amount = current transaction amount
            erase the control keys message
            display the new control keys message
            get the new transaction date
            get the new transaction description
            get the new transaction amount
            save the new transaction date
            save the new transaction description
            save the new transaction amount
            break
        default
            continue
        }
        break
    }
}
```

Function Description: ca_func

The **ca_func** prints a chart of accounts. Its implementation is illustrated by the following pseudocode:

```
if (ledger is empty) {
    return to the pull-down menu system
}
set the report title
start the report

        continued...
```

```
for (i = 0; i < number of accounts; i+ +) {
    print the account's number, name, balance, and description
}
do a form feed
```

Function Description: tb_func

The **tb_func** function prints a trial balance. Its implementation is illustrated by the following pseudocode:

```
debits = 0
credits = 0
if (ledger is empty) {
    return to the pull-down menu system
}
set the report title
start the report
for (i = 0; i < number of accounts; i+ +) {
    if (account isn't an ending inventory account) {
        if (account has a debit balance) {
            debits + = account balance
            print the account's number, name and balance
        }
    }
}
for (i = 0; i < number of accounts; i+ +) {
    if (account isn't an ending inventory account) {
        if (account has a credit balance) {
            credits + = account balance
            print the account's number, name, and balance
        }
    }
}
print the total debits and credits
do a form feed
```

Function Description: glar_func

The **glar_func** function prints a general ledger activity report, posts the transactions to their respective accounts, and closes out the transactions file. Its implementation is illustrated by the following pseudocode:

```
if (ledger is empty || there aren't any transactions) {
    return to the pull-down menu system
}
set the report title
start up the report
for (i = 0; i < number of transactions; i+ +) {
    print the transaction's number and amount
}
do a form feed
close the report window
set the report title
start up the report
for (i = 0; i < number of accounts; i+ +) {
    updated account balance = current account balance
    for (j = 0; j < number of transactions; j+ +) {
        if (account number = = transaction's account number) {
            print the account number
            print the account name
            print the beginning balance
            for (k = j; k < number of transactions; k+ +) {
                if (account number = = transaction's account number) {
                    updated account balance + = transaction amount
                    print the transaction's date, description, amount,
                        and the updated account balance
                }
            }
            print the ending account balance
        }
    }
}
do a form feed
save the new account balances
number of transactions = 0
save the updated data files
```

Function Description: fs_func

The **fs_func** function prints an income statement and a balance sheet. Its implementation is illustrated by the following pseudocode:


```
if (ledger is empty) {
     return to the pull-down menu system
}
set the report title
start the report
print the revenue accounts
print the total revenues
print the beginning inventory accounts
print the total beginning inventories
print the purchase accounts
print the total goods available for sale
print the ending inventory accounts
print the total cost of goods sold
print the gross profit
print the expense accounts
print the total operating expenses
print the income from operations
print the other revenue and expense accounts
print the total other revenues and expenses
print the net income
close the report window
set the new report title
start the report
print the current asset accounts
print the ending inventory accounts
print the total current assets
print the plant asset accounts
print the total plant assets
print the total assets
print the current liability accounts
print the total current liabilities
print the long-term liability accounts
print the total long-term liabilities
print the total liabilities
print the capital accounts
print the net income
print the total capital
print the total liabilities and capital
```

Function Description: compare

The **compare** function is used by the **qsort** and **bsearch** functions to compare account structures. Its implementation is illustrated by the following pseudocode:

```
if (first account number < second account number) {
    return(-1)
}
if (first account number > second account number) {
    return(1)
}
return(0)
```

Function Description: savenums

The **savenums** function saves the number of accounts and the number of transactions to the company data file. Its implementation is illustrated by the following pseudocode:

```
set the file position to the number of accounts offset
write the number of accounts
write the number of transactions
```

Function Description: saveaccts

The **saveaccts** function saves the general ledger accounts to the accounts file. Its implementation is illustrated by the following pseudocode:

```
set the file position to the start of the accounts file
write the accounts
```

Function Description: savetrans

The **savetrans** function saves the general ledger transactions to the transactions file. Its implementation is illustrated by the following pseudocode:

set the file position to the start of the transactions file
write the transactions

Function Description: start_report

The **start_report** function opens the report window and prints the first page's report heading. Its implementation is illustrated by the following pseudocode:

set the report window message
open the report window
display the report message
set the page number
print the report heading

Function Description: print_heading

The **print_heading** function prints a report heading. Its implementation is illustrated by the following pseudocode:

print a carriage return
print the company name
print the report title
print the date
print the page number
set the initial number of printed lines

Function Description: print_line

The **print_line** function prints a report line. Its implementation is illustrated by the following pseudocode:

```
print the report line
if (page is full) {
    do a form feed
    print a report heading
}
```

Function Description: print_accounts

The **print_accounts** function is used by the **fs_func** function to print account groups. Its implementation is illustrated by the following pseudocode:

```
total = 0
for (i = 0; i < number of accounts; i + +) {
    if (account number is in the specified range) {
        print the account's name and balance
        total + = account balance
    }
}
if (not printing current asset or capital accounts) {
    print an underline
}
```

Function Description: display_error

The **display_error** function displays error messages. Its implementation is illustrated by the following pseudocode:

```
display the error message in a dialog box
```

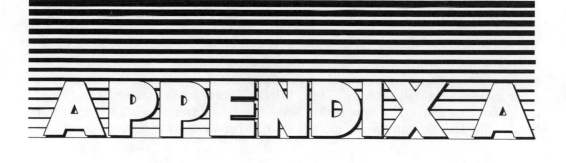

WINDOWS REFERENCE GUIDE

This appendix presents a complete reference guide for the WINDOWS toolbox. It defines and describes the global variables, standard data types, and objects included in WINDOWS and gives a syntax summary, description of purpose, and coding example for each of the WINDOWS functions.

GLOBAL VARIABLES

As mentioned in Chapter 3, the WINDOWS toolbox defines a number of global variables in the **windows.hpp** header file. These global variables are used by the application programmer to change many of the WINDOWS operating environment's default settings. Thus, WINDOWS is easily customized to meet the needs of a variety of application programs. Additionally, the **windows.hpp** header file defines a number of global variables for a variety of mouse operations.

__left__button

Defined As: int _left_button;

Description: After a call to the **read_mouse** function, the **_left_button** variable holds the mouse's left button status. If the left button is being held down, **_left_button** will be set to TRUE (1). Otherwise, **_left_button** will be set to FALSE (0) to indicate a released left button.

__menu__att

Defined As: int _menu_att;

Description: The **_menu_att** variable is used by the WINDOWS operating environment as the default display attribute for the dialog box and the pop-up and pull-down menu objects. Initially, **_menu_att** is set in **menus.cpp** to a value of 0x70 (black characters on a white background). However, the **_menu_att** variable can be changed to suit a particular application program's needs.

__menu__highlight

Defined As: int _menu_highlight;

Description: The **_menu_highlight** variable is used by the WINDOWS operating environment as the default display attribute for highlighting menu selections. Initially, **_menu_highlight** is set in **menus.cpp** to a value of 0x07 (white characters on a black background). However, the **_menu_highlight** variable can be changed to suit a particular application program's needs.

__menu__hotkey

Defined As: int _menu_hotkey;

Description: The **_menu_hotkey** variable is used by the WINDOWS operating environment as the default display attribute for menu item hotkeys. Initially, **_menu_hotkey** is set in **menus.cpp** to a value of 0x7f (intense white characters on a white background). However, the **_menu_hotkey** variable can be changed to suit a particular application program's needs.

mouse

Defined As: pointer mouse;

Description: The **mouse** variable is a globally defined **pointer** object. Because **mouse** is a globally defined object, mouse routines can easily be incorporated into an application program by simply accessing the **mouse** object through its related functions.

__mouse__x

Defined As: int _mouse_x;

Description: After a call to the **read_mouse** function, the **_mouse_x** variable holds the mouse's x-coordinate. Because the Microsoft mouse driver translates the mouse's text coordinates to their equivalent graphic coordinates, **_mouse_x** will hold the value of (mouse pointer's text column - 1) * 8.

__mouse__y

Defined As: int _mouse_y;

Description: After a call to the **read_mouse** function, the **_mouse_y** variable holds the mouse's y-coordinate. Because the Microsoft mouse driver translates the mouse's text coordinates to their equivalent graphic coordinates, **_mouse_y** will hold the value of (mouse's text row - 1) * 8.

__nonibm

Defined As: int _nonibm;

Description: The **_nonibm** variable is used by the WINDOWS operating environment to eliminate snow on an IBM CGA. When it is called, the **settext80** function determines the current display adapter's type. If a CGA adapter is present, **settext80** sets the **_nonibm** variable to FALSE (0). If an MDA or EGA adapter is present, **settext80** sets the **_nonibm** variable to TRUE (1). If the current display adapter is a non-IBM CGA, it is the program's responsibility to manually set the **_nonibm** variable to TRUE. Although this is strictly optional, manually setting the **_nonibm** variable will considerably speed up display input/output.

__right__button

Defined As: int _right_button;

Description: After a call to the **read_mouse** function, the **_right_button** variable holds the mouse's right button status. If the right button is being held down, **_right_button** will be set to TRUE (1). Otherwise, **_right_button** will be set to FALSE (0) to indicate a released right button.

STANDARD DATA TYPES

In **windows.hpp**, the WINDOWS toolbox defines a number of useful data types.

boolean

Defined As: typedef int boolean;

Description: The **boolean** data type is used to define logical variables. To assist in the use of the boolean data type, the following two constants are defined in **windows.hpp**:

Constant	Value
TRUE	1
FALSE	0

date

Defined As: typedef struct {
        int *month, day, year*;
    } date;

Description: The **date** structure is used to define dates for the **date_string**, **display_date**, and **input_date** functions. The **date** structure is used as follows:

Data Type	Description
month	The date's month.
day	The date's day of the month.
year	The date's year.

MENU

Defined As:
```
typedef struct {
        char *string;
        int hotkey;
        void (*function)(void);
        void (*help)(void);
} MENU;
```

Description: The **MENU** structure is used to define menu items for the WINDOWS toolbox menu objects. The **MENU** structure is used as follows:

Data Type	Description
string	Pointer to a string, which defines the menu item.
hotkey	Position in *string* of the menu item's hotkey character.
(*function*)()	Pointer to a function, which is executed if the menu item is selected.
(*help*)()	Pointer to a function, which is executed if help is requested for the highlighted menu item.

MENU__HEAD

Defined As:
```
typedef struct {
        char *heading;
        int hotkey, number;
        MENU *mptr;
} MENU_HEAD;
```

Description: The **MENU_HEAD** structure is used to define menus for pull-down menu objects. The **MENU_HEAD** structure is used as follows:

Data Type	Description
heading	Pointer to a string, which defines the menu's heading.
hotkey	Position in *heading* of the menu's pull-down hotkey character.
number	Number of items in the pull-down menu.
mptr	Pointer to an array of **MENU** structures, which defines the pull-down menu.

phone

Defined As:
```
typedef struct {
        int area, exchange, no;
} phone;
```

Description: The **phone** structure is used to define phone numbers for the **display_phone**, **input_phone**, and **phone_string** functions. The **phone** structure is used as follows:

Data Type	Description
area	The phone number's area code.
exchange	The phone number's exchange.
no	The phone number's final four digits.

ssn

Defined As:

```
typedef struct {
        int no1, no2, no3;
} ssn;
```

Description: The **ssn** structure is used to define Social Security numbers for the **display_ssn**, **input_ssn**, and **ssn_string** functions. The **ssn** structure is used as follows:

Data Type	Description
no1	The Social Security number's first three digits.
no2	The Social Security number's middle two digits.
no3	The Social Security number's final four digits.

OBJECTS

In **windows.hpp**, the WINDOWS toolbox defines a variety of objects. These objects are used to implement such features as display screen pointers, dynamic text windows, and a variety of menu systems.

dialog

Defined As:

```
class dialog {
private:
        int row, col;
        boolean ESC_flag;
public:
        dialog(int, int, boolean e = FALSE);
        dialog(dialog &);
        int get(int, MENU *, int, ...);
};
```

Description: **dialog** objects are used to implement dialog box style menus. The **dialog** constructor is used to define a dialog box menu's display screen position and to optionally define the menu's **ESC** key flag (*ESC_flag*).

pointer

Defined As:

```
class pointer {
public:
        pointer();
        ~pointer();
        void on(void);
        void off(void);
        void read(void);
        int row(void);
        int col(void);
        boolean lbutton(void);
        boolean rbutton(void);
};
```

Description: **pointer** objects are used to implement display screen pointing devices. The **pointer** constructor is used to reset a pointing device's driver. The **pointer** destructor is used to ensure that a pointing device's display screen pointer is turned off when the object goes out of scope.

popup

Defined As:
```
class popup {
private:
        int row, col1;
        boolean ESC_flag;
public:
        popup(int, int, boolean e = FALSE);
        popup(popup &);
        int get(int, MENU *);
};
```

Description: **popup** objects are used to implement pop-up style menus. The **popup** constructor is used to define a pop-up menu's upper left corner and to optionally define the menu's **ESC** key flag (*ESC_flag*).

pulldown

Defined As:
```
class pulldown {
private:
        int row, number, *tabs;
        char *hotkeys;
        MENU_HEAD *menus;
        void (*menu_help)(void);
public:
        pulldown(int, int, MENU_HEAD *, void(*m_h)(void) = NULL);
        pulldown(pulldown &);
        void display(void);
        int get(int);
};
```

Description: **pulldown** objects are used to implement pull-down style menus. The **pulldown** constructor is used to define a pull-down menu's menu bar row (*row*), the number (*number*) of the menu's pull-down menus, a pointer to the menu's array of MENU_HEAD structures, and to optionally define the menu's general help function (*menu_help*).

window

Defined As:

```
class window {
private:
        int row1, col1, row2, col2, watt, bflg;
        char *buffer;
        boolean oflag, sflag;
        int orow, ocol, ostart, oend;
        int crow, ccol;
        int b_adj(int cols);
        int urow();
        int lcol();
        int brow();
        int rcol();
public:
        window(int r1 = 1, int c1 = 1, int r2 = 25, int c2 = 80, int
            w = 7, int b = _NO_BORDER, int s = _NO_SCROLL);
        window(window &);
        ~window();
        void draw(void);
        void open(void);
        void close(void);
        void setcurpos(void);
        int currow(void);
        int curcol(void);
        int p_row(int);
        int p_col(int);
        void cls(void);
        void clreol(void);
        void scroll(int, int, boolean);
        void horizontal_bar(int, int);
        void vertical_bar(int, int);
```

continued...

```
                    void print(char *);
                    void println(char *);
                    void printat(int, int, char *);
                    void printlnat(int, int, char *);
              };
```

Description: **window** objects are used to define dynamic text windows. The **window** constructor is used to specify a text window's upper left corner (*row1*, *col1*), lower right corner (*row2*, *col2*), color attribute (*watt*), border type (*bflg*), and scroll type (*sflag*). If *watt* is equal to 0, the text window will not be drawn when it is opened. The *bflg* parameter can be one of the following constants (defined in **windows.hpp**):

Constant	Action
_NO_BORDER	When the window is opened, it is drawn without a border.
_SINGLE_LINE	When the window is opened, it is drawn with a single-lined border.
_DOUBLE_LINE	When the window is opened, it is drawn with a double-lined border.

The *sflag* parameter can be one of the following constants (defined in **windows.hpp**):

Constant	Action
_SCROLL	Scrolls text sent to the window by the **window::print**, **window::println**, **window::printat**, and **window::printlnat** functions.
_NO_SCROLL	Truncates text sent to the window by the **window::print**, **window::println**, **window::printat**, and **window::printlnat** functions.

FUNCTIONS

The WINDOWS toolbox contains a wide variety of functions. To facilitate their use in application programs, this section describes the WINDOWS functions in the following format:

Summary: Presents an exact syntactic model for each of the WINDOWS functions.

Description: Describes a function's purpose and how it is used in an application program.

Return Value: Explains any of the possible return values for a WINDOWS function.

See Also: Lists any similar or related WINDOWS functions.

Example: Illustrates how a WINDOWS function could actually be used in an application program.

clearone

Summary: #include "windows.hpp"
void clearone(*row*, *col*, *att*);
int *row*, *col*;   (character position)
int *att*;   (character attribute)

Description: The **clearone** macro displays a space at the position defined by
(*row*, *col*). Additionally, the position's attribute is set to *att*.

Return Value: No value is returned.

Example: The following program displays a message and demonstrates the
clearone macro by erasing the **T** at the start of the message.

```
//
// clearone Demo
//
#include <stdlib.h>
#include "windows.hpp"

main()
{
        save_initial_video();
        printstring(1, 1, "This is a demo of the clearone macro");
        waitkey();
        clearone(1, 1, 7);
        waitkey();
        exit(0);
}
```

clearscreen

Summary: #include "windows.hpp"
void clearscreen(*row1*, *col1*, *row2*, *col2*, *att*);
int *row1*, *col1*;   (upper left corner of the text window)
int *row2*, *col2*;   (lower right corner of the text window)
int *att*;   (text window attribute)

Description: The **clearscreen** macro clears an area of the display screen defined by the coordinates (*row1*, *col1*) and (*row2*, *col2*). Additionally, the cleared text window's attributes are set to *att*.

Return Value: No value is returned.

Example: The following program demonstrates the **clearscreen** macro by clearing the display screen.

```
//
// clearscreen Demo
//
#include <stdlib.h>
#include "windows.hpp"

main()
{
        settext80();
        clearscreen(1, 1, 25, 80, 7);
        printstring(1, 1, "The screen has been cleared!");
        waitkey();
        exit(0);
}
```

cursoroff, cursoron

Summary: #include "windows.hpp"
void cursoroff(void);
void cursoron(void);

Description: The **cursoroff** function turns the cursor off. The **cursoron** function turns the cursor on.

Return Value: No value is returned.

Example: The following program demonstrates the **cursoroff** and **cursoron** functions by first turning the cursor off and then turning the cursor back on again.

```
//
// cursoroff/cursoron Demo
//
#include <stdlib.h>
#include "windows.hpp"

main()
{
        settext80();
        clearscreen(1, 1, 25, 80, 7);
        cursoroff();
        printstring(1, 1, "Press a key to turn the cursor back on.....");
        waitkey();
        cursoron();
        exit(0);
}
```

date__string

Summary: #include "windows.hpp"
char *date_string(*string*, *date*);
char **string*;   (storage location for the date string)
date &*date*;   (date structure)

Description: The **date_string** function constructs an eight-character date string (*string* = "mm/dd/yy") for the date defined by *date*.

Return Value: The **date_string** function returns a pointer to the resulting date string.

See Also: **display_date** and **input_date**

Example: The following program demonstrates the **date_string** function by displaying a constructed date string at the upper left corner of the video display.

```
//
// date_string Demo
//
#include <stdlib.h>
#include "windows.hpp"

main()
{
        static date d = {10, 3, 61};
        char line[80];

        save_initial_video();
        printstring(1, 1, date_string(line, d));
        waitkey();
        exit(0);
}
```

dialog::get

Summary:

```
#include "windows.hpp"
object.get(nitems, menu, ntitles, [title, ....]);
dialog object;          (dialog box menu object)
int nitems;             (number of menu items)
MENU *menu;             (pointer to an array of MENU structures)
int ntitles;            (number of titles)
char *title;            (title pointer)
```

Description: The **dialog::get** function displays the dialog box menu defined by (*object*). If any titles are specified, they are displayed above the menu items pointed to by *menu*. A menu item can be selected by pressing the indicated hotkey. Furthermore, the double-lined menu item can be selected by simply pressing **ENTER**. Help, if it's available, can be requested for the highlighted menu item by pressing **F1**. The double-lined highlighting is moved from one menu item to the next by pressing either **LEFT ARROW** or **RIGHT ARROW**.

Return Value: If the menu item has a NULL function pointer, the **dialog::get** function returns the value of the selected item's hotkey. Otherwise, the **dialog::get** function returns a value of zero.

Example: The following program demonstrates the **dialog::get** function by asking whether or not a file should be saved. If instructed to do so, the **dialog::get** function executes the simulated save file function.

```
//
// dialog::get Demo
//
#include <stdlib.h>
#include "windows.hpp"

void save_file(void);

static MENU menu[3] = { {"Yes", 0, save_file, NULL},
                        {"No", 0, NULL, NULL},
                        {"Cancel", 0, NULL, NULL} };
```

continued...

```
main()
{
        int key;

        save_initial_video();
        mouse.on();
        do {
                key = dialog(13, 40, TRUE).get(3, menu, 2,
                "The file hasn't been saved!",
                "Do you want me to save it?");
        } while (key != 27 && key != 'C');
        exit(0);
}

void save_file(void)
{
        printcenter(13, 40, "The file has been saved");
        waitkey();
        clearscreen(13, 1, 13, 80, 7);
}
```

display__date

Summary: #include "windows.hpp"
void display_date(*row*, *col*, *date*);
int *row*, *col*;   (screen position)
date &*date*;   (date structure)

Description: The **display_date** function displays a date (*date*) at the display screen position defined by (*row*, *col*).

Return Value: No value is returned.

See Also: **date_string** and **input_date**

Example: The following program demonstrates the **display_date** function by displaying a variety of dates on the display screen.

```
//
// display_date Demo
//
#include <stdlib.h>
#include "windows.hpp"

main()
{
        static date d1 = {02, 04, 81} ;
        static date d2 = {03, 12, 83} ;

        save_initial_video();
        display_date(1, 10, d1);
        display_date(1, 20, d2);
        waitkey();
        exit(0);
}
```

display__dollar

Summary:
```
#include "windows.hpp"
void display_dollar(row, col, length, dollar);
int row, col;                    (screen position)
int length;                      (field length)
double &dollar;                  (dollar value)
```

Description: The **display_dollar** function displays a right-justified dollar value (*dollar*) with a field length of *length* at the display screen position defined by (*row, col*).

Return Value: No value is returned.

See Also: **input_dollar**

Example: The following program demonstrates the **display_dollar** function by displaying a variety of dollar values on the display screen.

```
//
// display_dollar Demo
//
#include <stdlib.h>
#include "windows.hpp"

main()
{
        double n1 = 32.376, n2 = -55.23;

        save_initial_video();
        display_dollar(1, 1, 10, n1);
        display_dollar(1, 40, 10, n2);
        display_dollar(2, 1, 10, 67.328);
        waitkey();
        exit(0);
}
```

display__number

Summary: #include "windows.hpp"
void display_number(*row, col, length, number*);
int *row, col*;   (screen position)
int *length*;   (field length)
unsigned long &*number*;   (numeric value)

Description: The **display_number** function displays a right-justified, unsigned numeric value (*number*) with a field length of *length* at the display screen position defined by (*row, col*).

Return Value: No value is returned.

See Also: **input_number**

Example: The following program demonstrates the **display_number** function by displaying a variety of numeric values on the display screen.

```
//
// display_number Demo
//
#include <stdlib.h>
#include "windows.hpp"

main()
{
        unsigned long n1 = 456789, n2 = 6789999;

        save_initial_video();
        display_number(1, 1, 10, n1);
        display_number(1, 40, 10, 32767);
        display_number(2, 1, 10, n2);
        waitkey();
        exit(0);
}
```

display_phone

Summary:

```
#include "windows.hpp"
void display_phone(row, col, number)
int row, col;                    (screen position)
phone &number                    (phone number structure)
```

Description: The **display_phone** function displays a phone number (*number*) at the display screen position defined by (*row*, *col*).

Return Value: No value is returned.

See Also: **input_phone** and **phone_string**

Example: The following program demonstrates the **display_phone** function by displaying an assortment of phone numbers on the display screen.

```
//
// display_phone Demo
//
#include <stdlib.h>
#include "windows.hpp"

main()
{
        static phone pn1 = {800, 555, 6678} ;
        static phone pn2 = {207, 555, 3277} ;

        save_initial_video();
        display_phone(1, 1, pn1);
        display_phone(1, 40, pn2);
        waitkey();
        exit(0);
}
```

display__ssn

Summary:
```
#include "windows.hpp"
void  display_ssn(row, col, number);
int row, col;              (screen position)
ssn &number;               (Social Security number structure)
```

Description: The **display_ssn** function displays a Social Security number (*number*) at the display screen position defined by (*row, col*).

Return Value: No value is returned.

See Also: **input_ssn** and **ssn_string**

Example: The following program demonstrates the **display_ssn** function by displaying an assortment of Social Security numbers on the display screen.

```
//
// display_ssn Demo
//
#include <stdlib.h>
#include "windows.hpp"

main()
{
        static ssn sn1 = {007, 25, 5687} ;
        static ssn sn2 = {101, 55, 3535} ;

        save_initial_video();
        display_ssn(1, 1, sn1);
        display_ssn(1, 40, sn2);
        waitkey();
        exit(0);
}
```

display__string

Summary:

```
#include "windows.hpp"
void display_string(row, col, length, string);
int row, col;                (screen position)
int length;                  (field length)
char *string;                (string pointer)
```

Description: The **display_string** function displays a left-justified alphanumeric string (*string*) with a field length of *length* at the display screen position defined by (*row, col*).

Return Value: No value is returned.

See Also: **input_string**

Example: The following program demonstrates the **display_string** function by displaying an assortment of strings on the display screen.

```
//
// display_string Demo
//
#include <stdlib.h>
#include "windows.hpp"

main()
{
        char *s1 = "This is demo string 1";
        char *s3 = "This is demo string 3";

        save_initial_video();
        display_string(1, 1, 25, s1);
        display_string(1, 40, 25, "This is demo string 2");
        display_string(2, 1, 25, s3);
        waitkey();
        exit(0);
}
```

drawbox

Summary:

```
#include "windows.hpp"
void drawbox(row1, col1, row2, col2, btype, att);
int row1, col1;        (upper left corner of the text window)
int row2, col2;        (lower right corner of the text window)
int btype;             (border type flag)
int att;               (border attribute)
```

Description: The **drawbox** function draws a border around a text window in which coordinates are defined by the points (*row1*, *col1*) and (*row2*, *col2*). Additionally, the border's attributes are set to *att*.

The *btype* parameter can be one of the following constants (defined in **windows.hpp**):

Constant	Action
_SINGLE_LINE	Draws a single-lined border around the text window.
_DOUBLE_LINE	Draws a double-lined border around the text window.

Return Value: No value is returned.

Example: The following program demonstrates the **drawbox** function by drawing a double-lined box around the right half of the display screen.

```
//
// drawbox Demo
//
#include <stdlib.h>
#include "windows.hpp"

main()
{
        save_initial_video();
        drawbox(1, 41, 25, 80, _DOUBLE_LINE, 0x70);
        waitkey();
        exit(0);
}
```

fillone

Summary:
```
#include "windows.hpp"
void fillone(row, col, chr, att);
int row, col;              (screen position)
int chr;                   (character)
int att;                   (attribute)
```

Description: The **fillone** function sets the display screen position defined by (*row*, *col*) to the specified character/attribute pair (*chr/att*).

Return Value: No value is returned.

Example: The following program demonstrates the **fillone** function by displaying a black-on-white **M** at screen position (4, 10).

```
//
// fillone Demo
//
#include <stdlib.h>
#include "windows.hpp"

main()
{
        save_initial_video();
        fillone(4, 10, 'M', 0x70);
        waitkey();
        exit(0);
}
```

fillscreen

Summary:	#include "windows.hpp"

```
void fillscreen(row1, col1, row2, col2, chr, att);
int row1, col1;        (upper left corner of the text window)
int row2, col2;        (lower right corner of the text window)
int chr;               (text window character)
int att;               (text window attribute)
```

Description: The **fillscreen** function fills the text window defined by the coordinates (*row1*, *col1*) and (*row2*, *col2*) with the character/attribute pair specified by (*chr*/*att*).

Return Value: No value is returned.

Example: The following program demonstrates the **fillscreen** function by filling the left half of the display screen with **R**s.

```
//
// fillscreen Demo
//
#include <stdlib.h>
#include "windows.hpp"

main()
{
        save_initial_video();
        fillscreen(1, 1, 25, 40, 'R', 7);
        waitkey();
        exit(0);
}
```

getcurpos

Summary: #include "windows.hpp"
void getcurpos(*row*, *col*, *sline*, *eline*);
int *row*; (cursor row position)
int *col*; (cursor column position)
int *sline*; (cursor starting line)
int *eline*; (cursor ending line)

Description: The **getcurpos** function retrieves the cursor values by returning the cursor's row position in *row*, the cursor's column position in *col*, the cursor character's starting line in *sline*, and the cursor character's ending line in *eline*.

Return Value: No value is returned.

Example: The following program demonstrates the **getcurpos** function by retrieving and displaying the current cursor values.

```
//
// getcurpos Demo
//
#include <stdio.h>
#include <stdlib.h>
#include "windows.hpp"

main()
{
    int row, col, sline, eline;

    settext80();
    getcurpos(&row, &col, &sline, &eline);
    clearscreen(1, 1, 25, 80, 7);
    setcurpos(1, 1);
    printf("Row: %2d  Column: %2d  Starting Line: %2d  Ending Line: %2d\n",
            row, col, sline, eline);
    waitkey();
    exit(0);
}
```

hide_mouse

Summary:
```
#include "windows.hpp"
void hide_mouse(void);
```

Description: The **hide_mouse** function turns off the mouse pointer.

Return Value: No value is returned.

See Also: **show_mouse**

Example: The following program demonstrates the **hide_mouse** function by turning off the mouse pointer.

```
//
// hide_mouse Demo
//
#include <stdlib.h>
#include <bios.h>
#include "windows.hpp"

main()
{
        save_initial_video();
        reset_mouse();
        show_mouse();
        do {
        read_mouse();
        } while (!_bios_keybrd(1) && !_left_button);
        hide_mouse();
        if (_bios_keybrd(1))
                waitkey();
        exit(0);
}
```

hotstring

Summary: #include "windows.hpp"
void hotstring(*row*, *col*, *hotkey*, *string*);
int *row*, *col*;   (screen position)
int *hotkey*;   (hotkey position)
char **string*;   (string pointer)

Description: The **hotstring** function displays a string at the display screen
position defined by (*row*, *col*). Additionally, the string's *hotkey*
character's attribute is set to **_menu_hotkey**.

Return Value: No value is returned.

Example: The following program demonstrates the **hotstring** function by
displaying a hotstring at the beginning of the tenth display screen
line.

```
//
// hotstring Demo
//
#include <stdlib.h>
#include "windows.hpp"

main()
{
        save_initial_video();
        hotstring(10, 1, 10, "This is a HOTSTRING test!");
        waitkey();
        exit(0);
}
```

input__date

Summary: #include "windows.hpp"
int input_date(*row*, *col*, *date*);
int *row*, *col*;   (screen position)
date &*date*;   (data entry field's contents)

Description: The **input_date** function displays and inputs an eight-character date (*date* = "mm/dd/yy") at the display screen position defined by (*row*, *col*). The following control keys are active during the **input_date** function:

Control Key	Action
HOME	Move to the first character in the data entry field.
END	Move to the last character in the data entry field.
LEFT ARROW	Move to the previous character in the data entry field.
RIGHT ARROW	Move to the next character in the data entry field.

Return Value: The **input_date** function returns the value of the last key pressed.

See Also: **date_string** and **display_date**

Example: The following program demonstrates the **input_date** function by requesting the current date.

```
//
// input_date Demo
//
#include <stdlib.h>
#include "windows.hpp"

main()
{
        static date d;

        save_initial_video();
        printstring(10, 1, "Please Enter Today's Date:");
        while (input_date(10, 28, d) != 27) ;
        exit(0);
}
```

input__dollar

Summary: #include "windows.hpp"
int input_dollar(*row*, *col*, *length*, *dollar*);
int *row*, *col*;   (screen position);
int *length*;   (data entry field's length)
int *dollar*;   (date entry field's contents)

Description: The **input_dollar** function displays and inputs a right-justified dollar value (*dollar*) with a field length of *length* at the display screen position defined by (*row*, *col*). The following control keys are active during the **input_dollar** function:

Control Key	Action
HOME	Clear the data entry field's contents.
BACKSPACE	Erase the last digit entered.

Return Value: The **input_dollar** function returns the value of the last key pressed.

See Also: **display_dollar**

Example: The following program demonstrates the **input_dollar** function by requesting an account balance.

```
//
// input_dollar Demo
//
#include <stdlib.h>
#include "windows.hpp"

main()
{
        double n = 0;

        save_initial_video();
        printstring(10, 1, "Please Enter The Account Balance:");
        while (input_dollar(10, 35, 10, n) != 27) ;
        exit(0);
}
```

input_number

Summary:
```
#include "windows.hpp"
int input_number(row, col, length, number);
int row, col;              (screen position)
int length;                (data entry field's length)
int number;                (data entry field's contents)
```

Description: The **input_number** function displays and inputs a right-justified numeric value (*number*) with a field length of *length* at the display screen position defined by (*row, col*). The following control keys are active during the **input_number** function:

Control Key	Action
HOME	Clear the data entry field's contents.
BACKSPACE	Erase the last digit entered.

Return Value: The **input_number** function returns the value of the last key pressed.

See Also: **display_number**

Example: The following program demonstrates the **input_number** function by requesting an account number.

```
//
// input_number Demo
//
#include <stdlib.h>
#include "windows.hpp"

main()
{
        unsigned long n = 0;

        save_initial_video();
        printstring(10, 1, "Please Enter the Account Number:");
        while (input_number(10, 34, 6, n) != 27) ;
        exit(0);
}
```

input__phone

Summary: #include "windows.hpp"
int input_phone(*row*, *col*, *number*);
int *row*, *col*;   (screen position)
phone &*number*;   (data entry field's contents)

Description: The **input_phone** function displays and inputs a 14-character telephone number (*number* = "(xxx) xxx-xxxx") at the display screen position defined by (*row*, *col*). The following keys are active during the **input_phone** function:

Control Key	Action
HOME	Move to the first character in the data entry field.
END	Move to the last character in the data entry field.
LEFT ARROW	Move to the previous character in the data entry field.
RIGHT ARROW	Move to the next character in the data entry field.

Return Value: The **input_phone** function returns the value of the last key pressed.

See Also: **display_phone** and **phone_string**

Example: The following program demonstrates the **input_phone** function by requesting the operator's telephone number.

```
//
// input_phone Demo
//
#include <stdlib.h>
#include "windows.hpp"

main()
{
        static phone n;

        save_initial_video();
        printstring(10, 1, "Please Enter Your Phone Number:");
        while (input_phone(10, 33, n) != 27) ;
        exit(0);
}
```

input__ssn

Summary:	#include "windows.hpp" int input_ssn(*row*, *col*, *number*); int *row*, *col*; (screen position) ssn &*number*; (data entry field's contents)

Description: The **input_ssn** function displays and inputs an 11-character Social Security number (*number* = "xxx-xx-xxxx") at the display screen position defined by (*row*, *col*). The following control keys are active during the **input_ssn** function:

Control Key	Action
HOME	Move to the first character in the data entry field.
END	Move to the last character in the data entry field.
LEFT ARROW	Move to the previous character in the data entry field.
RIGHT ARROW	Move to the next character in the data entry field.

Return Value: No value is returned.

See Also: **display_ssn** and **ssn_string**

Example: The following program demonstrates the **input_ssn** function by requesting the operator's Social Security number.

```
//
// input_ssn Demo
//
#include <stdlib.h>
#include "windows.hpp"

main()
{
        static ssn n;

        save_initial_video();
        printstring(10, 1, "Please Enter Your Social Security Number:");
        while (input_ssn(10, 43, n) != 27) ;
        exit(0);
}
```

input__string

Summary:
```
#include "windows.hpp"
int input_string(row, col, length, string);
int row, col;                    (screen position)
int length;                      (data entry field's length)
char *string;                    (data entry field's contents)
```

Description: The **input_string** function displays and inputs a left-justified alphanumeric string (*string*) with a field length of *length* at the display screen position defined by (*row, col*). The following control keys are active during the **input_string** function:

Control Key	Action
HOME	Erase the data entry field's contents.
BACKSPACE	Erase the last character entered.

Return Value: No value is returned.

See Also: **display_string**

Example: The following program demonstrates the **input_string** function by requesting the operator's name.

```
//
// input_string Demo
//
#include <stdlib.h>
#include "windows.hpp"

main()
{
        static char string[31];

        save_initial_video();
        printstring(10, 1, "Please Enter Your Name:");
        while (input_string(10, 25, 30, string) != 27) ;
        exit(0);
}
```

max

Summary:
```
#include "windows.hpp"
int max(first, second);
int first;                          (integer value);
int second;                         (integer value);
```

Description: The **max** function compares two integer values (*first*, *second*) to see which one is the largest.

Return Value: The **max** function returns the largest of the two integer values.

See Also: **min**

Example: The following program demonstrates the **max** function by determining the longest string in an array of strings.

```
//
// max Demo
//
#include <stdio.h>
#include <stdlib.h>
#include <string.h>
#include "windows.hpp"

static char *test[3] = {"This is the first string",
    "This is the second string",
    "This is the third string"};

main()
{
    int i, longest = 0;

    for (i = 0; i < 3; i++)
            longest = max(longest, strlen(test[i]));
    printf("The longest string has a length of %d characters.\n", longest);
    exit(0);
}
```

min

Summary: #include "windows.hpp"
int min(*first*, *second*);
int *first*;   (integer value)
int *second*;   (integer value)

Description: The **min** function compares two integer values (*first*, *second*) to
see which one is the smallest.

Return Value: The **min** function returns the smallest of the two integer values.

See Also: **max**

Example: The following program demonstrates the **min** function by determining the shortest string in an array of strings.

```
//
// min Demo
//
#include <stdio.h>
#include <stdlib.h>
#include <string.h>
#include "windows.hpp"

static char *test[3] = {"This is the first string",
    "This is the second string",
    "This is the third string"};

main()
{
    int i, shortest = 9999;

    for (i = 0; i < 3; i++)
            shortest = min(shortest, strlen(test[i]));
    printf("The longest string has a length of %d characters.\n", shortest);
    exit(0);
}
```

phone__string

Summary: #include "windows.hpp"
char *phone_string(*string*, *number*);
char *string*;   (storage location for phone number string)
phone &*number*;   (phone number structure)

Description: The **phone_string** function constructs a 14-character phone number string (*string* = "(xxx) xxx-xxxx") for the phone number defined by *number*.

Return Value: The **phone_string** function returns a pointer to the resulting phone number string.

See Also: **display_phone** and **input_phone**

Example: The following program demonstrates the **phone_string** function by displaying a constructed phone number string on the tenth line of the display screen.

```
//
// phone_string Demo
//
#include <stdlib.h>
#include "windows.hpp"

main()
{
        static phone n = {207, 555, 3235};
        char line[80];

        save_initial_video();
        printstring(10, 1, phone_string(line, n));
        waitkey();
        exit(0);
}
```

pointer::col

Summary:
```
#include "windows.hpp"
int object.col(void);
pointer object;                    (text pointer object)
```

Description: The **pointer::col** function determines a text pointer's (*object*) column position. (**Note:** To obtain the text pointer's current column position, a call to the **pointer::read** function must be performed before a call to the **pointer::col** function.)

Return Value: The **pointer::col** function returns the text pointer's column position.

See Also: **pointer::read**

Example: The following program demonstrates the **pointer::col** function by continuously displaying the text pointer's column position.

```
//
// pointer::col Demo
//
#include <stdio.h>
#include <stdlib.h>
#include <bios.h>
#include "windows.hpp"

main()
{
    save_initial_video();
    mouse.on();
    do {
            mouse.read();
            setcurpos(1, 1);
            printf("Pointer Column: %3d", mouse.col());
    } while (!_bios_keybrd(1) && !mouse.lbutton() && !mouse.rbutton()) ;
    if (_bios_keybrd(1))
            waitkey();
    exit(0);
}
```

pointer::lbutton

Summary: #include "windows.hpp"
int *object*.lbutton(void);
pointer *object*;   (text pointer object)

Description: The **pointer::lbutton** function determines a text pointer's (*object*) left button status. (**Note:** To obtain the text pointer's current left button status, a call to the **pointer::read** function must be performed before a call to the **pointer::lbutton** function.)

Return Value: The **pointer::lbutton** function returns the text pointer's left button status. If the text pointer's left button is being pressed, the **pointer::lbutton** function will return TRUE (1). Otherwise, the **pointer::lbutton** function will return FALSE (0) to indicate a released left button.

See Also: **pointer::read**

Example: The following program demonstrates the **pointer::lbutton** function by continuously displaying the text pointer's left button status.

```
//
// pointer::lbutton Demo
//
#include <stdio.h>
#include <stdlib.h>
#include <bios.h>
#include "windows.hpp"

main()
{
        save_initial_video();
        mouse.on();
        do {
                mouse.read();
                setcurpos(1, 1);
                printf("Pointer Left Button Status: %d", mouse.lbutton());
        } while (!_bios_keybrd(1) && !mouse.rbutton()) ;
        if (_bios_keybrd(1))
                waitkey();
        exit(0);
}
```

pointer::off

Summary: #include "windows.hpp"
void *object*.off(void)
pointer *object*;   (text pointer object)

Description: The **pointer::off** function turns off a text pointer (*object*).

Return Value: No value is returned.

See Also: **pointer::on**

Example: After waiting for a key or the text pointer's left button to be pressed, the following program demonstrates the **pointer::off** function by turning the text pointer off.

```
//
// pointer::off Demo
//
#include <stdio.h>
#include <stdlib.h>
#include <bios.h>
#include "windows.hpp"

main()
{
        save_initial_video();
        mouse.on();
        do {
                mouse.read();
        } while (!_bios_keybrd(1) && !mouse.lbutton()) ;
        mouse.off();
        if (_bios_keybrd(1))
                waitkey();
        exit(0);
}
```

pointer::on

Summary: #include "windows.hpp"
void *object*.on(void);
pointer *object*;   (text pointer object)

Description: The **pointer::on** function turns on a text pointer (*object*).

Return Value: No value is returned.

See Also: **pointer::off**

Example: The following program demonstrates the **pointer::on** function by turning the text pointer on.

```
//
// pointer::on Demo
//
#include <stdio.h>
#include <stdlib.h>
#include <bios.h>
#include "windows.hpp"

main()
{
        save_initial_video();
        mouse.on();
        do {
                mouse.read();
        } while (!_bios_keybrd(1) && !mouse.lbutton()) ;
        if (_bios_keybrd(1))
                waitkey();
        exit(0);
}
```

pointer::rbutton

Summary:
#include "windows.hpp"
int *object*.rbutton(void);
pointer *object*;   (text pointer object)

Description: The **pointer::rbutton** function determines a text pointer's (*object*) right button status. (**Note:** To obtain the text pointer's current right button status, a call to the **pointer::read** function must be performed before a call to the **pointer::rbutton** function.)

Return Value: The **pointer::rbutton** function returns the text pointer's right button status. If the text pointer's right button is being pressed, the **pointer::rbutton** function will return TRUE (1). Otherwise, the **pointer::rbutton** function will return FALSE (0) to indicate a released right button.

See Also: **pointer::read**

Example: The following program demonstrates the **pointer::rbutton** function by continuously displaying the text pointer's right button status.

```
//
// pointer::rbutton Demo
//
#include <stdio.h>
#include <stdlib.h>
#include <bios.h>
#include "windows.hpp"

main()
{
    save_initial_video();
    mouse.on();
    do {
            mouse.read();
            setcurpos(1, 1);
            printf("Pointer Right Button Status: %d", mouse.rbutton());
    } while (!_bios_keybrd(1) && !mouse.lbutton()) ;
    if (_bios_keybrd(1))
            waitkey();
    exit(0);
}
```

pointer::read

Summary:

```
#include "windows.hpp"
void object.read(void);
pointer object;                    (text pointer object)
```

Description: The **pointer::read** function determines a text pointer's (*object*) row position, column position, left button status, and right button status.

Return Value: No value is returned.

See Also: **pointer::col**, **pointer::lbutton**, **pointer::rbutton**, and **pointer::row**

Example: The following program demonstrates the **pointer::read** function by continuously displaying the text pointer's row position, column position, left button status, and right button status.

```
//
// pointer::read Demo
//
#include <stdio.h>
#include <stdlib.h>
#include <bios.h>
#include "windows.hpp"

main()
{
    save_initial_video();
    mouse.on();
    do {
            mouse.read();
            setcurpos(1, 1);
            printf("Pointer Row: %3d\n", mouse.row());
            printf("Pointer Column: %3d\n", mouse.col());
            printf("Pointer Left Button Status: %d\n", mouse.lbutton());
            printf("Pointer Right Button Status: %d", mouse.rbutton());
    } while (!_bios_keybrd(1)) ;
            waitkey();
    exit(0);
}
```

pointer::row

Summary: #include "windows.hpp"
int *object*.row(void);
pointer *object*;   (text pointer object)

Description: The **pointer::row** function determines a text pointer's (*object*) row position. (**Note:** To obtain the text pointer's current row position, a call to the **pointer::read** function must be performed before a call to the **pointer::row** function.)

Return Value: The **pointer::row** function returns the text pointer's row position.

See Also: **pointer::read**

Example: The following program demonstrates the **pointer::row** function by continuously displaying the text pointer's row position.

```
//
// pointer::row Demo
//
#include <stdio.h>
#include <stdlib.h>
#include <bios.h>
#include "windows.hpp"

main()
{
    save_initial_video();
    mouse.on();
    do {
            mouse.read();
            setcurpos(1, 1);
            printf("Pointer Row: %3d", mouse.row());
    } while (!_bios_keybrd(1) && !mouse.lbutton() && !mouse.rbutton()) ;
    if (_bios_keybrd(1))
            waitkey();
    exit(0);
}
```

popup::get

Summary:
```
#include "windows.hpp"
int object.popup(nitems, menu);
popup object;                    (pop-up menu object)
int nitems;                      (number of menu items)
MENU *menu;                      (pointer to an array of MENU
                                 structures)
```

Description: The **popup::get** function displays the pop-up menu defined by *object*. Selection of a menu item is accomplished by pressing that item's indicated hotkey. Furthermore, the highlighted menu item can be selected by pressing the **ENTER** key. Help, if it's available, can be requested for the highlighted menu item by pressing **F1**. The highlighting can be moved by pressing the **UP ARROW** or **DOWN ARROW** key.

Return Value: If the pop-up menu object's **ESC_flag** is TRUE and the **ESC** key is pressed, the **popup::get** function returns a value of 27. Otherwise, the **popup::get** function will return a value of 0.

Example: The following program demonstrates the **popup::get** function by displaying a three-item pop-up menu. The pop-up menu will be continuously displayed until the "Exit the Program" menu item is selected by the operator.

```
//
// popup Demo
//
#include <stdlib.h>
#include "windows.hpp"

void save_file(void);
void load_file(void);
void exit_prog(void);
void sf_help(void);
void lf_help(void);
void ep_help(void);

static MENU menu[3] = { {"Save the File", 0, save_file, sf_help},
                        {"Load the File", 0, load_file, lf_help},
                        {"Exit the Program", 0, exit_prog, ep_help} };
```

continued...

```
main()
{
        save_initial_video();
        mouse.on();
        while (!((popup)popup(3, 30, TRUE)).get(3, menu)) ;
        exit(0);
}

void save_file(void)
{
        printcenter(19, 40, "Save File Function");
        waitkey();
        clearscreen(19, 1, 19, 80, 7);
}

void load_file(void)
{
        printcenter(19, 40, "Load File Function");
        waitkey();
        clearscreen(19, 1, 19, 80, 7);
}

void exit_prog(void)
{
        exit(0);
}

void sf_help(void)
{
        printcenter(19, 40, "Save File Help Function");
        waitkey();
        clearscreen(19, 1, 19, 80, 7);
}

void lf_help(void)
{
        printcenter(19, 40, "Load File Help Function");
        waitkey();
        clearscreen(19, 1, 19, 80, 7);
}

void ep_help(void)
{
        printcenter(19, 40, "Exit Program Help Function");
        waitkey();
        clearscreen(19, 1, 19, 80, 7);
}
```

printcenter

Summary:
```
#include "windows.hpp"
void printcenter(row, col, string);
int row;                    (screen row)
int col;                    (column to center the string on)
char *string;               (string pointer)
```

Description: The **printcenter** function displays a string (*string*) on the display screen row defined by *row* and centered on the column defined by *col*.

Return Value: No value is returned.

Example: The following program demonstrates the **printcenter** function by centering a string on the top line of the display screen.

```
//
// printcenter Demo
//
#include <stdlib.h>
#include "windows.hpp"

main()
{
    save_initial_video();
    printcenter(1, 40, "This message is centered on the top display line");
    waitkey();
    exit(0);
}
```

printone

Summary:
```
#include "windows.hpp"
void printone(row, col, chr);
int row, col;                    (screen position)
int chr;                         (character)
```

Description: The **printone** function displays a character (*chr*) at the display screen position defined by (*row*, *col*).

Return Value: No value is returned.

Example: The following program demonstrates the **printone** function by displaying a **Z** at display screen position (5, 40).

```
//
// printone Demo
//
#include <stdlib.h>
#include "windows.hpp"

main()
{
        save_initial_video();
        printone(5, 40, 'Z');
        waitkey();
        exit(0);
}
```

printstring

Summary:
```
#include "windows.hpp"
void printstring(row, col, string);
int row, col;                    (screen position)
char *string;                    (string pointer)
```

Description: The **printstring** function displays a string (*string*) at the display screen position defined by (*row*, *col*).

Return Value: No value is returned.

Example: The following program demonstrates the **printstring** function by displaying a string at display screen position (2, 10).

```
//
// printstring Demo
//
#include <stdlib.h>
#include "windows.hpp"

main()
{
        save_initial_video();
        printstring(2, 10, "This message starts at row 2, column 10");
        waitkey();
        exit(0);
}
```

pulldown::display

Summary: #include "windows.hpp"
void *object*.display(void);
pulldown *object*;   (pull-down menu object)

Description: The **pulldown::display** function displays a pull-down menu bar for the pull-down menu defined by (*object*).

Return Value: No value is returned.

See Also: **pulldown::get**

Example: For a complete demonstration of the pull-down menu functions, see the example under **pulldown::get**.

pulldown::get

Summary: #include "windows.hpp"
int *object*.get(*ikey*);
pulldown *object*;   (pull-down menu object)
int *ikey*;   (initial key value)

Description: The **pulldown::get** function is used to implement multiple pull-down menus. The **pulldown::get** function recognizes the following control keys:

Control Key	Action
ALT + Heading Hotkey	Pulls down the indicated menu.
ESC	Removes the current menu from the display screen.
LEFT ARROW	Removes the current menu from the display screen and pulls down the next menu to the left.
RIGHT ARROW	Removes the current menu from the display screen and pulls down the next menu to the right.
Menu Item Hotkey	Executes the selected menu item's function.
ENTER	Executes the highlighted menu item's function.
F1	If a menu hasn't been pulled down, executes the overall help function. Otherwise, executes the highlighted menu item's help function.
UP ARROW	Moves the highlight bar up to the previous menu item.
DOWN ARROW	Moves the highlight bar down to the next menu item.

An initial key value can be sent to the **pulldown::get** function by placing the appropriate value in the *ikey* parameter. Otherwise, the *ikey* parameter must equal zero to indicate no initial key.

Return Value: If a menu item isn't selected, the **pulldown::get** function returns the value of the last key pressed. Otherwise, the **pulldown::get** function returns a value of 0.

See Also: **pulldown::display**

Example: The following program demonstrates the **pulldown::display** and **pulldown::get** functions by implementing a series of pull-down menus for a simple general ledger program.

```
//
// pulldown::get Demo
//
#include <stdio.h>
#include <stdlib.h>
#include "windows.hpp"

void save_file(void);
void read_file(void);
void exit_prog(void);
void add_acc(void);
void del_acc(void);
void add_tra(void);
void del_tra(void);
void prt_coa(void);
void led_upd(void);
void fin_stat(void);
void sf_help(void);
void rf_help(void);
void aa_help(void);
void da_help(void);
void at_help(void);
void dt_help(void);
void pc_help(void);
void lu_help(void);
void fs_help(void);
void main_help(void);

static MENU file[3] = { {"Save the File", 0, save_file, sf_help},
 {"Read the File", 0, read_file, rf_help},
 {"Exit the Program", 0, exit_prog, NULL} };

static MENU accounts[2] = { {"Add an Account", 0, add_acc, aa_help},
        {"Delete an Account", 0, del_acc, da_help} };

static MENU transact[2] = { {"Add a Transaction", 0, add_tra, at_help},
        {"Delete a Transaction", 0, del_tra, dt_help} };
```

continued...

```
static MENU print[3] = { {"Print a Chart of Accounts", 8, prt_coa, pc_help},
        {"Print a Ledger Update", 15, led_upd, lu_help},
        {"Print Financial Statements", 6, fin_stat, fs_help} };

static MENU_HEAD heads[4] = { {"File", 0, 3, file},
        {"Accounts", 0, 2, accounts},
        {"Transactions", 0, 2, transact},
        {"Print", 0, 3, print} };

main()
{
        pulldown menu(1, 4, heads, main_help);

        save_initial_video();
        mouse.on();
        setcurpos(15, 1);
        cursoron();
        menu.display();
        while (TRUE) {
                int key = menu.get(0);
                setcurpos(15, 1);
                printf("%4d\n", key);
        }

}

void save_file(void)
{
        printcenter(19, 40, "Save File Function");
        waitkey();
        clearscreen(19, 1, 19, 80, 7);
}

void read_file(void)
{
        printcenter(19, 40, "Read File Function");
        waitkey();
        clearscreen(19, 1, 19, 80, 7);
}

void exit_prog(void)
{
        exit(0);
}

void add_acc(void)
{
        printcenter(19, 40, "Add Account Function");
        waitkey();
        clearscreen(19, 1, 19, 80, 7);
}
```

continued...

237

```
void del_acc(void)
{
        printcenter(19, 40, "Delete Account Function");
        waitkey();
        clearscreen(19, 1, 19, 80, 7);
}

void add_tra(void)
{
        printcenter(19, 40, "Add Transaction Function");
        waitkey();
        clearscreen(19, 1, 19, 80, 7);
}

void del_tra(void)
{
        printcenter(19, 40, "Delete Transaction Function");
        waitkey();
        clearscreen(19, 1, 19, 80, 7);
}

void prt_coa(void)
{
        printcenter(19, 40, "Print Chart of Accounts Function");
        waitkey();
        clearscreen(19, 1, 19, 80, 7);
}

void led_upd(void)
{
        printcenter(19, 40, "Ledger Update Function");
        waitkey();
        clearscreen(19, 1, 19, 80, 7);
}

void fin_stat(void)
{
        printcenter(19, 40, "Financial Statements Function");
        waitkey();
        clearscreen(19, 1, 19, 80, 7);
}

void sf_help(void)
{
        printcenter(20, 40, "Save File Help Function");
        waitkey();
        clearscreen(20, 1, 20, 80, 7);
}
```

continued...

```
void rf_help(void)
{
        printcenter(20, 40, "Read File Help Function");
        waitkey();
        clearscreen(20, 1, 20, 80, 7);
}

void aa_help(void)
{
        printcenter(20, 40, "Add Account Help Function");
        waitkey();
        clearscreen(20, 1, 20, 80, 7);
}

void da_help(void)
{
        printcenter(20, 40, "Delete Account Help Function");
        waitkey();
        clearscreen(20, 1, 20, 80, 7);
}

void at_help(void)
{
        printcenter(20, 40, "Add Tranaction Help Function");
        waitkey();
        clearscreen(20, 1, 20, 80, 7);
}

void dt_help(void)
{
        printcenter(20, 40, "Delete Tranoaction Help Function");
        waitkey();
        clearscreen(20, 1, 20, 80, 7);
}

void pc_help(void)
{
        printcenter(20, 40, "Print Chart of Accounts Help Function");
        waitkey();
        clearscreen(20, 1, 20, 80, 7);
}

void lu_help(void)
{
        printcenter(20, 40, "Ledger Update Help Function");
        waitkey();
        clearscreen(20, 1, 20, 80, 7);
}
```

continued...

239

```
void fs_help(void)
{
        printcenter(20, 40, "Financial Statements Help Function");
        waitkey();
        clearscreen(20, 1, 20, 80, 7);
}

void main_help(void)
{
        printcenter(20, 40, "Main Help Function");
        waitkey();
        clearscreen(20, 1, 20, 80, 7);
}
```

read__mouse

Summary: #include "windows.hpp"
void read_mouse(void);

Description: The **read_mouse** function determines the mouse's row position, column position, left button status, and right button status.

Return Value: No value is returned.

See Also: **_left_button**, **_mouse_x**, **_mouse_y**, and **_right_button**

Example: The following program demonstrates the **read_mouse** function by continuously displaying the mouse's row position, column position, left button status, and right button status.

```
//
// read_mouse Demo
//
#include <stdio.h>
#include <stdlib.h>
#include <bios.h>
#include "windows.hpp"

main()
{
        save_initial_video();
        reset_mouse();
        show_mouse();
        do {
                read_mouse();
                setcurpos(1, 1);
                printf("Mouse Row: %3d\n", _mouse_y);
                printf("Mouse Column: %3d\n", _mouse_x);
                printf("Mouse Left Button Status: %d\n", _left_button);
                printf("Mouse Right Button Status: %d", _right_button);
        } while (!_bios_keybrd(1)) ;
        hide_mouse();
        waitkey();
        exit(0);
}
```

reset__mouse

Summary: #include "windows.hpp"
void reset_mouse(void);

Description: The **reset_mouse** function resets the mouse driver.

Return Value: No value is returned.

Example: The following program demonstrates the **reset_mouse** function by resetting the mouse driver.

```
//
// reset_mouse Demo
//
#include <stdlib.h>
#include <bios.h>
#include "windows.hpp"

main()
{
        save_initial_video();
        reset_mouse();
        show_mouse();
        do {
        read_mouse();
        } while (!_bios_keybrd(1) && !_left_button);
        hide_mouse();
        if (_bios_keybrd(1))
                waitkey();
        exit(0);
}
```

restorescreen

Summary:

```
#include "windows.hpp"
void restorescreen(row1, col1, row2, col2, buffer);
int row1, col1;        (upper left corner of the text window)
int row2, col2;        (lower right corner of the text window)
char *buffer;          (buffer pointer)
```

Description: The **restorescreen** function displays a text window, which has been previously saved in *buffer*, at the coordinates defined by (*row1*, *col1*) and (*row2*, *col2*). Because each of the text window's characters consists of a character/attribute pair, the buffer must be ((*row2* - *row1* + 1) * (*col2* - *col1* + 1) * 2) bytes long.

Return Value: No value is returned.

See Also: **savescreen**

Example: The following program demonstrates the **restorescreen** function by displaying a previously saved text window.

```
//
// restorescreen Demo
//
#include <stdlib.h>
#include "windows.hpp"

static char vbuff[4000];

main()
{
        settext80();
        savescreen(1, 1, 25, 80, vbuff);
        clearscreen(1, 1, 25, 80, 7);
        waitkey();
        restorescreen(1, 1, 25, 80, vbuff);
        waitkey();
        exit(0);
}
```

save__initial__video

Summary: #include "windows.hpp"
void save_initial_video(void);

Description: The **save_initial_video** function is called at the start of an application program to initialize the WINDOWS operating environment, save the cursor's position and type, save a copy of the display screen, and clear the display screen. When the application program is finished executing, the **save_initial_video** function will automatically restore the display screen's initial contents and cursor settings.

Return Value: No value is returned.

See Also: **settext80**

Example: The following program demonstrates the **save_initial_video** function by saving and restoring the original screen contents.

```
//
// save_initial_video Demo
//
#include <stdlib.h>
#include "windows.hpp"

main()
{
        save_initial_video();
        printcenter(13, 40, "This is a save_initial_video demo");
        waitkey();
        exit(0);
}
```

savescreen

Summary:
```
#include "windows.hpp"
void savescreen(row1, col1, row2, col2, buffer);
int row1, col1;        (upper left corner of the text window)
int row2, col2;        (lower right corner of the text window)
char *buffer;          (buffer pointer)
```

Description: The **savescreen** function buffers a text window at the coordinates defined by (*row1*, *col1*) and (*row2*, *col2*). Because each of the text window's characters consists of a character/attribute pair, *buffer* must be ((*row2* - *row1* + 1) * (*col2* - *col1* + 1) * 2) bytes long.

Return Value: No value is returned.

See Also: **restorescreen**

Example: The following program demonstrates the **savescreen** function by duplicating the left half of the display screen onto the right half of the display screen.

```
//
// savescreen Demo
//
#include <stdlib.h>
#include "windows.hpp"

static char vbuff[2000];

main()
{
        settext80();
        savescreen(1, 1, 25, 40, vbuff);
        restorescreen(1, 41, 25, 80, vbuff);
        waitkey();
        exit(0);
}
```

setattrib

Summary: #include "windows.hpp"
void setattrib(*row1*, *col1*, *row2*, *col2*, *att*);
int *row1*, *col1*;   (upper left corner of the text window)
int *row2*, *col2*;   (lower right corner of the text window)
int *att*;   (text window attribute)

Description: The **setattrib** function sets an entire text window's attributes to *att*. The text window is defined by the coordinates (*row1*, *col1*) and (*row2*, *col2*).

Return Value: No value is returned.

Example: The following program demonstrates the **setattrib** function by setting the right half of the display screen to black characters on a white background.

```
//
// setattrib Demo
//
#include <stdlib.h>
#include "windows.hpp"

main()
{
        save_initial_video();
        setattrib(1, 41, 25, 80, 0x70);
        waitkey();
        exit(0);
}
```

setcurpos

Summary: #include "windows.hpp"
void setcurpos(*row*, *col*);
int *row*, *col*;   (cursor position)

Description: The **setcurpos** function moves the cursor to the display screen position defined by (*row*, *col*).

Return Value: No value is returned.

Example: The following program demonstrates the **setcurpos** function by moving the cursor to the right half of the display screen's center line.

```
//
// setcurpos Demo
//
#include <stdio.h>
#include <stdlib.h>
#include "windows.hpp"

main()
{
    save_initial_video();
    setcurpos(13, 41);
    printf("This message starts at the right half of the center line");
    waitkey();
    exit(0);
}
```

setcursor

Summary:	#include "windows.hpp" void setcursor(*sline*, *eline*); int *sline*;　　　　　　　　　　(cursor starting line) int *eline*;　　　　　　　　　　(cursor ending line)
Description:	The **setcursor** function sets the cursor character's starting (*sline*) and ending (*eline*) lines.
Return Value:	No value is returned.
Example:	The following program demonstrates the **setcursor** function by setting the cursor character to a completely filled block.

```
//
// setcursor Demo
//
#include <stdlib.h>
#include "windows.hpp"

main()
{
        save_initial_video();
        setcurpos(1, 1);
        setcursor(0, 7);
        cursoron();
        waitkey();
        exit(0);
}
```

setone

Summary:
```
#include "windows.hpp"
void setone(row, col, att);
int row, col;                    (screen position)
int att;                         (attribute)
```

Description: The **setone** function sets the attribute for the display screen position defined by (row, col) to att.

Return Value: No value is returned.

Example: The following program demonstrates the **setone** function by setting the attribute for position (23, 2) to a black character on a white background.

```
//
// setone Demo
//
#include <stdlib.h>
#include "windows.hpp"

main()
{
        save_initial_video();
        setone(23, 2, 0x70);
        waitkey();
        exit(0);
}
```

settext80

Summary: `#include "windows.hpp"`
`void settext80(void);`

Description: The **settext80** function initializes the WINDOWS operating environment. The **settext80** function should always be called before using any of the WINDOWS toolbox functions.

Return Value: No value is returned.

See Also: **save_initial_video**

Example: The following program demonstrates the **settext80** function by initializing the WINDOWS operating environment.

```
//
// settext80 Demo
//
#include <stdlib.h>
#include "windows.hpp"

main()
{
        settext80();
        clearscreen(1, 1, 25, 80, 7);
        setcurpos(1, 1);
        waitkey();
        exit(0);
}
```

show__mouse

Summary:

```
#include "windows.hpp"
void show_mouse(void);
```

Description: The **show_mouse** function turns on the mouse pointer.

Return Value: No value is returned.

See Also: **hide_mouse**

Example: The following program demonstrates the **show_mouse** function by turning on the mouse pointer.

```
//
// show_mouse Demo
//
#include <stdlib.h>
#include <bios.h>
#include "windows.hpp"

main()
{
        save_initial_video();
        reset_mouse();
        show_mouse();
        do {
        read_mouse();
        } while (!_bios_keybrd(1) && !_left_button);
        hide_mouse();
        if (_bios_keybrd(1))
                waitkey();
        exit(0);
}
```

ssn__string

Summary: #include "windows.hpp"
char *ssn_string(*string, number*);
char **string*;   (storage location for the Social Security
                                number string)
ssn &*number*;   (Social Security number structure)

Description: The **ssn_string** function constructs an 11-character Social Security number string (*string* = "xxx-xx-xxxx") for the Social Security number defined by *number*.

Return Value: The **ssn_string** function returns a pointer to the resulting Social Security number string.

See Also: **display_ssn** and **input_ssn**

Example: The following program demonstrates the **ssn_string** function by displaying a constructed Social Security number string on the tenth line of the display screen.

```
//
// ssn_string Demo
//
#include <stdlib.h>
#include "windows.hpp"

main()
{
        static ssn n = {007, 55, 3535};
        char line[80];

        save_initial_video();
        printstring(10, 1, ssn_string(line, n));
        waitkey();
        exit(0);
}
```

waitkey

Summary: #include "windows.hpp"
int waitkey(void);

Description: The **waitkey** function waits for the operator to press a key.

Return Value: The **waitkey** function returns the ASCII code for all nonextended-keyboard keys. Extended-keyboard keys return a value of their scan code + 256.

Example: The following program demonstrates the **waitkey** function by returning the values of an assortment of key presses. Program execution will continue until the **ESC** key is pressed.

```
//
// waitkey Demo
//
#include <stdio.h>
#include <stdlib.h>
#include "windows.hpp"

main()
{
        int key;

        save_initial_video();
        while (TRUE) {
                if ((key = waitkey()) == 27)
                        exit(0);
                printf("%d\n", key);
        }
}
```

window::close

Summary: #include "windows.hpp"
void *object*.close(void);
window *object*;   (dynamic text window object)

Description: The **window::close** function closes the previously opened text window defined by *object*.

Return Value: No value is returned.

See Also: **window::open**

Example: The following program demonstrates the **window::close** function by closing a text window at the coordinates (1, 20) and (15, 50).

```
//
// window::close Demo
//
#include <stdlib.h>
#include "windows.hpp"

main()
{
        window w(1, 20, 15, 50, 0x70, _SINGLE_LINE);

        save_initial_video();
        w.open();
        waitkey();
        w.close();
        exit(0);
}
```

window::clreol

Summary:
#include "windows.hpp"
void *object*.clreol(void);
window *object*;   (dynamic text window object)

Description:
The **window::clreol** clears the current text window line from the cursor's current column position to the text window's right border. The text window is defined by *object*.

Return Value: No value is returned.

Example:
The following program demonstrates the **window::clreol** function by erasing a portion of a text window's top line.

```
//
// window::clreol Demo
//
#include <stdlib.h>
#include "windows.hpp"

main()
{
        int i;
        window w(1, 20, 15, 50, 0x70, _SINGLE_LINE);

        save_initial_video();
        w.open();
        for (i = 0; i < 10; i++)
            w.println("This is another string");
        waitkey();
        w.setcurpos(1, 2);
        w.clreol();
        waitkey();
        exit(0);
}
```

window::cls

Summary:
```
#include "windows.hpp"
void object.cls(void);
window object;                    (dynamic text window object)
```

Description: The **window::cls** function clears the dynamic text window defined by *object*.

Return Value: No value is returned.

Example: The following program demonstrates the **window::cls** function by clearing the contents of a text window.

```
//
// window::cls Demo
//
#include <stdlib.h>
#include "windows.hpp"

main()
{
        int i;
        window w(1, 20, 15, 50, 0x70, _SINGLE_LINE);

        save_initial_video();
        w.open();
        for (i = 0; i < 10; i++)
            w.println("This is another string");
        waitkey();
        w.cls();
        waitkey();
        exit(0);
}
```

window::curcol

Summary: #include "windows.hpp"
int *object*.curcol(void);
window *object*;   (dynamic text window object)

Description: The **window::curcol** function retrieves a dynamic text window's (*object*'s) cursor column.

Return Value: The **window::curcol** returns the dynamic text window's cursor column.

See Also: **window::currow**

Example: The following program demonstrates the **window::curcol** function by displaying a dynamic text window's cursor column.

```
//
// window::curcol Demo
//
#include <stdio.h>
#include <stdlib.h>
#include "windows.hpp"

main()
{
        int i;
        window w(1, 20, 15, 50, 0x70, _SINGLE_LINE);

        save_initial_video();
        w.open();
        w.setcurpos(10, 5);
        setcurpos(20, 1);
        printf("Current Window Column: %d", w.curcol());
        waitkey();
        exit(0);
}
```

window::currow

Summary: #include "windows.hpp"
int *object*.currow(void);
window *object*;   (dynamic text window object)

Description: The **window::currow** function retrieves a dynamic text window's (*object*'s) cursor row.

Return Value: The **window::currow** returns the dynamic text window's cursor row.

See Also: **window::curcol**

Example: The following program demonstrates the **window::currow** function by displaying a dynamic text window's cursor row.

```
//
// window::currow Demo
//
#include <stdio.h>
#include <stdlib.h>
#include "windows.hpp"

main()
{
        int i;
        window w(1, 20, 15, 50, 0x70, _SINGLE_LINE);

        save_initial_video();
        w.open();
        w.setcurpos(10, 5);
        setcurpos(20, 1);
        printf("Current Window Row: %d", w.currow());
        waitkey();
        exit(0);
}
```

window::draw

Summary:	#include "window.hpp" void *object*.draw(void); window *object*; (dynamic text window object)
Description:	The **window::draw** function draws the dynamic text window defined by *object*.
Return Value:	No value is returned.
See Also:	**window::open**
Example:	The following program demonstrates the **window::draw** function by drawing a double-lined text window at the coordinates (10, 30) and (15, 50).

```
//
// window::draw Demo
//
#include <stdlib.h>
#include "windows.hpp"

main()
{
        save_initial_video();
        window(10, 30, 15, 50, 0x70, _DOUBLE_LINE).draw();
        waitkey();
        exit(0);
}
```

window::horizontal__bar

Summary:
```
#include "windows.hpp"
void object.horizontal_bar(curpos, total);
window object;                    (dynamic text window object)
int curpos;                       (current line position)
int total;                        (line length)
```

Description: The **window::horizontal_bar** function draws a horizontal scroll bar on the bottom line of a dynamic text window (*object*). The scroll bar setting is derived by dividing *curpos* by *total*.

Return Value: No value is returned.

See Also: **window::open** and **window::vertical_bar**

Example: The following program demonstrates the **window::horizontal_bar** function by displaying a variety of line positions.

```
//
// window::horizontal_bar Demo
//
#include <stdlib.h>
#include "windows.hpp"

main()
{
        window w(1, 30, 10, 70, 7, _SINGLE_LINE);

        save_initial_video();
        w.open();
        w.horizontal_bar(0, 100);
        waitkey();
        w.horizontal_bar(50, 100);
        waitkey();
        w.horizontal_bar(100, 100);
        waitkey();
        exit(0);
}
```

window::open

Summary:
```
#include "windows.hpp"
void object.open(void);
window object;                    (dynamic text window object)
```

Description: The **window::open** function dynamically opens and draws the dynamic text window defined by *object*.

Return Value: No value is returned.

See Also: **window::close** and **window::draw**

Example: The following program demonstrates the **window::open** function by opening and drawing a dynamic text window at the coordinates (1, 20) and (15, 50).

```
//
// window::open Demo
//
#include <stdlib.h>
#include "windows.hpp"

main()
{
        window w(1, 20, 15, 50, 0x70, _DOUBLE_LINE);

        save_initial_video();
        w.open();
        waitkey();
        w.close();
        exit(0);
}
```

window::p__col

Summary: #include "windows.hpp"
int *object*.p_col(*column*);
window *object*;   (dynamic text window object)
int *column*;   (logical column)

Description: The **window::p_col** determines the physical display screen
column for a dynamic text window's (*object*'s) logical column
(*column*).

Return Value: The **window::p_col** returns the logical column's corresponding
physical display screen column.

See Also: **window::p_row**

Example: The following program demonstrates the **window::p_col** function
by displaying the physical display screen column for a dynamic
text window's logical column.

```
//
// window::p_col Demo
//
#include <stdio.h>
#include <stdlib.h>
#include "windows.hpp"

main()
{
        int i;
        window w(1, 20, 15, 50, 0x70, _SINGLE_LINE);

        save_initial_video();
        w.open();
        setcurpos(20, 1);
        printf("Logical Column: 5 = Physical Column: %d", w.p_col(5));
        waitkey();
        exit(0);
}
```

window::p__row

Summary:
```
#include "windows.hpp"
int object.p_row(row);
window object;              (dynamic text window object)
int row;                   (logical row)
```

Description: The **window::p_row** determines the physical display screen row for a dynamic text window's (*object*'s) logical row (*row*).

Return Value: The **window::p_row** returns the logical row's physical display screen row.

See Also: **window::p_col**

Example: The following program demonstrates the **window::p_row** function by displaying the physical display screen row for a dynamic text window's logical row.

```
//
// window::p_row Demo
//
#include <stdio.h>
#include <stdlib.h>
#include "windows.hpp"

main()
{
        int i;
        window w(1, 20, 15, 50, 0x70, _SINGLE_LINE);

        save_initial_video();
        w.open();
        setcurpos(20, 1);
        printf("Logical Row: 7 = Physical Row: %d", w.p_row(7));
        waitkey();
        exit(0);
}
```

window::print

Summary:
```
#include "windows.hpp"
void object.print(string);
window object;            (dynamic text window object)
char *string;             (string pointer)
```

Description: The **window::print** function displays a *string* at a dynamic text window's (*object's*) current cursor position.

Return Value: No value is returned.

See Also: **window::printat**, **window::println**, and **window::printlnat**

Example: The following program demonstrates the **window::print** function by displaying an assortment of strings in a dynamic text window.

```
//
// window::print Demo
//
#include <stdlib.h>
#include "windows.hpp"

main()
{
        int i;
        window w(1, 20, 15, 50, 0x70, _SINGLE_LINE, _SCROLL);

        save_initial_video();
        w.open();
        w.print("This is message 1");
        w.print("This is message 2");
        w.print("This is message 3");
        waitkey();
        exit(0);
}
```

window::printat

Summary:
#include "windows.hpp"
void *object*.printat(*row*, *col*, *string*);
window *object*;   (dynamic text window object)
int *row*, *col*;   (window position)
char **string*;   (string pointer)

Description: The **window::printat** function displays a *string* at the dynamic text window position defined by (*row*, *col*). The dynamic text window is defined by *object*.

Return Value: No value is returned.

See Also: **window::print**, **window::println**, and **window::printlnat**

Example: The following program demonstrates the **window::printat** function by displaying a variety of strings in a dynamic text window.

```
//
// window::printat Demo
//
#include <stdlib.h>
#include "windows.hpp"

main()
{
        int i;
        window w(1, 20, 15, 50, 0x70, _SINGLE_LINE, _SCROLL);

        save_initial_video();
        w.open();
        w.printat(2, 1, "This is message 1");
        w.printat(1, 1, "This is message 2");
        w.printat(5, 1, "This is message 3");
        waitkey();
        exit(0);
}
```

window::println

Summary: #include "windows.hpp"
void *object*.println(*string*);
window *object*;   (dynamic text window object)
char **string*;   (string pointer)

Description: The **window::println** function displays a *string* and a carriage
return at a dynamic text window's (*object*'s) current cursor position.

Return Value: No value is returned.

See Also: **window::print**, **window::printat**, and **window::printlnat**

Example: The following program demonstrates the **window::println** function by displaying an assortment of strings in a dynamic text
window.

```
//
// window::println Demo
//
#include <stdlib.h>
#include "windows.hpp"

main()
{
        int i;
        window w(1, 20, 15, 50, 0x70, _SINGLE_LINE, _SCROLL);

        save_initial_video();
        w.open();
        w.println("This is message 1");
        w.println("This is message 2");
        w.println("This is message 3");
        waitkey();
        exit(0);
}
```

window:: printlnat

Summary:	#include "windows.hpp"
	void *object*.printlnat(*row*, *col*, *string*);
	window *object*;　　　　　　　(dynamic text window object)
	int *row*, *col*;　　　　　　　(window position)
	char **string*;　　　　　　　(string pointer)

Description: The **window::printlnat** function displays a *string* and a carriage return at the dynamic text window position defined by (*row*, *col*). The dynamic text window is defined by *object*.

Return Value: No value is returned.

See Also: **window::print**, **window::printat**, and **window::println**

Example: The following program demonstrates the **window::printlnat** function by displaying a variety of strings in a dynamic text window.

```
//
// window::printlnat Demo
//
#include <stdlib.h>
#include "windows.hpp"

main()
{
        int i;
        window w(1, 20, 15, 50, 0x70, _SINGLE_LINE, _SCROLL);

        save_initial_video();
        w.open();
        w.printlnat(2, 1, "This is message 1");
        w.printlnat(1, 1, "This is message 2");
        w.printlnat(5, 1, "This is message 3");
        waitkey();
        exit(0);
}
```

window::scroll

Summary:

#include "windows.hpp"
void *object*.scroll(*nlines*, *direction*, *cflag*);
window *object*;   (dynamic text window object)
int *nlines*;   (number of lines to be scrolled)
int *cflag*;   (clear lines flag)

Description:

The **window::scroll** function scrolls the contents of the dynamic text window defined by *object*. If *cflag* is TRUE (1), the *nlines* at the beginning of the scroll are cleared. Otherwise, the beginning scroll lines are left intact. The *direction* parameter can be one of the following constants (defined in **window.hpp**):

Constant	Action
_UP	Scroll the dynamic text window's contents up *nlines*.
_DOWN	Scroll the dynamic text window's contents down *nlines*.
_LEFT	Scroll the dynamic text window's contents left *nlines*.
_RIGHT	Scroll the dynamic text window's contents right *nlines*.

Return Value: No value is returned.

Example: The following program demonstrates the **window::scroll** function by performing a variety of scroll operations.

```
//
// window::scroll Demo
//
#include <stdlib.h>
#include "windows.hpp"

main()
{
        int i;
        window w(1, 20, 15, 50, 0x70, _SINGLE_LINE);

        save_initial_video();
        w.open();
        for (i = 0; i < 10; i++)
            w.println("This is another string");
        waitkey();
        w.scroll(1, _UP, _CLEAR);
        waitkey();
        w.scroll(1, _DOWN, _CLEAR);
        waitkey();
        w.scroll(1, _LEFT, _CLEAR);
        waitkey();
        w.scroll(1, _RIGHT, _CLEAR);
        waitkey();
        exit(0);
}
```

window::setcurpos

Summary: #include "windows.hpp"
void *object*.setcurpos(*row*, *col*);
window *object*;   (dynamic text window object)
int *row*, *col*;   (text window position)

Description: The **window::setcurpos** function moves the cursor to the dynamic text window position defined by (*row*, *col*). The dynamic text window is defined by *object*.

Return Value: No value is returned.

Example: The following program demonstrates the **window::setcurpos** function by moving the cursor to a variety of positions.

```
//
// window::setcurpos Demo
//
#include <stdlib.h>
#include "windows.hpp"

main()
{
        int i;
        window w(1, 20, 15, 50, 0x70, _SINGLE_LINE);

        save_initial_video();
        w.open();
        cursoron();
        waitkey();
        w.setcurpos(10, 5);
        waitkey();
        w.setcurpos(6, 17);
        waitkey();
        exit(0);
}
```

window::vertical__bar

Summary: #include "windows.hpp"
void *object*.vertical_bar(*curpos*, *total*);
window *object*;   (dynamic text window object)
int *curpos*;   (current line position)
int *total*;   (line length)

Description: The **window::vertical_bar** function draws a vertical scroll bar on the right side of the dynamic text window defined by *object*. The scroll bar setting is derived by dividing *curpos* by *total*.

Return Value: No value is returned.

See Also: **window::open** and **window::horizontal_bar**

Example: The following program demonstrates the **window::vertical_bar** function by displaying a variety of file positions.

```
//
// window::vertical_bar Demo
//
#include <stdlib.h>
#include "windows.hpp"

main()
{
        window w(1, 30, 10, 70, 7, _SINGLE_LINE);

        save_initial_video();
        w.open();
        w.vertical_bar(0, 100);
        waitkey();
        w.vertical_bar(50, 100);
        waitkey();
        w.vertical_bar(100, 100);
        waitkey();
        exit(0);
}
```

APPENDIX B

THE IBM PC ROM BIOS VIDEO SERVICES

As explained in Chapter 1, the IBM PC ROM BIOS video services place a wide variety of display input/output routines at a programmer's disposal. This appendix presents a detailed look at the ROM BIOS video services that are common to all IBM PCs and compatibles. Although the ROM BIOSes contained in some members of the PC family (i.e., the AT and computers with EGA adapters) offer video functions not found in the original IBM PC ROM BIOS, they will not be covered here because of their lack of portability across the entire family of IBM PCs and compatibles.

Each of the ROM BIOS video functions is presented as follows:

- **Register Summary:** The register summary explains how the 8086 registers are used to pass parameters to a ROM BIOS video function and return values back to the calling program. An 8086 register model is presented for each of the ROM BIOS video functions. All of the shaded registers in the 8086 register summaries indicate registers that are used either by the calling program to pass parameters to the ROM BIOS video function or by the ROM BIOS video function to return values back to the calling program. Parameter passing is summarized in an appropriate **Call With** section. Returned values are summarized in an appropriate **Returns** section.

- **Function Description:** A description of the ROM BIOS function's purpose is presented for each of the ROM BIOS video functions. Furthermore, any notes of special interest are provided.

- **Suggested Macro Definition:** A suggested assembly language macro definition is presented for each of the ROM BIOS video functions. Although the use of such a macro is strictly optional, macros can save programmers a great deal of time in developing programs that continuously use the same function calls over and over.

- **Programming Example:** A program fragment is presented for each of the ROM BIOS video functions. These examples are intended to illustrate how each of the ROM BIOS video functions is used in an application program.

SET VIDEO MODE (FUNCTION 00H)

Register Summary:

AX: | AH | AL |
BX: | BH | BL |
CX: | CH | CL |
DX: | DH | DL |

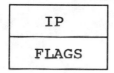

| SP |
| BP |
| SI |
| DI |

| IP |
| FLAGS |

| CS |
| DS |
| SS |
| ES |

Call With:

AH = 00H

AL = Video mode

Returns:

Nothing

Description: ROM BIOS video function 00H sets the currently active video mode as follows:

Display Mode	Description	Adapter(s)
00H	40 × 25 black-and-white text	CGA, EGA, PCjr
01H	40 × 25 color text	CGA, EGA, PCjr
02H	80 × 25 black-and-white text	CGA, EGA, PCjr
03H	80 × 25 color text	CGA, EGA, PCjr
04H	320 × 200 4-color graphics	CGA, EGA, PCjr
05H	320 × 200 4-color (color off)	CGA, EGA, PCjr
06H	640 × 200 2-color graphics	CGA, EGA, PCjr
07H	80 × 25 black-and-white text	MDA, EGA
08H	160 × 200 16-color graphics	PCjr
09H	320 × 200 16-color graphics	PCjr
0AH	640 × 200 4-color graphics	PCjr
0DH	320 × 200 16-color graphics	EGA
0EH	640 × 200 16-color graphics	EGA
0FH	640 × 350 2-color graphics	EGA
10H	640 × 350 4/16-color graphics	EGA

Suggested Macro Definition:

```
setvidmode      macro   vidmode
                mov     ah,0
                mov     al,vidmode
                int     10h
                endm
```

Example: The following program fragment demonstrates how ROM BIOS video function 00H is used to set the current video mode to the 80-column by 25-row color text mode:

```
        .
        .
        .
mov     ah,0            ;AH=Set video mode function code
mov     al,3            ;Set video mode to
int     10h             ; 80 x 25 color mode
        .
        .
        .
```

SET CURSOR TYPE (FUNCTION 01H)

Register Summary:

AX:	AH	AL
BX:	BH	BL
CX:	CH	CL
DX:	DH	DL

SP
BP
SI
DI

IP
FLAGS

CS
DS
SS
ES

Call With:

AH = 01H

CH = Starting cursor line

CL = Ending cursor line

Returns:

Nothing

Description: ROM BIOS function 01H sets the starting and ending lines for the blinking cursor character. The default values used by most application programs are as follows:

Cursor Type	Starting Line	Ending Line
Mode 07H	11	12
Modes 00H - 03H	6	7
Turn cursor off	32	0

Suggested Macro Definition:

```
setcurtype      macro   sline,eline
                mov     ah,1
                mov     ch,sline
                mov     cl,eline
                int     10h
                endm
```

Example: The following program fragment demonstrates how ROM BIOS video function 01H is used to turn the cursor off:

```
        .
        .
        .
        mov     ah,1            ;AH=Set cursor type function
        mov     cx,2000h        ;CX=Turn off cursor values
        int     10H             ;Turn off the cursor
        .
        .
        .
```

SET CURSOR POSITION (FUNCTION 02H)

Register Summary:

AX: | AH | AL |
BX: | BH | BL |
CX: | CH | CL |
DX: | DH | DL |

| SP |
| BP |
| SI |
| DI |

| IP |
| FLAGS |

| CS |
| DS |
| SS |
| ES |

Call With:

AH = 02H

BH = Page number

DH = Cursor row

DL = Cursor column

Returns:

Nothing

Description: ROM BIOS video function 02H sets the current cursor position. In graphics modes, the page number passed in BH must be zero. The upper left corner of the screen is 0,0. The lower right corner of the screen is 24,79 in 80-column modes and 24,39 in 40-column modes.

Suggested Macro Definition:

```
setcurpos       macro   page,row,column
                mov     ah,2
                mov     bh,page
                mov     dh,row
                mov     dl,column
                endm
```

Example: The following program fragment demonstrates how ROM BIOS video function 02H is used to home the cursor:

```
        .
        .
        .
        mov     ah,2        ;AH=Set cursor position function code
        mov     bh,0        ;BH=Page 0
        xor     dx,dx       ;Set cursor to upper left hand corner
        int     10h         ;Position the cursor
        .
        .
        .
```

READ CURSOR VALUES (FUNCTION 03H)

Register Summary:

AX: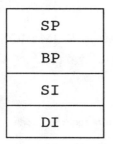

Call With:

AH = 03H

BH = Page number

Returns:

CH = Cursor starting line

CL = Cursor ending line

DH = Cursor row position

DL = Cursor column position

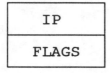

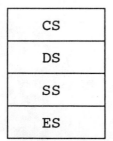

Description: ROM BIOS video function 03H retrieves the cursor character's starting line, the cursor character's ending line, the cursor row position, and the cursor column position. In graphics modes, the page number passed in BH must be zero.

Suggested Macro Definition:

```
readcurval      macro    page
                mov      ah,3
                mov      bh,page
                endm
```

Example: The following program fragment demonstrates how ROM BIOS video function 03H is used to retrieve the page zero cursor values:

```
        .
        .
        .
        mov     ah,3          ;AH=Read cursor values function code
        mov     bh,0          ;BH=Page 0
        int     10h           ;Go get the values
        .
        .
        .
```

READ LIGHT PEN VALUES (FUNCTION 04H)

Register Summary:

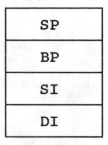

AX: | AH | AL |
BX: | BH | BL |
CX: | CH | CL |
DX: | DH | DL |

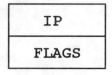

| SP |
| BP |
| SI |
| DI |

| IP |
| FLAGS |

| CS |
| DS |
| SS |
| ES |

Call With:

AH = 04H

Returns:

AH = 0 if light pen isn't triggered

   1 if light pen is triggered

CH = Pixel row

BX = Pixel column

DH = Character row

DL = Character column

Description: ROM BIOS video function 04H returns the light pen's trigger status, pixel position, and character position.

Suggested Macro Definition:

```
readpen      macro
             mov    ah,4
             int    10h
             int    10h
             endm
```

Example: The following program fragment demonstrates how ROM BIOS video function 04H is used to retrieve the light pen values. Note that the following code fragment will perform a continuous loop until the light pen is triggered:

```
             .
             .
             .
loop:        mov    ah,4        ;AH=Read light pen function code
             int    10h         ;Get the light pen values
             test   ah,1        ;Loop till the
             jz     loop        ; pen is triggered
             .
             .
             .
```

SELECT DISPLAY PAGE (FUNCTION 05H)

Register Summary:

AX:	AH	AL
BX:	BH	BL
CX:	CH	CL
DX:	DH	DL

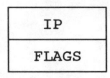

SP
BP
SI
DI

IP
FLAGS

CS
DS
SS
ES

Call With:

AH = 05H

AL = Page number

Returns:

Nothing

Description: ROM BIOS video function 05H selects the currently active display page. The maximum allowable page number varies according to the video mode and the display adapter as follows:

Mode(s)	Adapter	Allowable Page Numbers
00H and 01H	CGA	0 to 7
02H and 03H	CGA	0 to 3
02H, 03H, and 0DH	EGA	0 to 7
0EH	EGA	0 to 3
0FH and 10H	EGA	0 to 1

Suggested Macro Definition:

```
seldisppag      macro   page
                mov     ah,5
                mov     al,page
                int     10h
                endm
```

Example: The following program fragment demonstrates how ROM BIOS video function 05H is used to select display page 1:

```
        .
        .
        .
        mov     ah,5        ;AH=Select page function code
        mov     al,1        ;Select
        int     10h         ; page 1
        .
        .
        .
```

SCROLL WINDOW UP (FUNCTION 06H)

Register Summary:

AX:

BX:

CX:

DX:

SP
BP
SI
DI

IP
FLAGS

CS
DS
SS
ES

Call With:

AH = 06H

AL = Number of scroll lines

BH = Attribute for the cleared area

CH = Upper left row

CL = Upper left column

DH = Lower right row

DL = Lower right column

Returns:

Nothing

Description: ROM BIOS video function 06H scrolls a display screen window's contents upward. If the number of lines passed in AL is equal to zero, the entire window will be cleared. Otherwise, only the specified number of lines in AL will be scrolled and cleared.

Suggested Macro Definition:

```
windowup        macro   row1,col1,row2,col2,lines,att
                mov     ah,6
                mov     al,lines
                mov     bh,att
                mov     ch,row1
                mov     cl,col1
                mov     dh,row2
                mov     dl,col2
                int     10h
                endm
```

Example: The following program fragment demonstrates how ROM BIOS video function 06H is used to clear the left half of the display screen:

```
        .
        .
        .
        mov     ah,6            ;AH=Scroll window up function code
        mov     al,0            ;AL=Clear the whole window
        mov     bh,7            ;BH=Normal attribute
        mov     ch,0            ;CH=Upper left row
        mov     cl,0            ;CL=Upper left column
        mov     dh,24           ;DH=Lower right row
        mov     dl,39           ;DL=Lower right column
        int     10h             ;Clear the screen
        .
        .
        .
```

SCROLL WINDOW DOWN (FUNCTION 07H)

Register Summary:

AX: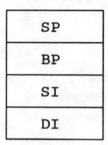

BX:

CX:

DX:

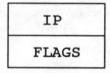

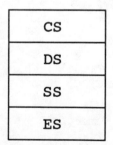

Call With:

AH = 07H

AL = Number of scroll lines

BH = Attribute for the cleared area

CH = Upper left row

CL = Upper left column

DH = Lower right row

DL = Lower right column

Returns:

Nothing

Description: ROM BIOS video function 07H scrolls a display screen window's contents downward. If the number of lines passed in AL is equal to zero, the window will be completely cleared. Otherwise, only the specified number of lines in AL will be scrolled and cleared.

Suggested Macro Definition:

```
windowdown      macro   row1,col1,row2,col2,lines,att
                mov     ah,7
                mov     al,lines
                mov     bh,att
                mov     ch,row1
                mov     cl,col1
                mov     dh,row2
                mov     dl,col2
                int     10h
                endm
```

Example: The following program fragment demonstrates how ROM BIOS video function 07H is used to clear the right half of the display screen's top ten lines:

```
        .
        .
        .
        mov     ah,7            ;AH=Scroll window down function code
        mov     al,0            ;AL=Clear the whole window
        mov     bh,7            ;BH=Normal attribute
        mov     ch,0            ;CH=Upper left row
        mov     cl,40           ;CL=Upper left column
        mov     dh,9            ;DH=Lower right row
        mov     dl,79           ;DL=Lower right column
        int     10h             ;Clear the window
        .
        .
        .
```

READ CHARACTER/ATTRIBUTE PAIR (FUNCTION 08H)

Register Summary:

AX: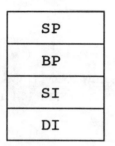

BX:

CX:

DX:

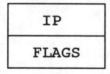

Call with:

AH = 08H

BH = Page number

Returns:

AH = Attribute

AL = ASCII code

Description: ROM BIOS video function 08H retrieves the character/attribute pair located at the current cursor position. While in graphics modes, the page number passed in BH must be zero.

Suggested Macro Definition:

```
readpair        macro   page
                mov     ah,8
                mov     bh,page
                int     10h
                endm
```

Example: The following program fragment demonstrates how ROM BIOS video function 08H is used to read the character/attribute pair in the upper left corner of the display screen:

```
        .
        .
        .
        mov     ah,2            ;AH=Set cursor function code
        mov     bh,0            ;BH=Page 0
        mov     dh,0            ;DH=Cursor row position
        mov     dl,0            ;DL=Cursor column position
        int     10h             ;Home the cursor
        mov     ah,8            ;AH=Read pair function code
        mov     bh,0            ;BH=Page 0
        int     10h             ;Get the char/att pair
        .
        .
        .
```

WRITE CHARACTER/ATTRIBUTE PAIR (FUNCTION 09H)

Register Summary:

AX: | AH | AL |
BX: | BH | BL |
CX: | CH | CL |
DX: | DH | DL |

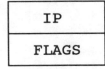

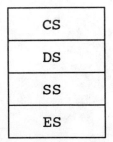

Call With:

AH = 09H

AL = ASCII code

BH = Page number

BL = Attribute

CX = Number of characters

Returns:

Nothing

Description: ROM BIOS video function 09H displays a specified number of character/attribute pairs, beginning at the current cursor position. The cursor position is not updated by ROM BIOS video function 09H. In graphics modes, the page number passed in BH must equal zero.

Suggested Macro Definition:

```
writepair      macro    page,char,att,number
               mov      ah,9
               mov      al,char
               mov      bh,page
               mov      bl,att
               mov      cx,number
               int      10h
               endm
```

Example: The following program fragment demonstrates how ROM BIOS video function 09H is used to completely fill the bottom line of the display screen with an underline character:

```
           .
           .
           .
     mov    ah,2           ;AH=Set cursor function code
     mov    bh,0           ;BH=Page 0
     mov    dh,24          ;DH=Cursor row position
     mov    dl,0           ;DL=Cursor column position
     int    10h            ;Move the cursor
     mov    ah,9           ;AH=Write pair function code
     mov    al,'_'         ;AL=Underline character
     mov    bh,0           ;BH=Page 0
     mov    bl,7           ;BL=Normal attribute
     mov    cx,80          ;CX=Line length
     int    10h            ;Display the line
           .
           .
           .
```

WRITE CHARACTERS (FUNCTION 0AH)

Register Summary:

AX: | AH | AL |
BX: | BH | BL |
CX: | CH | CL |
DX: | DH | DL |

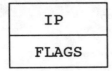

| SP |
| BP |
| SI |
| DI |

| IP |
| FLAGS |

| CS |
| DS |
| SS |
| ES |

Call With:

AH = 0AH

AL = ASCII code

BH = Page number

BL = Color (Graphics only)

CX = Number of characters

Returns:

Nothing

Description: ROM BIOS video function 0AH writes a specified number of characters, beginning at the current cursor position. The cursor position is not updated by ROM BIOS video function 0AH. In graphics modes, the page number passed in BH must be zero.

Suggested Macro Definition:

```
writechar       macro   page,char,number,color
                mov     ah,0ah
                mov     al,char
                mov     bh,page
                ifnb    <color>
                mov     bl,color
                endif
                mov     cx,number
                int     10h
                endm
```

Example: The following program fragment demonstrates how ROM BIOS video function 0AH is used to display 40 * (asterisk) characters, starting at the upper left corner of the display screen:

```
        .
        .
        .
        mov     ah,2            ;AH=Set cursor function code
        mov     bh,0            ;BH=Page 0
        mov     dh,0            ;DH=Cursor row position
        mov     dl,0            ;DL=Cursor column position
        int     10h            ;Home the cursor
        mov     ah,0ah          ;AH=Write characters function code
        mov     al,'*'          ;AL=Asterisk character
        mov     bh,0            ;BH=Page 0
        mov     cx,40          ;CX=Number of characters
        int     10h            ;Display the characters
        .
        .
        .
```

SET COLOR PALETTE (FUNCTION 0BH)

Register Summary:

AX: | AH | AL |

BX: | BH | BL |

CX: | CH | CL |

DX: | DH | DL |

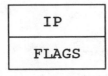

Call With:

AH = 0BH

BH = Function code

BL = Color or Palette code

| SP |
| BP |
| SI |
| DI |

| IP |
| FLAGS |

Returns:

Nothing

| CS |
| DS |
| SS |
| ES |

Description: ROM BIOS video function 0BH selects either a color palette or the background and border colors. If the function code in BH is equal to zero, ROM BIOS video function 0BH sets the background and border colors. While in graphics modes, the background and the border colors will be set to the color passed in BL. While in text modes, only the border color will be set to the color passed in BL. If the function code in BH is equal to one, the new color palette code is passed in BL as follows:

Palette	Pixel Value	Color
0	0	Current Background Color
	1	Green
	2	Red
	3	Brown
1	0	Current Background Color
	1	Cyan
	2	Magenta
	3	White

Suggested Macro Definition:

```
setpalette    macro    func,color
              mov      ah,0bh
              mov      bh,func
              mov      bl,color
              endm
```

Example: The following program fragment demonstrates how ROM BIOS video function 0BH is used to set a display screen's background to white:

```
          .
          .
          .
mov    ah,0bh         ;AH=Set palette function
mov    bh,0           ;BH=Set border color function
mov    bl,7           ;BL=White color value
int    10h            ;Set border to white
          .
          .
          .
```

WRITE GRAPHICS PIXEL (FUNCTION 0CH)

Register Summary:

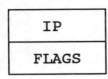

AX: | AH | AL |
BX: | BH | BL |
CX: | CH | CL |
DX: | DH | DL |

| SP |
| BP |
| SI |
| DI |

| IP |
| FLAGS |

| CS |
| DS |
| SS |
| ES |

Call With:

AH = 0CH

AL = Color value

CX = Pixel column

DX = Pixel row

Returns:

Nothing

Description: ROM BIOS video function 0CH sets a graphics pixel to the color passed in AL. For video modes 04H and 05H, the legitimate range for color values is 0 to 3. Video mode 06H allows only color values 0 and 1. Whenever bit 7 of the color value is set, the color value is xored with the pixel's current color value.

Suggested Macro Definition:

```
writepixel      macro   pixelx,pixely,color
                mov     ah,0ch
                mov     al,color
                mov     cx,pixelx
                mov     dx,pixely
                endm
```

Example: The following program fragment demonstrates how ROM BIOS video function 0CH is used to draw a graphics line across the center of the display screen:

```
                .
                .
                .
                mov     cx,0        ;CX=Starting x-coordinate
                mov     dx,120      ;DX=Y-coordinate
loop:           mov     ah,0ch      ;AH=Write pixel function code
                mov     al,1        ;AL=Color value
                int     10h         ;Turn on the pixel
                inc     cx          ;Bump the x-coordinate
                cmp     cx,640      ;Loop
                jb      loop        ; till done
                .
                .
                .
```

READ GRAPHICS PIXEL (FUNCTION 0DH)

Register Summary:

AX:	AH	AL
BX:	BH	BL
CX:	CH	CL
DX:	DH	DL

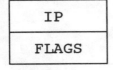

SP
BP
SI
DI

IP
FLAGS

CS
DS
SS
ES

Call With:

AH = 0DH

CX = Pixel column

DX = Pixel row

Returns:

AL = Color value

Description: ROM BIOS video function 0DH retrieves the color value for a specified graphics pixel. The range of the retrieved color value is dependent upon the current video mode.

Suggested Macro Definition:

```
readpixel      macro    pixelx,pixely
               mov      ah,0dh
               mov      cx,pixelx
               mov      dx,pixely
               int      10h
               endm
```

Example: The following program fragment demonstrates how ROM BIOS video function 0DH is used to retrieve the color value of pixel 0,25:

```
               .
               .
               .
               mov      ah,0dH       ;AH=Read pixel function code
               mov      cx,0         ;CX=Pixel x-coordinate
               mov      dx,25        ;DX=Pixel y-coordinate
               int      10h          ;Retrieve the color value
               .
               .
               .
```

WRITE CHARACTER IN TELETYPE MODE (FUNCTION 0EH)

Register Summary:

AX: | AH | AL |
BX: | BH | BL |
CX: | CH | CL |
DX: | DH | DL |

| SP |
| BP |
| SI |
| DI |

| IP |
| FLAGS |

| CS |
| DS |
| SS |
| ES |

Call With:

AH = 0EH

AL = ASCII code

BH = Page number

BL = Color value for graphics modes

Returns:

Nothing

Description: ROM BIOS video function 0EH displays a character by using a teletype mode. The ASCII codes for bell, backspace, carriage return, and linefeed are all recognized by the teletype mode. All other ASCII codes display their corresponding characters.

Suggested Macro Definition:

```
writetty        macro   char,page,color
                mov     ah,0eh
                mov     al,char
                mov     bh,page
                ifnb    <color>
                mov     bl,color
                endif
                int     10h
                endm
```

Example: The following program fragment demonstrates how ROM BIOS video function 0EH is used to perform a carriage return.

```
                .
                .
                .
                mov     ah,0eh          ;AH=Write teletype function code
                mov     al,13           ;AL=Carriage return
                mov     bh,0            ;BH=Page number
                int     10h             ;Do a carriage return
                .
                .
                .
```

GET VIDEO MODE (FUNCTION 0FH)

Register Summary:

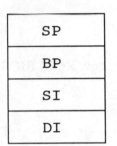

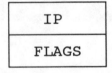

Call With:

AH = 0FH

Returns:

AH = Line length

AL = Video Mode

BH = Page Number

Description: ROM BIOS video function 0FH retrieves the number of columns per display line, the currently active page number, and the current video mode as follows:

Display Mode	Description	Adapter(s)
00H	40 × 25 black-and-white text	CGA, EGA, PCjr
01H	40 × 25 color text	CGA, EGA, PCjr
02H	80 × 25 black-and-white text	CGA, EGA, PCjr
03H	80 × 25 color text	CGA, EGA, PCjr
04H	320 × 200 4-color graphics	CGA, EGA, PCjr
05H	320 × 200 4-color (color off)	CGA, EGA, PCjr
06H	640 × 200 2-color graphics	CGA, EGA, PCjr
07H	80 × 25 black-and-white text	MDA, EGA
08H	160 × 200 16-color graphics	PCjr
09H	320 × 200 16-color graphics	PCjr
0AH	640 × 200 4-color graphics	PCjr
0DH	320 × 200 16-color graphics	EGA
0EH	640 × 200 16-color graphics	EGA
0FH	640 × 350 2-color graphics	EGA
10H	640 × 350 4/16-color graphics	EGA

Suggested Macro Definition:

```
getvidmode      macro
                mov     ah,0fh
                int     10h
                endm
```

Example: The following program fragment demonstrates how ROM BIOS video function 0FH is used to retrieve the current video mode, the current display page, and the number of columns per line:

```
        .
        .
        .
mov     ah,0fh              ;AH=Get video mode function code
int     10h                 ;Get the video mode
        .
        .
        .
```

APPENDIX C

THE MICROSOFT MOUSE DRIVER ROUTINES

As explained in Chapter 4, the Microsoft mouse driver offers a wide variety of routines for controlling a Microsoft compatible mouse. This appendix presents a detailed look at the routines that are contained in the Microsoft mouse driver.

Each of the Microsoft mouse driver functions is presented as follows:

Register Summary: The register summary explains how the 8086 registers are used to pass parameters to a mouse driver function and return values back to the calling program. An 8086 register model is presented for each of the mouse driver functions. All of the shaded registers in the 8086 register summaries indicate registers that are used either by the calling program to pass parameters to the mouse driver function or by the mouse driver function to return values back to the calling program. Parameter passing is summarized in an appropriate **Call With** section. Returned values are summarized in an appropriate **Returns** section.

Function Description: A description of the mouse driver function's purpose is presented for each of the mouse driver functions. Furthermore, notes of special interest are provided.

Suggested Macro Definition: A suggested assembly language macro definition is presented for each of the mouse driver functions. Although the use of such a macro is strictly optional, macros can save programmers a great deal of time in developing programs that continuously use the same function calls over and over.

Programming Example: A program fragment is presented for each of the mouse driver functions. These examples are intended to illustrate how each of the mouse driver functions is used in an application program.

RESET MOUSE DRIVER (FUNCTION 00H)

Register Summary:

AX: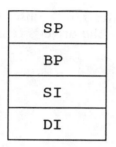

BX:

CX:

DX:

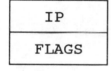

Call With:

AX = 00H

Returns:

AX = Mouse status

BX = Number of mouse buttons

Description: Mouse driver function 00H resets the mouse driver by turning off the mouse pointer and disabling any event handlers. If a mouse is available, function 00H will return a value of 0FFFFH in register AX. Otherwise, function 00H will return a value of 0000H in register AX.

Suggested Macro Definition:

```
resetdriver     macro
                mov     ax,0
                int 33h
                endm
```

Example: The following program fragment demonstrates how mouse driver function 00H is used to reset the mouse driver and save the driver's returned status:

```
        .
        .
        .
        mov     ax,0            ;Reset the
        int     33h             ; mouse driver
        mov     mstatus,ax      ;Save the driver's status
        .
        .
        .
```

TURN ON MOUSE POINTER (FUNCTION 01H)

Register Summary:

AX: | AH | AL |

BX: | BH | BL |

CX: | CH | CL |

DX: | DH | DL |

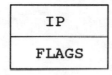

SP
BP
SI
DI

IP
FLAGS

CS
DS
SS
ES

Call With:

AX = 0001H

Returns:

Nothing

Description: Mouse driver function 01H turns on the mouse pointer.

Suggested Macro Definition:

```
pointeron     macro
              mov     ax,1
              int     33h
              endm
```

Example: The following program fragment demonstrates mouse driver function 01H by turning on the mouse pointer:

```
        .
        .
        .
        mov     ax,1            ;Turn on the
        int     33h             ; mouse pointer
        .
        .
        .
```

TURN OFF MOUSE POINTER (FUNCTION 02H)

Register Summary:

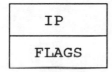

AX:	AH	AL
BX:	BH	BL
CX:	CH	CL
DX:	DH	DL

SP
BP
SI
DI

IP
FLAGS

CS
DS
SS
ES

Call With:

AX = 0002H

Returns:

Nothing

Description: Mouse driver function 02H turns off the mouse pointer.

Suggested Macro Definition:

```
pointeroff      macro
                mov     ax,2
                int     33h
                endm
```

Example: The following program fragment demonstrates mouse driver function 02H by turning off the mouse pointer:

```
                .
                .
                .
                mov     ax,2            ;Turn off the
                int     33h             ; mouse pointer
                .
                .
                .
```

GET BUTTON STATUS AND
POINTER POSITION (FUNCTION 03H)

Register Summary:

AX: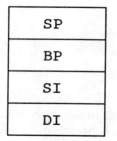

BX:

CX:

DX:

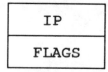

Call With:

AX = 0003H

Returns:

BX = Button status

CX = Pointer x-coordinate

DX = Pointer y-coordinate

Description: Mouse driver function 03H returns the mouse pointer's x-coordinate in register CX, the mouse pointer's y-coordinate in register DX, and the mouse buttons' status in register BX as follows:

Bit	True (1)	False(0)
0	Left button down	Left button released
1	Right button down	Right button released
2	Center button down	Center button released

Suggested Macro Definition:

```
getstatus       macro
                mov     ax,3
                int     33h
                endm
```

Example: The following program fragment demonstrates mouse driver function 03H by continuously looping until the left mouse button is pressed:

```
                .
                .
                .
loop:           mov     ax,3        ;Get the
                int     33h         ; mouse status
                and     bx,1        ;Loop till the
                jz      loop        ; left button is pressed
                .
                .
                .
```

SET POINTER POSITION (FUNCTION 04H)

Register Summary:

AX: | AH | AL |
BX: | BH | BL |
CX: | CH | CL |
DX: | DH | DL |

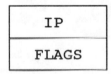

| SP |
| BP |
| SI |
| DI |

| IP |
| FLAGS |

| CS |
| DS |
| SS |
| ES |

Call With:

AX = 0004H

CX = X-coordinate

DX = Y-coordinate

Returns:

Nothing

Description: Mouse driver function 04H moves the mouse pointer to the coordinates defined by registers CX and DX.

Suggested Macro Definition:

```
setpointerpos    macro    x,y
                 mov      cx,x
                 mov      dx,y
                 mov      ax,4
                 int      33h
                 endm
```

Example: The following program fragment demonstrates mouse driver function 04H by moving the mouse pointer to the upper left corner of the display screen:

```
        .
        .
        .
        mov     cx,0            ;X-coordinate = 0
        mov     dx,0            ;Y-coordinate = 0
        mov     ax,4            ;Move the
        int     33h             ; mouse pointer
        .
        .
        .
```

GET BUTTON PRESS STATUS (FUNCTION 05H)

Register Summary:

AX: | AH | AL |

BX: | BH | BL |

CX: | CH | CL |

DX: | DH | DL |

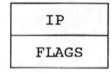

| SP |
| BP |
| SI |
| DI |

| IP |
| FLAGS |

| CS |
| DS |
| SS |
| ES |

Call With:

AX = 0005H

BX = Button number

Returns:

AX = Mouse buttons' status

BX = Button press count

CX = X-coordinate of last press

DX = Y-coordinate of last press

Description: Mouse driver function 05H returns the press count since function 05H was previously called and the pointer position of the last press for the mouse button specified in register BX as follows:

Button	Value
Left button	0
Right button	1
Center button	2

Additionally, mouse driver function 05H returns the mouse buttons' status in register AX as follows:

Bit	True (1)	False(0)
0	Left button down	Left button released
1	Right button down	Right button released
2	Center button down	Center button released

Suggested Macro Definition:

```
buttonpress    macro   button
               mov     bx,button
               mov     ax,5
               int     33h
               endm
```

Example: The following program fragment demonstrates mouse driver function 05H by continuously looping until the left button is pressed with the mouse pointer located on the top line of the display screen:

```
                .
                .
                .
loop:           mov     bx,0            ;Get the
                mov     ax,5            ; left
                int     33h             ;  button values
                and     ax,1            ;Loop if
                jz      loop            ; button not pressed
                cmp     dx,8            ;Loop if not
                jb      loop            ; on top line
                .
                .
                .
```

GET BUTTON RELEASE STATUS (FUNCTION 06H)

Register Summary:

AX: | AH | AL |
BX: | BH | BL |
CX: | CH | CL |
DX: | DH | DL |

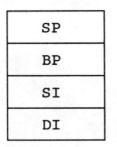

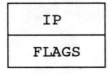

Call With:

AX = 0006H

BX = Button number

Returns:

AX = Mouse buttons' status

BX = Button release count

CX = X-coordinate of last release

DX = Y-coordinate of last release

Description: Mouse driver function 06H returns the release count since function 06H was previously called and the pointer position of the last release for the mouse button specified in register BX as follows:

Button	Value
Left button	0
Right button	1
Center button	2

Additionally, mouse driver function 05H returns the mouse buttons' status in register AX as follows:

Bit	True (1)	False(0)
0	Left button down	Left button released
1	Right button down	Right button released
2	Center button down	Center button released

Suggested Macro Definition:

```
buttonrelease   macro   button
                mov     bx,button
                mov     ax,6
                int     33h
                endm
```

Example: The following program fragment demonstrates mouse driver function 06H by continuously looping until the left button is released with the mouse pointer located on the top line of the display screen:

```
        .
        .
        .
loop:       mov     bx,0        ;Get the
            mov     ax,6        ; left
            int     33h         ;  button values
            and     ax,1        ;Loop if
            jnz     loop        ; button is pressed
            cmp     dx,8        ;Loop if not
            jb      loop        ; on top line
        .
        .
        .
```

SET HORIZONTAL LIMITS (FUNCTION 07H)

Register Summary:

AX:

AH	AL

BX:

BH	BL

CX:

CH	CL

DX:

DH	DL

SP
BP
SI
DI

IP
FLAGS

CS
DS
SS
ES

Call With:

AX = 0007H

CX = Minimum x-coordinate

DX = Maximum x-coordinate

Returns:

Nothing

Description: Mouse driver function 07H limits the mouse pointer's display area to the horizontal coordinates specified in registers CX and DX.

Suggested Macro Definition:

```
horlimits    macro    min,max
             mov      cx,min
             mov      dx,max
             mov      ax,7
             int      33h
             endm
```

Example: The following program fragment demonstrates mouse driver function 07H by limiting the mouse pointer to the right half of the display screen:

```
        .
        .
        .
   mov     cx,320          ;CX = Minimum x-coordinate
   mov     dx,639          ;DX = Maximum x-coordinate
   mov     ax,7            ;Go set
   int     33h             ; the limits
        .
        .
        .
```

SET VERTICAL LIMITS (FUNCTION 08H)

Register Summary:

AX: | AH | AL |
BX: | BH | BL |
CX: | CH | CL |
DX: | DH | DL |

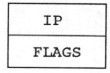

SP
BP
SI
DI

IP
FLAGS

CS
DS
SS
ES

Call With:

AX = 0008H

CX = Minimum y-coordinate

DX = Maximum y-coordinate

Returns:

Nothing

Description: Mouse driver function 08H limits the mouse pointer's display area to the vertical coordinates specified in registers CX and DX.

Suggested Macro Definition:

```
verlimits       macro   min,max
                mov     cx,min
                mov     dx,max
                mov     ax,8
                int     33h
                endm
```

Example: The following program fragment demonstrates mouse driver function 08H by limiting the mouse pointer to the top thirteen lines of the display screen:

```
        .
        .
        .
        mov     cx,0            ;CX = Minimum y-coordinate
        mov     dx,103          ;DX = Maximum y-coordinate
        mov     ax,8            ;Go set
        int     33h             ; the limits
        .
        .
        .
```

SET GRAPHIC SHAPE (FUNCTION 09H)

Register Summary:

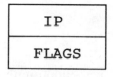

AX:

BX:

CX:

DX:

SP

BP

SI

DI

IP

FLAGS

CS

DS

SS

ES

Call With:

AX   = 0009H

BX   = Hot spot's left offset

CX   = Hot spot's top offset

ES:DX = Shape buffer pointer

Returns:

Nothing

331

Description: Mouse driver function 09H changes the graphic pointer's shape to the shapes defined in the buffer pointed to by ES:DX as follows:

Buffer Bytes	Type of Mask
00H to 20H	ANDed with the display screen's image
21H to 40H	XORed with the display screen's image

Additionally, mouse driver function 09H defines the graphic pointer's hot spot to the relative offsets passed in registers BX and CX. These offsets are relative to the upper left corner of the graphic pointer's image and must be in the range -16 to 16.

Suggested Macro Definition:

```
setgraphic    macro    left,top,buffer
              mov      bx,left
              mov      cx,right
              mov      ax,seg buffer
              mov      es,ax
              mov      dx,offset buffer
              mov      ax,9
              int      33h
              endm
```

Example: The following program demonstrates mouse driver function 09H by setting the graphic pointer to a new shape:

```
    .
    .
    .
    mov    bx,0              ;BX = Hot spot's left offset
    mov    cx,0              ;CX = Hot spot's right offset
    mov    ax,seg pointer    ;AX = Pointer buffer's segment
    mov    es,ax             ;Put it into ES
    mov    dx,offset pointer ;ES:DX = Pointer buffer pointer
    mov    ax,9              ;Set the
    int    33h               ; new pointer
    .
    .
    .
```

SET TEXT POINTER TYPE (FUNCTION 0AH)

Register Summary:

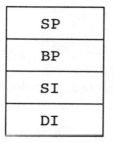

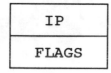

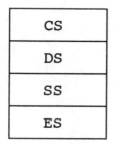

Call With:

AX = 000AH

BX = Pointer type

CX = AND mask or starting cursor line

DX = XOR mask or ending cursor line

Returns:

Nothing

Description: Mouse driver function 0AH sets the type and shape for the mouse's text pointer. If register BX = 1, the mouse's text pointer will be set to the hardware text cursor and the cursor's starting and ending lines will be set to the values passed in registers CX and DX, respectively. Otherwise, the mouse's text pointer will be set to a software cursor, and the cursor's character/attribute AND and XOR bit masks will be set to the values passed in registers CX and DX, respectively.

Suggested Macro Definition:

```
settext          macro     type,amask,xmask
                 mov       bx,type
                 mov       cx,amask
                 mov       dx,xmask
                 mov       ax,0ah
                 int       33h
                 endm
```

Example: The following program fragment demonstrates mouse driver function 0AH by setting the mouse's text pointer to the hardware cursor:

```
        .
        .
        .
        mov       bx,1         ;Hardware cursor flag
        mov       cx,6         ;CX = Starting cursor line
        mov       dx,7         ;DX = Ending cursor line
        mov       ax,0ah       ;Set the new
        int       33h          ; text pointer
        .
        .
        .
```

GET MOTION COUNT (FUNCTION 0BH)

Register Summary:

AX: | AH | AL |

BX: | BH | BL |

CX: | CH | CL |

DX: | DH | DL |

| SP |
| BP |
| SI |
| DI |

| IP |
| FLAGS |

| CS |
| DS |
| SS |
| ES |

Call With:

AX = 000BH

Returns:

CX = Horizontal mickey count

DX = Vertical mickey count

Description: Mouse driver function 0BH returns the number of **mickeys** (1/200")
the mouse has moved since function 0BH was last called.

Suggested Macro Definition:

```
getmotion       macro
                mov     ax,0bh
                int     33h
                endm
```

Example: The following program fragment demonstrates mouse driver function
0BH by continuously looping until the mouse is moved up and to the left:

```
            .
            .
            .
loop:       mov     ax,0bh          ;Get the
            int     33h             ; motion count
            cmp     cx,0            ;Loop if mouse
            jge     loop            ; hasn't move left
            cmp     dx,0            ;Loop if mouse
            jge     loop            ; hasn't move up
            .
            .
            .
```

SET USER-DEFINED EVENT HANDLER (FUNCTION 0CH)

Register Summary:

AX: | AH | AL |

BX: | BH | BL |

CX: | CH | CL |

DX: | DH | DL |

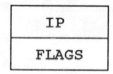

| SP |
| BP |
| SI |
| DI |

| IP |
| FLAGS |

| CS |
| DS |
| SS |
| ES |

Call With:

AX   = 000CH

CX   = Event mask

ES:DX = Address of the event
           handler

Returns:

Nothing

Description: Mouse driver function 0CH sets a user-defined event handler to the address passed in registers ES:DX. The user-defined event handler is called whenever one of the events specified in the event mask occurs. The event mask is passed in register CX as follows:

Bit	Event
0	Mouse movement
1	Left button pressed
2	Left button released
3	Right button pressed
4	Right button released
5	Center button pressed
6	Center button released

Upon entry to the event handler, the mouse driver will pass values to the event handler in the following registers:

Register	Contents
AX	Event flags
BX	Button status
CX	Mouse pointer's x-coordinate
DX	Mouse pointer's y-coordinate
SI	Vertical mickey count
DI	Horizontal mickey count
DS	Mouse driver data segment

Suggested Macro Definition:

```
userhandler    macro    mask,handler
               mov      cx,mask
               mov      ax,seg handler
               mov      es,ax
               mov      dx,offset handler
               mov      ax,0ch
               int      33h
               endm
```

Example: The following program fragment demonstrates mouse driver function 0CH by setting a "left button pressed" event handler:

```
        .
        .
        .
        mov      cx,2                    ;CX = Left button pressed mask
        mov      ax,seg handler          ;AX = Handler's segment
        mov      es,ax                   ;Put it into ES
        mov      dx,offset handler       ;ES:DX = Handler's address
        mov      ax,0ch                  ;Set the
        int      33h                     ; event handler
        .
        .
        .
```

TURN ON LIGHT PEN EMULATION (FUNCTION 0DH)

Register Summary:

AX: | AH | AL |
BX: | BH | BL |
CX: | CH | CL |
DX: | DH | DL |

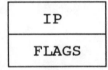

| SP |
| BP |
| SI |
| DI |

| IP |
| FLAGS |

| CS |
| DS |
| SS |
| ES |

Call With:

AX = 000DH

Returns:

Nothing

Description: Mouse driver function 0DH turns on light pen emulation. While light pen emulation is on, pressing both the left and right buttons at the same time will be interpreted as a "pen down" event.

Suggested Macro Definition:

```
lightpenon    macro
              mov     ax,0dh
              int     33h
              endm
```

Example: The following program fragment demonstrates mouse driver function 0DH by turning the light pen emulation on:

```
       .
       .
       .
       mov     ax,0dh          ;Turn the light
       int     33h             ; pen emulation on
       .
       .
       .
```

TURN OFF LIGHT PEN EMULATION (FUNCTION OEH)

Register Summary:

AX:

AH	AL

BX:

BH	BL

CX:

CH	CL

DX:

DH	DL

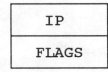

SP
BP
SI
DI

IP
FLAGS

CS
DS
SS
ES

Call With:

AX = 000EH

Returns:

Nothing

Description: Mouse driver function 0EH turns off light pen emulation.

Suggested Macro Definition:

```
lightpenoff    macro
               mov     ax,0eh
               int     33h
               endm
```


Example: The following program fragment demonstrates mouse driver function 0EH by turning the light pen emulation off:

```
        .
        .
        .
        mov     ax,0eh          ;Turn the light
        int     33h             ; pen emulation off
        .
        .
        .
```

SET MICKEYS:PIXELS RATIOS (FUNCTION 0FH)

Register Summary:

AX: | AH | AL |

BX: | BH | BL |

CX: | CH | CL |

DX: | DH | DL |

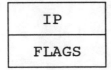

| SP |
| BP |
| SI |
| DI |

| IP |
| FLAGS |

| CS |
| DS |
| SS |
| ES |

Call With:

AX = 000FH

CX = Horizontal mickeys

DX = Vertical mickeys

Returns:

Nothing

Description: Mouse driver function 0FH sets the horizontal and vertical mickeys-to-eight-pixels ratio to the values passed in registers CX and DX, respectively. The default horizontal ratio is 8:8 and the default vertical ratio is 16:8.

Suggested Macro Definition:

```
setratios       macro   horizontal,vertical
                mov     cx,horizontal
                mov     dx,vertical
                mov     ax,0fh
                int     33h
                endm
```

Example: The following program fragment demonstrates mouse driver function 0FH by setting the horizontal ratio to 16:8 and the vertical ratio to 32:8.

```
                .
                .
                .
                mov     cx,16           ;CX = 16:8 horizontal ratio
                mov     dx,32           ;DX = 32:8 vertical ratio
                mov     ax,0fh          ;Set the
                int     33h             ; ratios
                .
                .
                .
```

SET EXCLUSION AREA (FUNCTION 10H)

Register Summary:

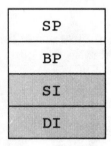

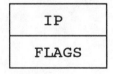

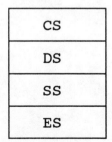

Call With:

AX = 0010H

CX = Upper left x-coordinate

DX = Upper left y-coordinate

SI = Lower right x-coordinate

DI = Lower right y-coordinate

Returns:

Nothing

Description: Mouse driver function 10H defines an area of the display screen in which the mouse pointer is not displayed.

Suggested Macro Definition:

```
setexclusion    macro   x1,y1,x2,y2
                mov     cx,x1
                mov     dx,y1
                mov     si,x2
                mov     di,y2
                mov     ax,10h
                int     33h
                endm
```

Example: The following program fragment demonstrates mouse driver function 10H by defining the right half of the display screen as an exclusion area:

```
        .
        .
        .
        mov     cx,320      ;CX = Upper left x-coordinate
        mov     dx,0        ;DX = Upper left y-coordinate
        mov     si,639      ;SI = Lower right x-coordinate
        mov     di,199      ;DI = Lower right y-coordinate
        mov     ax,10h      ;Set the
        int     33h         ; exclusion area
        .
        .
        .
```

SET DOUBLE-SPEED THRESHOLD (FUNCTION 13H)

Register Summary:

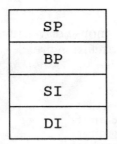

AX: | AH | AL |
BX: | BH | BL |
CX: | CH | CL |
DX: | DH | DL |

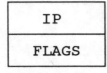

| SP |
| BP |
| SI |
| DI |

| IP |
| FLAGS |

| CS |
| DS |
| SS |
| ES |

Call With:

AX = 0013H

DX = Double-speed threshold
(mickeys:second)

Description: Mouse driver function 13H sets the double-speed threshold to the value passed in register DX. The default double-speed threshold is 64 mickeys per second.

Suggested Macro Definition:

```
setdouble       macro   threshold
                mov     dx,threshold
                mov     ax,13h
                int     33h
                endm
```

Example: The following program fragment demonstrates mouse driver function 13H by setting the double-speed threshold to 200 mickeys per second:

```
        .
        .
        .
mov     dx,200          ;DX = New threshold
mov     ax,13h          ;Set the new
int     33h             ; double speed threshold
        .
        .
        .
```

SWAP USER-DEFINED EVENT HANDLERS (FUNCTION 14H)

Register Summary:

AX: | AH | AL |

BX: | BH | BL |

CX: | CH | CL |

DX: | DH | DL |

| SP |
| BP |
| SI |
| DI |

| IP |
| FLAGS |

| CS |
| DS |
| SS |
| ES |

Call With:

AX   = 0014H

CX   = Event mask

ES:DX = Address of the event handler

Returns:

CX   = Old event mask

ES:DX = Old event handler's address

Description: Mouse driver function 14H swaps a previously installed user-defined event handler with a new user-defined event handler.

Suggested Macro Definition:

```
swapuserhandler  macro   mask,handler
                 mov     cx,mask
                 mov     ax,seg handler
                 mov     es,ax
                 mov     dx,offset handler
                 mov     ax,14h
                 int     33h
                 endm
```

Example: The following program fragment demonstrates mouse driver function 14H by swapping the current event handler with a new event handler:

```
        .
        .
        .
        mov     cx,2                    ;CX = Left button pressed mask
        mov     ax,seg newhandler       ;AX = New handler's segment
        mov     es,ax                   ;Put it into ES
        mov     dx,offset newhandler    ;ES:DX = New handler's address
        mov     ax,14h                  ;Swap the
        int     33h                     ; event handlers
        .
        .
        .
```

GET MOUSE STATUS BUFFER SIZE (FUNCTION 15H)

Register Summary:

AX: | AH | AL |
BX: | BH | BL |
CX: | CH | CL |
DX: | DH | DL |

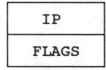

| SP |
| BP |
| SI |
| DI |

| IP |
| FLAGS |

| CS |
| DS |
| SS |
| ES |

Call With:

AX = 0015H

Returns:

BX = Buffer size

Description: Mouse driver function 15H returns the size of the mouse driver's status buffer in register BX.

Suggested Macro Definition:

```
getbuffersize    macro
                 mov     ax,15h
                 int     33h
                 endm
```

Example: The following program fragment demonstrates mouse driver function 15H by retrieving the size of the mouse driver's status buffer:

```
        .
        .
        .
        mov     ax,15h          ;Get the
        int     33h             ; buffer size
        .
        .
        .
```

SAVE MOUSE DRIVER STATUS (FUNCTION 16H)

Register Summary:

AX: | AH | AL |

BX: | BH | BL |

CX: | CH | CL |

DX: | DH | DL |

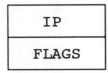

| SP |
| BP |
| SI |
| DI |

| IP |
| FLAGS |

| CS |
| DS |
| SS |
| ES |

Call With:

AX   = 0016H

ES:DX = Buffer address

Returns:

Nothing

Description: Mouse driver function 16H saves the mouse driver's status buffer in a buffer at the address specified by registers ES:DX.

Suggested Macro Definition:

```
savestatus      macro   buffer
                mov     ax,seg buffer
                mov     es,ax
                mov     dx,offset buffer
                mov     ax,16h
                int     33h
                endm
```

Example: The following program fragment demonstrates mouse driver function 16H by saving the mouse driver's status buffer:

```
        .
        .
        .
        mov     ax,seg buffer           ;AX = Status buffer's segment
        mov     es,ax                   ;Put it into ES
        mov     dx,offset buffer        ;ES:DX = Status buffer's address
        mov     ax,16h                  ;Save the
        int     33h                     ; status buffer
        .
        .
        .
```

RESTORE MOUSE DRIVER STATUS (FUNCTION 17H)

Register Summary:

AX: | AH | AL |

BX: | BH | BL |

CX: | CH | CL |

DX: | DH | DL |

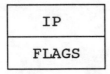

SP

BP

SI

DI

IP

FLAGS

CS

DS

SS

ES

Call With:

AX   = 0017H

ES:DX = Buffer address

Returns:

Nothing

Description: Mouse driver function 17H restores the mouse driver's status buffer to the values in the buffer at the address specified in registers ES:DX.

Suggested Macro Definition:

```
restorestatus    macro    buffer
                 mov      ax,seg buffer
                 mov      es,ax
                 mov      dx,offset buffer
                 mov      ax,17h
                 int      33h
                 endm
```

Example: The following program fragment demonstrates mouse driver function 17H by restoring the mouse driver's status buffer:

```
        .
        .
        .
        mov    ax,seg buffer      ;AX = Status buffer's segment
        mov    es,ax              ;Put it into ES
        mov    dx,offset buffer   ;ES:DX = Status buffer's address
        mov    ax,17h             ;Restore the
        int    33h                ; status buffer
        .
        .
        .
```

SET ALTERNATE EVENT HANDLER (FUNCTION 18H)

Register Summary:

AX: | AH | AL |
BX: | BH | BL |
CX: | CH | CL |
DX: | DH | DL |

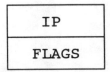

| SP |
| BP |
| SI |
| DI |

| IP |
| FLAGS |

| CS |
| DS |
| SS |
| ES |

Call With:

AX   = 0018H

CX   = Event mask

ES:DX = Address of the event
         handler

Returns:

AX   = Success flag

Description: Mouse driver function 18H sets one of three alternate event handlers to the address passed in registers ES:DX. The alternate event handler is called whenever one of the events specified in the event mask occurs. The event handler's event mask is passed in register CX as follows:

Bit	Event
0	Mouse movement
1	Left button pressed
2	Left button released
3	Right button pressed
4	Right button released
5	**SHIFT** key pressed during a mouse button event
6	**CTRL** key pressed during a mouse button event
7	**ALT** key pressed during a mouse button event

At least one of bits five through seven must be set in the event mask. If the alternate event handler is successfully set, register AX will return with a value of 0018H. Otherwise, register AX will return with a value of 0FFFFH. Upon entry to the event handler, the mouse driver will pass the following values:

Register	Contents
AX	Event flags
BX	Button status
CX	Mouse pointer's x-coordinate
DX	Mouse pointer's y-coordinate
SI	Vertical mickey count
DI	Horizontal mickey count
DS	Mouse driver data segment

Suggested Macro Definition:

```
setalthandler  macro  mask,handler
               mov    cx,mask
               mov    ax,seg handler
               mov    es,ax
               mov    dx,offset handler
               mov    ax,18h
               int    33h
               endm
```

Example: The following program fragment demonstrates mouse driver function 18H by setting an alternate event handler:

```
           .
           .
           .
    mov    cx,22h                 ;CX = Left button/Shift key mask
    mov    ax,seg handler         ;AX = Handler's segment
    mov    es,ax                  ;Put it into ES
    mov    dx,offset handler      ;ES:DX = Handler's address
    mov    ax,18h                 ;Set the
    int    33h                    ; event handler
           .
           .
           .
```

GET ALTERNATE EVENT HANDLER'S ADDRESS (FUNCTION 19H)

Register Summary:

AX:

AH	AL
BH	BL
CH	CL
DH	DL

AX:

BX:

CX:

DX:

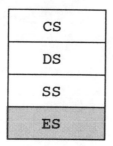

SP
BP
SI
DI

IP
FLAGS

CS
DS
SS
ES

Call With:

AX = 0019H

CX = Event mask

Returns:

CX = Event mask

ES:DX = Address of the event
        handler

Description: Mouse driver function 19H returns the address of an alternate event handler in registers ES:DX. If an alternate event handler hasn't been established or a matching event mask can't be found, mouse driver function 19H will return register CX with a value of 0000H.

Suggested Macro Definition:

```
getalthandler    macro    mask
                 mov      cx,mask
                 mov      ax,19h
                 int      33h
                 endm
```

Example: The following program fragment demonstrates mouse driver function 19H by retrieving an event handler's address:

```
        .
        .
        .
        mov     cx,22h          ;CX = Left button/Shift key mask
        mov     ax,19h          ;Get the event
        int     33h             ; handler's address
        .
        .
        .
```

SET SENSITIVITY (FUNCTION 1AH)

Register Summary:

AX: | AH | AL |

BX: | BH | BL |

CX: | CH | CL |

DX: | DH | DL |

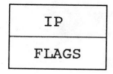

| SP |
| BP |
| SI |
| DI |

| IP |
| FLAGS |

| CS |
| DS |
| SS |
| ES |

Call With:

AX = 001AH

BX = Horizontal mickeys

CX = Vertical mickeys

DX = Double-speed threshold
(mickeys:second)

Returns:

Nothing

Description: Mouse driver function 1AH sets the horizontal and vertical mickey-to-eight-pixel ratios and the double-speed threshold.

Suggested Macro Definition:

```
setsensitivity  macro   horizontal,vertical,threshold
                mov     bx,horizontal
                mov     cx,vertical
                mov     dx,threshold
                mov     ax,1ah
                int     33h
                endm
```

Example: The following program fragment demonstrates mouse driver function 1AH by setting the mouse sensitivity values:

```
        .
        .
        .
        mov     bx,32       ;BX = 32:8 horizontal ratio
        mov     cx,32       ;CX = 32:8 horizontal ratio
        mov     dx,100      ;DX = 100 mickeys/second threshold
        mov     ax,1ah      ;Set the new
        int     33h         ; sensitivity values
        .
        .
        .
```

GET SENSITIVITY (FUNCTION 1BH)

Register Summary:

AX: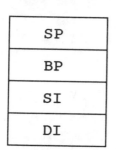

BX:

CX:

DX:

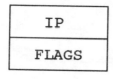

Call With:

AX = 001BH

Returns:

BX = Horizontal mickeys

CX = Vertical mickeys

DX = Double-speed threshold

Description: Mouse driver function 1BH retrieves the horizontal and vertical mickeys-to-pixels ratios and the double-speed threshold.

Suggested Macro Definition:

```
getsensitivity    macro
                  mov     ax,1bh
                  int     33h
                  endm
```

Example: The following program fragment demonstrates mouse driver function 1BH by retrieving the sensitivity values:

```
        .
        .
        .
        mov     ax,1bh          ;Get the
        int     33h             ; sensitivity values
        .
        .
        .
```

SET INTERRUPT RATE (FUNCTION 1CH)

Register Summary:

AX: | AH | AL |
BX: | BH | BL |
CX: | CH | CL |
DX: | DH | DL |

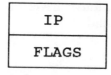

| SP |
| BP |
| SI |
| DI |

| IP |
| FLAGS |

| CS |
| DS |
| SS |
| ES |

Call With:

AX = 001CH

BX = Interrupt rate

Returns:

Nothing

Description: Mouse driver function 1CH sets the mouse driver's interrupt rate. The interrupt rate is passed in register BX as follows:

Bit	Number of Interrupts per Second
0	0
1	30
2	50
3	100
4	200

Suggested Macro Definition:

```
setintrate      macro   rate
                mov     bx,rate
                mov     ax,1ch
                int     33h
                endm
```

Example: The following program fragment demonstrates mouse driver function 1CH by setting the interrupt rate to 100 interrupts per second:

```
        .
        .
        .
        mov     bx,8        ;BX = 100 interrupts/second value
        mov     ax,1ch      ;Set the new
        int     33h         ; interrupt rate
        .
        .
        .
```

SET POINTER DISPLAY PAGE (FUNCTION 1DH)

Register Summary:

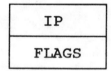

AX:

BX:

CX:

DX:

SP
BP
SI
DI

IP
FLAGS

CS
DS
SS
ES

Call With:

AX = 001DH

BX = Display page

Returns:

Nothing

Description: Mouse driver function 1DH sets the mouse pointer's video display page to the value passed in register BX.

Suggested Macro Definition:

```
setdisplaypage    macro    page
                  mov      bx,page
                  mov      ax,1dh
                  int      33h
                  endm
```

Example: The following program fragment demonstrates mouse driver function 1DH by setting the mouse pointer's display page to video page two:

```
      .
      .
      .
mov      bx,2        ;BX = Video display page number
mov      ax,1dh      ;Set the pointer's
int      33h         ; display page
      .
      .
      .
```

GET POINTER DISPLAY PAGE (FUNCTION 1EH)

Register Summary:

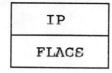

AX: | AH | AL |

BX: | BH | BL |

CX: | CH | CL |

DX: | DH | DL |

| SP |
| BP |
| SI |
| DI |

| IP |
| FLAGS |

| CS |
| DS |
| SS |
| ES |

Call With:

AX = 001EH

Returns:

BX = Display page

Description: Mouse driver function 1EH retrieves the mouse pointer's video display page.

Suggested Macro Definition:

```
getdisplaypage  macro
                mov     ax,1eh
                int     33h
                endm
```

Example: The following program fragment demonstrates mouse driver function 1EH by retrieving the mouse pointer's display page:

```
        .
        .
        .
        mov     ax,1eh          ;Get the pointer's
        int     33h             ; display page
        .
        .
        .
```

DISABLE MOUSE DRIVER (FUNCTION 1FH)

Register Summary:

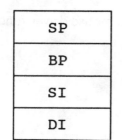

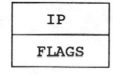

Call With:

AX = 001FH

Returns:

AX = Success flag

ES:BX = Previous contents of INT 33H

Description: Mouse driver function 1FH disables the mouse driver and returns the previous contents of the INT 33H interrupt vector. If the operation is successful, register AX will be returned with a value of 001FH. Otherwise, register AX will be returned with a value of 0FFFFH.

Suggested Macro Definition:

```
disabledriver    macro
                 mov     ax,1fh
                 int     33h
                 endm
```

Example: The following program fragment demonstrates mouse driver function 1FH by disabling the mouse driver:

```
        .
        .
        .
        mov     ax,1fh          ;Disable the
        int     33h             ; mouse driver
        .
        .
        .
```

ENABLE MOUSE DRIVER (FUNCTION 20H)

Register Summary:

AX:

AH	AL

BX:

BH	BL

CX:

CH	CL

DX:

DH	DL

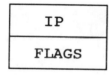

SP
BP
SI
DI

IP
FLAGS

CS
DS
SS
ES

Call With:

AX = 0020H

Returns:

Nothing

Description: Mouse driver function 20H enables the mouse driver.

Suggested Macro Definition:

```
enabledriver    macro
                mov     ax,20h
                int     33h
                endm
```

Example: The following program fragment demonstrates mouse driver function 20H by enabling the mouse driver:

```
        .
        .
        .
        mov     ax,20h          ;Enable the
        int     33h             ; mouse driver
        .
        .
        .
```

RESET MOUSE DRIVER (FUNCTION 21H)

Register Summary:

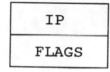

AX:

AH	AL

BX:

BH	BL

CX:

CH	CL

DX:

DH	DL

SP
BP
SI
DI

IP
FLAGS

CS
DS
SS
ES

Call With:

AX = 0021H

Returns:

AX = Success flag

BX = Number of buttons

Description: Mouse driver function 21H resets the mouse driver and returns the number of mouse buttons in register BX. If the function is successful, register AX will be returned with a value of 0FFFFH. Otherwise, register AX will be returned with a value of 0021H.

Suggested Macro Definition:

```
resetmouse      macro
                mov     ax,21h
                int     33h
                endm
```

Example: The following program fragment demonstrates mouse driver function 21H by resetting the mouse driver:

```
        .
        .
        .
        mov     ax,21h          ;Reset the
        int     21h             ; mouse driver
        .
        .
        .
```

SET LANGUAGE (FUNCTION 22H)

Register Summary:

AX: | AH | AL |
BX: | BH | BL |
CX: | CH | CL |
DX: | DH | DL |

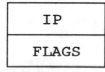

```
SP
BP
SI
DI
```

```
IP
FLAGS
```

```
CS
DS
SS
ES
```

Call With:

AX = 0022H

BX = Language code

Returns:

Nothing

Description: Mouse driver function 22H sets the language for the mouse driver's messages to the language code passed in register BX as follows:

Code Number	Language
0	English
1	French
2	Dutch
3	German
4	Swedish
5	Finnish
6	Spanish
7	Portuguese
8	Italian

Suggested Macro Definition:

```
setlanguage    macro   code
               mov     bx,code
               mov     ax,22h
               int     33h
               endm
```

Example: The following program fragment demonstrates mouse driver function 22H by changing the mouse driver's language to Italian:

```
        .
        .
        .
        mov     bx,8        ;BX = Italian language code
        mov     ax,22h      ;Set the mouse driver's
        int     33h         ; language to Italian
        .
        .
        .
```

GET LANGUAGE CODE (FUNCTION 23H)

Register Summary:

AX: | AH | AL |

BX: | BH | BL |

CX: | CH | CL |

DX: | DH | DL |

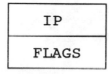

SP
BP
SI
DI

IP
FLAGS

CS
DS
SS
ES

Call With:

AX = 0023H

Returns:

BX = Language code

Description: Mouse driver function 23H returns the mouse driver's language code in register BX.

Suggested Macro Definition:

```
getlanguage     macro
                mov     ax,23h
                int     33h
                endm
```

Example: The following program fragment demonstrates mouse driver function 23H by retrieving the mouse driver's language code:

```
        .
        .
        .
        mov     ax,23h          ;Get the mouse driver's
        int     33h             ; language code
        .
        .
        .
```

GET MOUSE INFORMATION (FUNCTION 24H)

Register Summary:

AX: | AH | AL |
BX: | BH | BL |
CX: | CH | CL |
DX: | DH | DL |

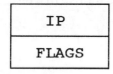

```
SP
BP
SI
DI
```

```
IP
FLAGS
```

```
CS
DS
SS
ES
```

Call With:

AX = 24H

Returns:

BH = Major version number

BL = Minor version number

CH = Mouse type

CL = IRQ number

Description: Mouse driver function 24H returns the mouse driver's version number, mouse type, and mouse adapter's IRQ setting. The mouse type returned in register CH is interpreted as follows:

Contents	Mouse Type
1	Bus mouse
2	Serial mouse
3	InPort mouse
4	PS/2 mouse
5	HP mouse

Suggested Macro Definition:

```
getinfo         macro
                mov     ax,24h
                int     33h
                endm
```

Example: The following program fragment demonstrates mouse driver function 24H by retrieving the mouse information:

```
        .
        .
        .
        mov     ax,24h          ;Get the
        int     33h             ; mouse information
        .
        .
        .
```

APPENDIX D

COMPILING THE WINDOWS TOOLBOX

This appendix explains how to compile the WINDOWS toolbox with either the Zortech C++ compiler or the Guidlelines C++ compiler (which is actually a translator).

COMPILING WINDOWS WITH ZORTECH C++

Batch File Listing: zortech.bat

Listing D.1 — **zortech.bat** — is a batch file for compiling the WINDOWS toolbox — **windows.lib**. In addition to constructing the WINDOWS toolbox, **zortech.bat** compiles and links SIMPLE LEDGER — **ledger.exe**.

Listing D.1: zortech.bat

```
rem
rem             zortech.bat
rem             Compile WINDOWS with Zortech C++
rem
masm /mx video,;
ztc -c lowlevel mouse pointer window menus popup dialog pulldown idate idollar inumber
iphone issn istring
rem
rem             Build WINDOWS library - windows.lib
rem
lib windows +video+lowlevel+mouse+pointer+window+menus+popup+dialog+pulldown+idate+
idollar+inumber+iphone+issn+istring;
rem
rem             Compile and Link SIMPLE LEDGER
rem
ztc ledger windows
rem
rem             Remove the Unwanted OBJ Files
rem
del *.obj
```

COMPILING WINDOWS WITH GUIDELINES C++

Although Guidelines C++ is a translator and not a true C++ compiler, it can still be used to construct the WINDOWS toolbox. Essentially, Guidelines C++ translates C++ source code into Microsoft-C-compatible source code. Once the C++ source code has been translated, it can be easily compiled with the Microsoft C compiler. Because the Guidelines C++ translator's execution is controlled by an assortment of batch files and MS-DOS doesn't provide a effective way to chain batch files, it isn't feasible to create a batch file that would automatically construct the WINDOWS toolbox. Accordingly, a Guidelines C++ version of the WINDOWS toolbox is created by assembling **video.asm** with MASM, compiling all of the WINDOWS C++ source files with the **cppobj.bat** translator batch file, and building **windows.lib** with LIB.

Header Files: bios.h, ctype.h, dos.h, and stdarg.h

Whereas Guidelines C++ does an effective job of translating C++ source code into Microsoft C compatible source code, the Guidelines C++ translator's header files do not provide support for many of the Microsoft C library functions. To provide the necessary Microsoft C library support, two of the Guidelines C++ translator's header files, **ctype.h** and **stdarg.h**, must be replaced and two new header files, **bios.h** and **dos.h**, must be added to the translator's INCLUDE directory.

Listing D.2: bios.h

```
/****************************************************************************
* bios.h - For Guidelines C++
****************************************************************************/
#ifndef BIOSH
#define BIOSH

/* function prototype */
unsigned _bios_keybrd(unsigned);

#endif
```

Listing D.3: ctype.h

```
/***************************************************************************
* ctype.h - For Guidelines C++
***************************************************************************/
#ifndef CTYPEH
#define CTYPEH

#define _U        01      /* Upper case */
#define _L        02      /* Lower case */
#define _N        04      /* Numeral (digit) */
#define _S        010     /* Spacing character */
#define _P        020     /* Punctuation */
#define _C        040     /* Control character */
#define _B        0100    /* Blank */
#define _X        0200    /* heXadecimal digit */

extern char       _ctype[];

#define isalpha(c)    ((_ctype + 1)[c] & (_U | _L))
#define isupper(c)    ((_ctype + 1)[c] & _U)
#define islower(c)    ((_ctype + 1)[c] & _L)
#define isdigit(c)    ((_ctype + 1)[c] & _N)
#define isxdigit(c)   ((_ctype + 1)[c] & _X)
#define isalnum(c)    ((_ctype + 1)[c] & (_U | _L | _N))
#define isspace(c)    ((_ctype + 1)[c] & _S)
#define ispunct(c)    ((_ctype + 1)[c] & _P)
#define isprint(c)    ((_ctype + 1)[c] & (_P | _U | _L | _N | _B))
#define isgraph(c)    ((_ctype + 1)[c] & (_P | _U | _L | _N))
#define iscntrl(c)    ((_ctype + 1)[c] & _C)
#define isascii(c)    (!((c) & ~0177))
#define _toupper(c)   ((c) - 'a' + 'A')
#define _tolower(c)   ((c) - 'A' + 'a')
#define toascii(c)    ((c) & 0177)

int toupper(int);
int tolower(int);

#endif
```

Listing D.4: dos.h

```
/*****************************************************************************
* dos.h - For Guidelines C++
*****************************************************************************/
#ifndef DOSH
#define DOSH

/* word registers */

struct WORDREGS {
    unsigned int ax;
    unsigned int bx;
    unsigned int cx;
    unsigned int dx;
    unsigned int si;
    unsigned int di;
    unsigned int cflag;
    };


/* byte registers */

struct BYTEREGS {
    unsigned char al, ah;
    unsigned char bl, bh;
    unsigned char cl, ch;
    unsigned char dl, dh;
    };


/* registers union */

union REGS {
    struct WORDREGS x;
    struct BYTEREGS h;
    };


/* segment registers */

struct SREGS {
    unsigned int es;
    unsigned int cs;
    unsigned int ss;
    unsigned int ds;
    };

/* function prototype */
int int86(int, union REGS *, union REGS *);

#endif
```

Listing D.5: stdarg.h

```
/*****************************************************************************
* stdarg.h - For Guidelines C++
*****************************************************************************/
#ifndef STDARGH
#define STDARGH

typedef char *va_list;

#define va_start(ap,v) ap = (va_list)&v + sizeof(v)
#define va_arg(ap,t) ((t *)(ap += sizeof(t)))[-1]
#define va_end(ap) ap = NULL

#endif
```

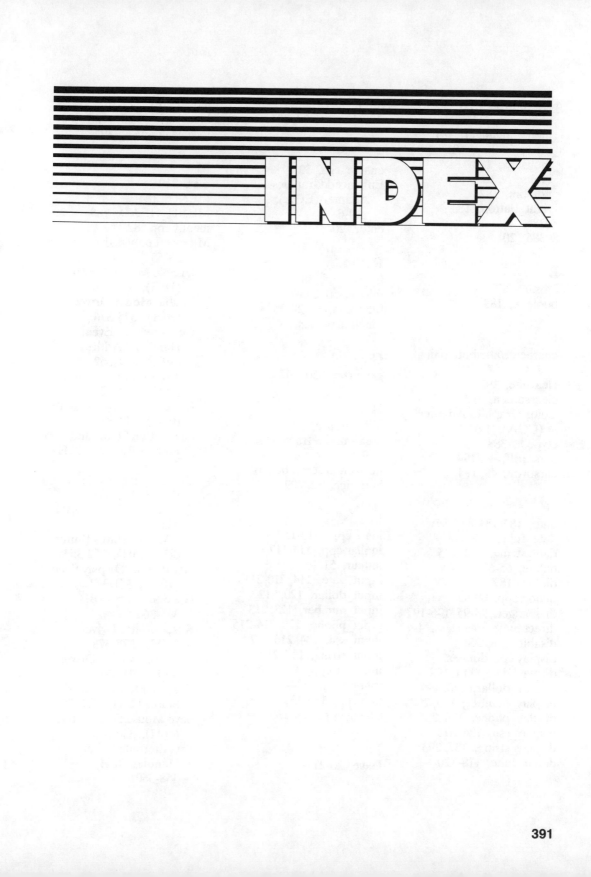

RELATED TITLES
FROM MIS:PRESS

ORDER FORM

PROGRAM LISTINGS ON DISKETTE

This diskette contains the complete program listings for all programs and applications contained in this book. By using this diskette, you will eliminate time spent typing in pages of program code.

If you did not buy this book with diskette, use this form to order now:

Only:
$26⁹⁵